ST PAUL'S
IN ITS GLORY

St. Paul's Cathedral: *The West Front from Ludgate Hill*, 1852.

ST PAUL'S IN ITS GLORY

A Candid History of the Cathedral
1831–1911

by

G. L. PRESTIGE, D.D.
Late Canon and Treasurer of St Paul's

LONDON
S·P·C·K
1955

First published in 1955 by
S · P · C · K
Northumberland Avenue, London, W.C.2
Printed and Bound in England by
Hazell Watson and Viney Ltd.
Aylesbury and London

ACKNOWLEDGEMENTS

WARM thanks for help of various sorts are due to many kind friends: especially to the staffs of the British Museum Reading Room, the Guildhall Library, the Church Commissioners, and the North Thames Gas Board; to Mr W. Godfrey Allen, Dr J. Dykes Bower, Mr E. T. Floyd Ewin, Captain G. G. Shadbolt, and Canon Charles Smyth; to the Reverend R. H. Collier and Mr A. R. B. Fuller; and beyond all to the Reverend W. M. Atkins, Librarian of St Paul's, who has a better knowledge of the Cathedral library and records than anyone else now living and than most of those now dead, and without whose resource in the continual discovery of new material this book would have been completed in a vastly shorter compass both of time and contents.

CONTENTS

	Acknowledgements	v
	Abbreviations	xi
	George Leonard Prestige: A Memoir, *by the Dean of St Paul's*	xv
	Foreword	xvii
1	The Old Establishment	1
2	The Liveliness of Mr Smith	17
3	The Energy of Mr Hale	39
4	Problems of Administration	58
5	The Invention of Dr Milman	73
6	The Resolution of Mr Gregory	92
7	Associates in Reform	105
8	Financial Reconstruction	117
9	Dome and Decoration	132
10	Choir and Music under Stainer	148
11	Pastoral Care	162
12	Virgers and Miscreants	174
13	The Chapter in the '80s	187
14	Byzantine Splendours	206
15	Religion and the Public	220
16	The End of an Era	236
	Appendix: Unpublished Letters of Sydney Smith	249
	Index	257

ILLUSTRATIONS

St Paul's Cathedral: The West Front from Ludgate Hill, 1852 *Frontispiece*
From a lithograph by E. Walker.
Reproduced by courtesy of the Dean and Chapter of St Paul's.

Sydney Smith, Canon 1831–45 *Facing page* 44
From a hitherto unpublished portrait by E. U. Eddis.
Reproduced by courtesy of the Dean and Chapter of St Paul's.

Charles James Blomfield, Bishop of London 1828–56 45
From a portrait by Samuel Lane at Fulham Palace.
Reproduced by courtesy of the Bishop of London.

St Paul's Cathedral from the South, *c.* 1842 76
From an engraving by C. W. Radclyffe.
Reproduced by courtesy of the Dean and Chapter of St Paul's.

Richard Harris Barham, Minor Canon 1822–45 77
From a drawing by R. J. Lane, *c.* 1842.
Reproduced by courtesy of the National Portrait Gallery.

Robert Russell Green, Dean's Virger 1871–99 77
From a crayon drawing by Sir William Richmond.
Reproduced by courtesy of the Dean and Chapter of St Paul's.

The Funeral of the 1st Duke of Wellington: The Scene under the Dome, 18 November 1852 156
From an engraving by E. T. Dolby.
Reproduced by courtesy of the Dean and Chapter of St Paul's.

The Choir Robing at St Paul's, *c.* 1852 157
From an engraving by Jules Arnout.
Reproduced by courtesy of the Dean and Chapter of St Paul's.

St Paul's Cathedral: In the Nave Looking towards the Organ, *c.* 1852 204
From an engraving by E. T. Dolby.
Reproduced by courtesy of the Dean and Chapter of St Paul's.

Richard William Church, Dean 1871–90 205
From a contemporary photograph.
Reproduced by courtesy of the Dean and Chapter of St Paul's.

Robert Gregory, Dean 1891–1911 205
From a contemporary photograph.
Reproduced by courtesy of the Dean and Chapter of St Paul's.

ABBREVIATIONS

Acta	*Chapter Minute Book* 1832–60
Acta B., C., D.	*Chapter Minute Book* 1860–74, 1879–91, 1889–1951
Barham	*Life and Letters of the Rev. Richard Harris Barham*, by R. H. Dalton Barham, 2 vols., 1870 (new ed., 1 vol., 1880)
Browne	*The Recollections of a Bishop*, by G. F. Browne, 1915
Bumpus	*The Organists and Composers of S. Paul's Cathedral*, by John S. Bumpus, 1891
Bundle	*A Bundle of Memories*, by H. S. Holland (Preface dated 1915)
Cathedral Decoration	The second of two vols. of MS. extracts and cuttings under this title, in Cathedral library
Charterhouse Report	*Report of Enquiry made by . . . Charity Commission in 1854 into the State and Management . . . of the Charterhouse* (House of Commons, December 1857)
Church	*Life and Letters of Dean Church*, by Mary C. Church, 1895
D.E.C.H.	*Dictionary of English Church History*, ed. Ollard, Crosse, and Bond, 3rd ed., 1948
D.N.B.	*Dictionary of National Biography* with supplements
E.C. Reports	*Reports* of Ecclesiastical Commission appointed Feb. 1835, reported March 1835, March, May, and June 1836

E.R.C. Report	*Report* of Ecclesiastical Revenues Commission appointed June 1832, reported June 1835
Frost	*Early Recollections of St Paul's Cathedral*, by W. A. Frost (Preface dated 1925)
Green	*Copies of various Memorandums and notes I have kept since I have been Virger in St Paul's Cathedral from 1852*, MS., by R. R. Green (Cathedral library)
Gregory	*Autobiography of Robert Gregory*, ed. (with much additional matter) by W. H. Hutton, 1912
Hale MSS.	A small collection of autograph letters addressed to Archdeacon Hale and of transcripts of letters written by him, made by his daughter in 1873 (Cathedral library)
Holland	*Memoir and Letters of the Rev. Sydney Smith*, Vol. I (Memoir), by his daughter Lady Holland, 1855
Hutton	*Letters of William Stubbs*, by W. H. Hutton, 1904
Johnston	*Life and Letters of Henry Parry Liddon*, by J. D. Johnston, 1904
Letter(s)	*The Letters of Sydney Smith*, ed. by Nowell C. Smith, 2 vols., 1953
Milman	*Henry Hart Milman*, by Arthur Milman, 1900
Min.	*Minute Books* of the Weekly Saturday Chapters from 1870
Muniments	*Chapter Muniment Books:* Vol. V, 1775–96; Vol. VI, 1796–1826; Vol. VII, 1826–54; Vol. VIII, 1854–1911

Newbolt	*Years that are Past,* by W. C. E. Newbolt (1920)
Paget	*Henry Scott Holland.* Memoir and Letters, ed. by Stephen Paget, 1921
Penrose	Obituary notices of F. C. Penrose (one from *Journal of the R.I.B.A.,* 9 May 1903, another signed "F.G.P.") (Cathedral library)
Plan	*Plan . . . in a letter to the Rt. Rev. the Dean and the Rev. the Prebendaries of St Paul's,* by a clergyman, 1839 (Copy in *Scrap Book,* pp. 807–26; British Museum Library T.2392 (4))
Preachers Book	*Register of Morning Preachers, 1726–1925* (Cathedral library)
Press Cuttings	Collections of cuttings in Cathedral library or registry
Prestige	*Life of Charles Gore,* by G. L. Prestige, 1935
R.C.I.M.	*Third Report of Royal Commission on Improving the Metropolis,* 1845
Reid	*Life and Times of Sydney Smith,* by Stuart J. Reid, 2nd ed., 1884
Russell	*St Paul's in the Early Nineteenth Century,* by William Russell, 1920 (based mainly on *Hale MSS.* and on Archdeacon Hale's unpublished diaries, with constant quotation of sources)
Russell *B.*	*St Paul's under Dean Church and his Associates,* by William Russell, 1922
S.C.N.M.	*Report from Select Committee* (of House of Commons) *on National Monuments and Works of Art,* 1841

Scrap Book	Scrap Book in 4 vols. (Cathedral library)
Simpson	*Memoir of the Rev. W. Sparrow Simpson, D.D.*, by W. J. Sparrow Simpson, 1899
Sinclair	*Memorials of St Paul's Cathedral*, by W. M. Sinclair, 1909
Singleton	*Letters* (I, 1837; II, 1838; III, 1839) *to Archdeacon Singleton*, by Sydney Smith (cited from the 3rd vol. of *The Works of the Rev. Sydney Smith*, 2nd ed., 1840)
Statt.	*Registrum Statutorum et Consuetudinum Ecclesiae Cathedralis S. Pauli Londiniensis*, ed. by W. Sparrow Simpson, 1873
Sumner	*The Organs of St Paul's Cathedral*, by W. L. Sumner, 1931
Suppl.	*Supplement* to *Statt.*, 1897

GEORGE LEONARD PRESTIGE

A MEMOIR

by the Dean of St Paul's

THIS book is, alas, the last that we shall have from George Leonard Prestige, who died before he could see his work in print, but not before he had prepared it for the press with his accustomed care. He had many gifts, all of which he devoted to the service of Christ and His Church, and it is fitting that some words should be written here as a tribute to his memory and a record of the respect and affection in which he was held by those who knew him and worked with him.

It is appropriate that his last book should be about St Paul's, for our great Cathedral was, as it were, his last love and his last enthusiasm. When he came to St Paul's as Canon in 1950 he had an established reputation as scholar and theologian and as an able editor. After a brilliant career at Oxford he became a Fellow of New College, where he remained until, in 1920, he accepted the living of Upper Heyford in the diocese of Oxford. During the twenty years which he spent in this rural parish he laid the foundation of his Patristic erudition, which was perhaps unequalled in this country, and began to contribute regularly to the columns of the *Church Times*, becoming its Assistant Editor in 1931. His *Life of Charles Gore*, which appeared in 1935, was a labour of love, and the favourable reception of that book, as well as the pleasure which he had in writing it, no doubt encouraged him to give shape and expression to his thoughts on Patristic theology. Two notable contributions in this field followed his biography of Gore—*God in Patristic Thought* in 1936 and *Fathers and Heretics* in 1940. He was appointed Editor of the *Church Times* in 1941 and found in this office scope for his power of lucid and pungent writing. He was happy in the opportunity of forming public opinion not only on Church affairs, but also on those of national and international concern and in the contact with many and various minds which his editorship brought him. When his tenure of this post was somewhat abruptly terminated in 1947, he undertook the responsible task of Acting General Secretary of the Church of England Council on Foreign Relations. Though he fulfilled the duties thus laid upon him with characteristic energy and competence, his friends were aware that at this time he suffered from a sense of frustration, and it is, therefore, all the more pleasant to know that his appointment to St Paul's was to him a source of happiness and contentment. He soon grew devoted to the Cathedral and, having been made Treasurer, he turned his thoughts continually to the preservation and enhancement of the "glory" of St Paul's. His colleagues in the Chapter deeply regret that his time was so short, but in the few years during which he was with us he contributed much to the solution of the many problems with which we are faced, and St Paul's will bear for many years marks of the influence of his sense of history and his sane aesthetic judgement. He was keenly interested in the Appeal for funds to restore and maintain the Cathedral and took a prominent part in the preparation of the Campaign; we must be glad that he lived to see the initial response which gave promise of ultimate success. To us it seems grievous that he will not be with us when the great Church which he loved is finally restored in more than its former beauty and majesty, but we may believe that, in some sense, he will be with us. In another Cathedral there is a quaint and moving epitaph on a former Treasurer which I will apply to him:

> "Formerly Treasurer of this Cathedral
> Church, now a part of its treasure."

W. R. Matthews

The Deanery,
St Paul's

FOREWORD

THE STORY to be unfolded in the following pages covers a period of exactly eighty years in the life of the Cathedral Church of St Paul in the diocese and city of London. That period has a historical unity all its own. At its beginning the air was filled with agitated cries for reform, extending not only to revision of the existing system of parliamentary representation (which issued in the Reform Bill, introduced in 1831 and passed in the following year) and to the redress of a number of grave social wrongs, but also to drastic improvements in the administration of the Church, with particular reference to the endowments of bishoprics and cathedrals. The opening of the present history therefore exhibits St Paul's in its unreformed condition of endowment and constitution, and shows something of the way in which its old and essentially medieval system worked. The lines of reform were laid down in the Cathedrals Act of 1840. But the new arrangements then envisaged were only brought into full operation by a long and gradual process. An immense amount of detailed change and improvement in the operations of the Cathedral had to be introduced in the course of the succeeding years, largely through the reforming action of the Cathedral authorities themselves. Thus the second phase of the Cathedral's life during these eighty years was transitional in character and assumes an extremely complicated pattern. But most of the problems that required solution had been settled, at least in principle, by the middle of the '70s. Thereafter a third phase opens, during which St Paul's is seen in full enjoyment of the benefits of an accomplished reformation, illustrated in the enormous expansion of its activities and influence.

It follows from the facts just mentioned that no small proportion of this book will be concerned with the mechanics of operating a great church. But pious readers need feel no shame if they should catch themselves attending to, or even taking interest in, a record of that kind. No large institution can be conducted satisfactorily, if at all, without paying a great deal of regard to administration and supply, and to the many departmental and personal responsibilities involved. A nation at war, or an expedition to the Himalayas, depends to a great extent on logistics for its hope of achieving success. It is still true that an army marches on its stomach, and not even a saint can long continue to march wholly otherwise. Study of the temporal organization of a cathedral may therefore contribute many points of interest. But all the time, behind the screen of material needs and practical administration, of rooted abuses and personal deficiencies, of struggle for improvement and opposition to change, the real work of St Paul's has continued without interruption. The daily worship according to the use of the Book of Common Prayer has been regularly maintained. The witness of the Cathedral to the glory of God has been constantly presented in music and architecture, in preaching and scholarship and in duty done (done not so badly on the whole), as well as in continual offering of praises. All this provides the background to a picture which in certain aspects may appear at times to belong less to a sacred subject than to the purely secular scene.

It also needs to be emphasized that the impulse to reform proceeded in great measure from within the Cathedral rather than from external pressure, and that for this fact St Paul's and all who benefit by its ministrations owe a great debt to the long line of great men who were called to serve it. There is no need to enlarge here on the importance to the Cathedral of its personal constituents, which will be apparent to all who read the history of its fortunes and development. From Sydney Smith, who was appointed to a canonry in

1831, to Robert Gregory, who relinquished the deanery in 1911, the Cathedral never lacked men of character and enterprise to govern, guide, and establish it. Here as everywhere personal qualities demand a liberal entry on the balance-sheet of real achievement.

I

THE OLD ESTABLISHMENT

On 2 October 1831 Sydney Smith was admitted to the canonry in St Paul's to which he had been nominated by his friend Lord Grey, the Whig Prime Minister. The prime inventor of that effective political engine, *The Edinburgh Review*, took his stall amid some murmurs of wonder and apprehension. But the preferment was not excessive recompense for his intellectual honesty and passion for social justice, his independence of mind, his magnificently lucid prose, his exuberant imagination and antiseptic irony, his conquering though somewhat hard and impervious common sense, and his devastatingly respectful disrespect of persons, not to mention a lifetime of practical service in country parishes not to a political party but to the poor. Six days later the House of Lords rejected the Reform Bill. But Sydney Smith had already returned to Somerset, and on 11 October he delivered to a delirious audience at Taunton the immortal parable in which he compared the efforts of the House of Lords to stop the progress of Reform to the attempt of Dame Partington of Sidmouth to counteract the rising flood of the Atlantic Ocean with a mop.[1] He was now 60 years of age. He had done as much as any man to promote the Whig parliamentary triumph, and alone, with precious little reward,[2] had kept the official Church of England prominently represented in the battalions of Reform, in spite of the Prince Archbishop of Canterbury and the hierarchy in general. But he was too independent to be given entire confidence. His friends revelled in his mockery of their political opponents, but were not so merry when he chaffed them-

[1] *Works*, III, 123 f. [2] *Singleton*, I, 204.

selves.[1] The furthest point to which they dared to let their gratitude run was a "snug" £2000 a year at St Paul's Cathedral.[2]

In those days the two most conspicuous features of the Cathedral were its vast emptiness and its encompassing dirt. A solid screen, surmounted by the organ, cut off about three-quarters of the chancel from the remainder of the church, and this enclosed portion, holding at most a few hundred worshippers, alone was regularly used for divine service; a pulpit was provided near the eastern section of stalls, on the northern side, as in a parish church, and the altar stood against the wall of the apse.[3] The area under the dome, together with the transepts and the nave, presented an echoing void; only later was it muted with matting, for the special services instituted in 1858.[4] It is recorded that busy Bishop Blomfield, whom Sydney Smith described as possessing an "ungovernable passion for business",[5] once stood on Ludgate Hill and said to Sir Robert Phillimore: "I look at that great Cathedral and think of its large revenues and great responsibilities, and ask myself what good it is doing to this great city; and I feel compelled to answer, not any to a single soul in it." [6] To a visitor entering (by one of the transepts, since the west doors were not used) [7] on an afternoon in winter, it appeared not only empty but murky; while Evensong progressed behind the choir-screen, "the lamps scattered few and far between throughout the vast space under the dome" succeeded merely in "making darkness visible and dimly revealing the immensity of the building".[8] The impressiveness of the marble waste can only have been strengthened by glimpses of the superhuman effigies of Nelson's post-captains and Wellington's major-generals lurking

[1] Cf. *Letter* 734; *Singleton*, I, 206; II, 233.
[2] Reid, 293; Holland, 282–5; *Letter* 59 n.
[3] Gregory, facing 155; *Scrap Book*, 164, 788.
[4] Cf. p. 80.
[5] *Singleton*, I, 205.
[6] Gregory, 182; cf. *Letter* 814 (p. 707 *ad fin.*).
[7] *S.C.N.M.*, qu. 6.
[8] Reid, 313, quoting Greville.

behind iron railings in the bays; for owing to overcrowding at Westminster Abbey, monumental tributes to departed heroes had first begun to invade St Paul's within the preceding forty years. Sydney Smith, after viewing the collection as it then was in 1819, wrote that "the national monuments in St Paul's" formed "a disgusting heap of trash", and that such artists ought not to be encouraged.[1]

As for the dirt, London was full of it. It accumulated in the ill-made streets and befogged the atmosphere. Nor was the Cathedral equipped to exclude it. Both below in the crypt and above on the staircases were openings unshuttered and unglazed through which the wind swept dust and soot into the church; "many loads of dirt" were removed from the vaulting over the aisles in 1842, and chronic filth apparently obscured the floors, walls, monuments, and ceilings.[2] Considering that the church outside the choir-screens was virtually unused, some faint excuse may be admitted for the condition in which it was left. But cold entered everywhere as freely as dirt and there was no system of general heating. "To go to St Paul's", wrote Sydney Smith in November 1833, "is certain death. The thermometer is several degrees below zero. My sentences are frozen as they come out of my mouth, and are thawed in the course of the summer, making strange noises and unexpected assertions in various parts of the church."[3] It was just as cold twenty years later. Robert Green, who was virger from 1852 to 1899 and followed the invaluable habit of taking and preserving notes, remarks under February 1853: "Cathedral very cold; thermom. inside down to freezing point, 32; at this time there were no means of heating the Cathedral."[4]

Frost and dirt, however, were so commonplace that they could still be disregarded. The services were well attended. In 1824, in the month of July, the congregation at Sunday Evensong was crowded; not a seat was to be got except in

[1] *Letter* 319.
[2] Russell, 60, 77, 86.
[3] *Letter* 643.
[4] Green, 2.

the galleries, and that only by slipping half-a-crown into the palm of the virger.[1] Sydney Smith claimed in 1839 that he had "very often" counted 150 people at the afternoon service on weekdays, and on Sundays the choir was "full to suffocation".[2] The average attendance on weekday afternoons in 1841 was about fifteen to twenty.[3] The music was good. "The service is exceedingly grand . . . and chanted with beautiful voices." [4] The organist was Thomas Attwood, who had been something of an infant prodigy, attracted the attention of the Prince of Wales, and was given by him the means to study abroad; so at the age of 17 he was dispatched first to Naples, then to Mozart at Vienna. He returned to England after four years, and was appointed organist at St Paul's in 1796, when he was 30, remaining there until his death in 1838. Having begun life as the favourite pupil of Mozart, in his old age Attwood was one of the first to recognize the merits of Mendelssohn, whom he entertained and befriended. Mendelssohn loved to come and play the Cathedral organ. On one Sunday afternoon in 1829 he played so long after the service that the congregation could not be dispersed, and the virgers, in despair of closing the Cathedral, made the blower let the air out of the organ in the middle of a Bach fugue.[5]

The eight choirboys were in the charge of an officer called the Almoner. This post had been held by William Hawes, one of the vicars-choral and a competent musician, since 1812; five years later he had also been given charge of the ten boys of the Chapel Royal. He boarded both choirs in a large house on Adelphi Terrace, though for many years only the four senior boys of St Paul's slept in, the four juniors being merely day-boarders. Hawes wrote many glees and madrigals, and from 1824 to 1836 was Director of Music at the English Opera House, better remembered as the Lyceum

[1] *The Times*, 9 July 1824. [2] *Singleton*, III, 240.
[3] *S.C.N.M.*, qu. 42. [4] Reid, 313 (quoting Greville, 1 Dec. 1834).
[5] Bumpus, 118 ff., 132 ff.

Theatre. His interest in secular music helps to explain the fact that he improved the somewhat meagre boarding fees paid by the Dean and Chapter in his earlier days by hiring the boys out to sing at public concerts and oratorios. He defended this course of action by the claim that it contributed an important part towards their musical education.[1] One of the first activities initiated by Copleston, who became Dean at the end of 1827, was to put the choir-school on a better financial footing, after fifteen years of controversy during which Miss Maria Hackett, the redoubtable champion of choirboys' rights, had bombarded Bishop, Dean, Chapter, and Cathedral officers of every degree with protests (and a suit in Chancery) against the alienation of ancient choir-school endowments.[2] Miss Hackett lived until November 1874, when the new Cathedral Choir School was in course of building; she was a constant worshipper at St Paul's, and a tablet was erected to her memory in the crypt.[3]

The men's voices in choir were supplied by a body of six professional singers known as vicars-choral. Originally the vicars were the thirty deputies (as their name implies) of the mainly absentee prebendaries, and were in Holy orders:[4] perhaps a lingering tradition of their clerical status may account for the fact that the vicars-choral were charged with reading the first lesson at the daily capitular services until Chapter transferred that duty to the minor canons in 1769.[5] By the fourteenth century the vicars had apparently ceased to be priests and become virtually choirmen.[6] By the beginning of the sixteenth century their number had dwindled to six and they were permitted to marry.[7] But, like the minor canons, they still formed an independent body (though without having a common seal of their own);[8] they possessed certain corporate estates, and each of the six enjoyed a freehold of his office. One had to be

[1] Bumpus, 137 ff.
[2] Bumpus, 102 ff.
[3] Green, 101.
[4] *Statt.*, xxxix f.
[5] *Statt.*, 282; *Suppl.*, 164.
[6] *Statt.*, 138.
[7] *Statt.*, 234.
[8] *Statt.*, xli; *Acta*, 263.

permanently represented by a deputy (paid by Chapter), since the basic stipend of the Cathedral organist was secured by making him a vicar-choral; this odd system continued until 1888. When Attwood died and Goss was making inquiries about the vacancy, he was somewhat taken aback on being informed by Sydney Smith that the basic salary was about £34 a year; but he soon learned that additional channels of income were open.[1]

Further to assist the canons and supply their deficiencies, whether in musical art or in leisure to attend divine service, the Cathedral enjoyed an establishment of twelve minor or petty canons. These officers were endowed, like the canons, with estates both individual and corporate, and again, like them, possessed a freehold of their office; they formed a distinct corporation or College with a Warden and Senior and Junior Cardinals (originally "Cardinals of the Choir", which means, presumably, the corner-men), and managed their own affairs under a charter granted by Richard II. They might also serve from time to time as Sub-Dean, Succentor (in charge of the music), Sacrist, or Librarian. But their emoluments were minute compared with those of the residentiary canons, so it was the regular practice for them to hold benefices in or near the City in addition to their minor canonries, an arrangement which happily associated the life and work of the Cathedral with the parochial clergy and the workaday Church. The twelve who happened to be in office in 1831 contributed an aggregate service of 493 years, an average of over 41 each. Several of them wrote musical compositions of some merit,[2] and three acquired the degree of D.D. But the best-known of them by far was Richard Harris Barham, author of the *Ingoldsby Legends*.

Barham was lucky in belonging to the days before the establishment of strict ecclesiastical caste. He was freely admitted to the society of his ecclesiastical betters, whether canons or Dean,[3] nor was there as yet any sense of social

[1] Bumpus, 159. [2] Bumpus, 140, 150–2. [3] Barham, I, 48.

impropriety in a minor canon cutting a gentlemanly figure in London literary circles or becoming an acknowledged wit. Barham had inherited a modest estate in Kent (the Tappington of the *Legends*), lived on terms of intimacy with the Dean and Chapter, breakfasted with Sir Walter Scott, dined with poets and peers, and exchanged hilarious anecdotes with the entire town. He was an original member of the Garrick Club and a diligent parish priest. As an undergraduate at Brasenose, when called upon by his tutor to explain his continued absence from morning chapel at 7 o'clock, he replied that the hour was too late: "I cannot sit up till seven o'clock in the morning: I am a man of regular habits, and unless I get to bed by four—or five at latest—I am really fit for nothing next day." So through life he worked hard at business all day and after nightfall sat up till 3 a.m., absorbed in conversation, reading, or scribbling with equal facility and felicity the anonymous compositions which delighted his wide public.

The *Legends,* which he fathered on the mythical Thomas Ingoldsby, first began to appear in Bentley's *Miscellany* in 1837, along with contributions of a different stamp from Charles Dickens. From the same year dates the important work Barham undertook for the Cathedral library, where he spent his afternoons rearranging the books and selecting damaged volumes for repair and rebinding. For this purpose the Chapter allowed him, to the end of his life, to expend an annual grant of £20 and to receive a warm annual vote of thanks. One day in 1839 he was working in the library with a book-binder's 'prentice and a printer's devil, in an old coat "which, from a foolish prejudice in the multitude against patched elbows, I wear nowhere else", his hands and face "encrusted with the dust of years", when in walked the City Swordbearer and the Lord Mayor "in full fig", with the lively little Queen of the Belgians on his arm. Barham was quite equal to the occasion, and "*heureusement pour moi,* she spoke excellent English".[1] Barham died, a few months after Sydney Smith, in 1845.

Barham and Sydney Smith got on well together, although towards the close of 1834 Sydney's insatiable habit of pursuing inquiries led to an "open feud" with the College of Minor Canons. Apparently he was conducting a private investigation, independently of Chapter, into the chances of inducing some members of the body to resign and make room for younger men, on promise of Cathedral livings. But the College suspected him of a design to put himself at the head of a Radical revolt of minor canons against Chapter, which always kept the best Cathedral livings for its own members. The minor canons, as sound Tories, refused to co-operate; they "begged to decline giving specific answers to hypothetical propositions", and relations with the Canon were considerably strained. Barham stood solidly with his brethren in this business, in which they almost certainly misunderstood Sydney's motives and object.[2] But the personal friendship of the two men does not seem to have been impaired. They were at one in their sanctified common sense, their hatred of superstition and fanaticism, their solid pastoral industry, their simple and unaffected Christian piety.

Barham was a Tory and Sydney was a Whig: but even that superficial difference was mitigated when Sydney's independence of judgement led him to assail his old political associates over their methods of enforcing Church reform. "Mr Smith himself", wrote Barham in 1836,[3] "is as lively as ever, though they tell me he is losing caste with his party for turning Tory! Certain it is that the language he now holds is to the full as Conservative as anything that ever dropped from Peel or Lyndhurst." Three years later Sydney Smith did Barham a kindness that was deeply appreciated. His residentiary house at No. 1 Amen Corner (the Corner had not yet been enlarged into a Court), was untenanted; appar-

[1] Barham, II, 88 f.; *Acta*, 59, etc. [2] Barham, I, 258, 265 ff.
[3] Barham, I, 286 f.

ently it had not been occupied since 1831, and was overrun with rats, cats, "and such small deer", accompanied by ten thousand unoffending aboriginal black beetles. It was a much better house than Barham's rather cramped quarters in St Paul's Churchyard, and Sydney Smith offered his colleague the use of the premises, which included (as Barham records) a miniature garden "capable of the greatest improvement", with an "extensive prospect of the back of the Oxford Arms, and a fine Hanging Wood (the New Drop at Newgate) in the distance". Barham accepted gratefully and lived there till his death. Sydney Smith retained one room, probably as a sort of office, since it was no part of his scheme of life to bury his social talents in the City; but in fact he never used it.[1]

Another distinguished member of the foundation was Thomas Gaisford, Regius Professor of Greek at Oxford since 1812 and Dean of Christ Church from 1831. The unreformed Cathedral had thirty prebends, endowed with estates of annual value varying from less than £10 to nearly £1500; of these, four were held by the residentiaries (that is to say, by the four prebendaries who had been elected into "residence" and controlled the affairs of the Cathedral) and the rest were sinecures. Gaisford held a small sinecure prebend from 1823 until his death in 1855, but he was very unlike most of his fellow prebendaries if he ever came near the place or did anything for it beyond preaching possibly once a year.

The three great dignities of Treasurer, Precentor, and Chancellor were also moderately endowed, and also sinecure. The Precentor of the time was more noteworthy than distinguished. This was the Reverend C. A. Belli, appointed Precentor by the Bishop of London in March 1819, in the third year after his ordination and on the eleventh day after the death of his predecessor; he died, still Precentor, in January 1886, aged 94. Thereupon Virger Green records, as if it were matter of strange interest, that Belli "was present officially at the Duke of Wellington's funeral, November

[1] Barham, II, 79, 86; cf. new ed. (1 vol., 1880), 310.

18th 1852; and again at the opening of the Great Organ in the south transept [on St Paul's Day, 1861], but not officially, he then occupied a reserved seat in the congregation." He subsequently attended the Thanksgiving Service for the recovery of the Prince of Wales in 1872, and it is to this occasion that an amusing tradition is attached; he had so seldom visited the Cathedral during his long Precentorship as to be unknown by sight to the authorities, and was at first refused access to his stall because the Dean's Virger did not recognize him. Even in his earlier days the Precentor was so inconspicuous that Sydney Smith thought a better title for him would have been "the Absenter". The Bishop who so promptly promoted so immature a candidate was the amiable Howley, translated in 1828 to Canterbury. The reason for Mr. Belli's promotion was that he was Mrs Howley's younger brother.[1]

There were four residentiary canons, of whom the Dean was one. The person nominated to the deanery, if not already a prebendary of St Paul's, first had a prebend conferred on him by the Bishop, then was admitted residentiary, and finally was elected Dean by the Greater Chapter.[2] This ancient procedure, together with the obligation of the Dean to keep residence as canon, was swept away by the Cathedrals Act of 1840, after which no subsequent dean or canon of St Paul's held a prebend.

The technical obligations of residence were not exacting. Mattins and Evensong were sung daily in choir at 9.45 and 3.15. Mattins was also said earlier in the Morning Prayer Chapel (renamed St Dunstan's in 1905) before business opened in the City.[3] Holy Communion was celebrated in choir after Mattins on Sundays and Holy Days. From this impressive total, something considerable has to be subtracted. The early Mattins was the sole responsibility of the minor

[1] Green, 190 f.; cf. 19; Russell *B.*, 91; Frost, 29; Bumpus, 6; *D.N.B.*, "Howley"; *Fasti Oxonienses*, "Belli"; Sinclair, 344.

[2] Cf. *Acta*, 268 ff. [3] *Suppl.*, 3; *Acta D.*, 203; *Min.*, 24 April 1905.

canons and by this date hardly anybody attended; the hour at which it was said had been progressively retarded and was now fixed at 7 in summer and 8 in winter.[1] Sydney Smith tried, and failed, to get the service abolished in 1836, and it lingered on (from 1877 in the crypt chapel at 8 o'clock) until 1901. But the nine minor canons who were responsible for it (the Warden and Cardinals being exempt) only performed the duty by deputy, hiring a Morning Reader to conduct the service on their behalf; in 1755 they were paying him £10 a year, but a century or so later the rate had risen to 50 guineas.[2]

The capitular Mattins and Evensong were sung, and the lessons were read, by minor canons. It is clear that a conscientious residentiary like Sydney Smith was not infrequently present on weekdays, at least at Evensong; [3] but a minor canon was allowed to preside on behalf of the residentiary, and in that case occupied his stall, even if the absentee were the Dean.[4] He might deputize in the same way even on a Sunday, but this the Dean thought to be somewhat repugnant both to his own feelings and to the rules and practice of the Cathedral. According to correspondents in *The Times*, no member of Chapter had been present for the first fortnight of January 1829 except on Sundays, but during the previous December a residentiary "attended the service of the church regularly, week-days as well as Sundays, without the omission of a single day".[5] The morning sermon was preached on festivals and Holy Days by the holder of one of the dignities or the prebends, either personally or by deputy; on ordinary Sundays the Bishop nominated

[1] *Suppl.*, 3; cf. *S.C.N.M.*, qu. 5 (Bumpus, 189 n., is in error, as Mattins was said at 8 o'clock in 1853); *Acta*, 250; *Suppl.*, 7.

[2] Barham, I, 288; *Suppl.*, 7; Green, 128, 130; *minor canons' minutes*, 27 Oct. 1755, 11 June 1888, 1 Oct. 1901.

[3] *Singleton*, III, 240.

[4] *Acta*, 76, 95; Russell, 43; cf. Green, 198 (1887).

[5] *The Times*, 15 and 21 Jan. 1829.

a preacher. But, as reported to the Cathedral Commissioners in 1853, the Cathedral had on its staff a Divinity Lecturer, usually a minor canon, whose principal task was "to be ready and in attendance to preach" on all Holy Days in case the dignitary or prebendary on duty failed to put in an appearance.[1] After the sermon, when the bulk of the congregation departed, it was the duty of a minor canon, in the absence of Dean or residentiary, to complete the celebrations of the Communion; now and again he found it convenient to plead that the persons remaining were too few to comply with the requirements of the rubric, and to disappear before he could be stopped.[2] But members of the public raised complaints that they had thus been prevented from communicating, and Chapter in 1841 expressly forbade the minor canons so to disappear.

The residual duty of the canon-in-residence might thus amount to nothing more than preaching a sermon on Sunday afternoon; and even that could be evaded in case of sickness or laziness. It should be added that the residentiary was obliged to give dinner on Sunday between the morning and afternoon services to those minor canons and vicars-choral who had officiated in the forenoon. Sydney Smith tried to persuade the beneficiaries in 1839 to commute their customary right to Sunday dinner for a money payment. They refused his offer, which had the support of Chapter, on the ground that they esteemed the privilege of dining with the Canon too highly. He therefore proposed to pay for a dinner between services, without attending it himself, as he found the time extremely inconvenient; and invited the whole body of eighteen minor canons and vicars to dine with him in his own house once in every residence. This offer was also declined. However, in 1843, with the consent of the

[1] *Acta B.*, 340 ff.; *Statt.*, 283, 312; *Acta*, 251.

[2] Russell, 45, 48; *minor canons' minutes*, 16 Dec. 1841; cf. Russell, 80.

recipients, Chapter abolished the Sunday dinner and added £15 a year to their stipends by way of compensation.[1]

Throughout Sydney Smith's tenure of his canonry his Dean was Edward Copleston. Unlike most of the clerics associated with the Cathedral, Copleston was a man of great distinction. Elected to a Fellowship at Oriel in 1795, under the reforming Provost Eveleigh (the chief promoter of the new system of examination for degrees), he promptly became an outstanding figure in Oxford and the right-hand man of his Provost. He is said to have had a fine presence and a ready wit. He was a scholar, a hard worker, a man of affairs and man of the world, and the principal creator of the "Noetic" common room of Oriel, which contained "such a company of Fellows as had hardly ever been assembled in one College",[2] including successively Keble, Whately, Hawkins, Hampden, Arnold, Newman, Pusey, and Hurrell Froude. Even before he was made Provost in December 1814 (he was then nearly 39) Copleston dominated the College, insisting on the election of men of intellectual ability even though they might not have shone in the "routine of public examinations".[3] He had already held a tiny sinecure prebend in St Paul's since 1812. In 1827 he was nominated to the See of Llandaff, worth about £900 a year. To eke it out he was also appointed to the deanery of St Paul's, worth about £5200; the Dean received the same "dividend", or share of the annual balance in the common fund, as did each of the other residentiaries, amounting to about £2250, and enjoyed separate estates in addition which brought him in almost £3000.[4] Copleston was thus the tenth, and last, successive Dean of St Paul's to hold the deanery in conjunction with one of the less lucrative bishoprics, the custom having been started exactly a century

[1] *Letter* 591; *Acta*, 102; Russell, 84; *minor canons' minutes*, 12 July 1839; cf. *infra*, pp. 249 ff.

[2] Mallet, *History of the University of Oxford*, III, 214.

[3] Quoted in Faber, *Oxford Apostles*, 62.

[4] *E.R.C. Report*; cf. *Acta*, 81.

before his appointment. At Llandaff he showed himself an active bishop, devoting himself to the restoration of churches and erection of parsonages, and doing what he could to secure the presence in every parish of at least one clergyman who could speak Welsh.[1] His vital faculties were so robust that he survived till 1849.

In spite of his activity in his bishopric, Copleston proved himself a faithful and vigorous Dean of St Paul's. He did occasionally call in a deputy for his month of residence; but such evidence as exists points to his having normally done his own work. He regularly preached in person at the great festivals.[2] He was hardly ever absent from meetings of Chapter, though they often took place outside his own months of residence. In the last two years of his life they were usually held at the deanery, and were coming to be more frequent; but of the ninety-eight meetings minuted between June 1832 and his death in October 1849 he seems only to have missed eight or nine, and four of these occurred during the last two years. It is a good record. Sydney Smith was also very regular at Chapter; meetings were in fact commonly held in or near his turns of duty, and that for the reason that when any practical business needed to be done it was to him, either alone or jointly with the Dean, that Chapter turned for executive action. None of his colleagues possessed his springs of energy. Thomas Hughes (namesake and grandfather of the novelist and social worker) had been Clerk of the Closet to George III and George IV; he was infirm, and died in 1833. His successor, James Tate, was actively employed in a large parish at Edmonton. The other canon, Dr Blomberg, Vicar of St Giles', Cripplegate, also rose through close association with the Court. He seems to have enjoyed languid health, and his principal interest was fiddling; he had three violins, which were stolen by a

[1] *D.E.C.H.*, *sub* Llandaff; *D.N.B.*

[2] Russell, 43, also 40 (the December residence there referred to was the Dean's); *Preachers Book.*

discharged servant; one, a Stradivarius, was recovered for him from a Smithfield pawnshop by Barham, to his inexpressible comfort.[1]

It did not occur to Sydney Smith, any more than to his colleagues, to regard his services to the Cathedral as providing full-time employment. He still retained his Somersetshire living of Combe Florey, six or seven miles from Taunton, and spent two-thirds of his time in its congenial occupations and surroundings. In spite of the restlessness which grew upon him with increasing age, and of his jokes about the deadly unreality of an existence passed anywhere but in London, he loved his country home, especially when friends or grandchildren were staying in the parsonage, and the roses were in bloom or a good fire was burning in the grate.[2] By an odd coincidence his doctor, who lived at Taunton, had a nephew who was also destined to throw lustre on St Paul's; the child was aged 2 in 1831, and his name was Henry Parry Liddon.[3]

In order to keep his residence at the Cathedral in 1832 Sydney expected to be in London during February, March, and July; he also was in fact on duty in June.[4] This was only a temporary arrangement, as it is clear from his correspondence and other data that from the beginning of 1833 he took March, July, and November; he was often in town for a week or so before and after his term of duty. Faithfully did he do his work in St Paul's Churchyard. But his ideas of sociability, though boisterous, were not so Bohemian as to make him want to dine and breakfast regularly at the wrong end of the social metropolis. His prime friends revolved round Holland House and the two Houses of Parliament; his earthly paradise lay between Regent Street and Hyde Park. In earlier days, on his usual spring holiday in London, he had commonly stayed with his elder brother in this region; he lodged there for his installation. Now that he had regular business in

[1] Barham, I, 55, 56 f.
[2] Holland, 302 n.; cf. *Letters* 927, 929.
[3] Reid, 278.
[4] *Letters* 591, 608, 609.

London he took one or another furnished house. But at the end of 1835 he purchased a house of his own in Charles Street, Berkeley Square, on a short lease; and in the autumn of 1839 he bought a larger house in Green Street, Grosvenor Square.[1] It was about the same time that he offered Barham the use of the residentiary house which he himself was now in no probable circumstance likely to require.

[1] Holland, 242; *Letters* 704, 791.

2

THE LIVELINESS OF MR SMITH

IN THE present age, when personal publicity is so largely dependent on the trivialities or the irregularities of human life, it is difficult to conceive the immense European reputation won by Sydney Smith by sheer powers of thought, writing, and conversation. He was not even wealthy: he inherited comfortable legacies from an aunt in 1821 and his father in 1827, but the fortune that fell to him on the death of his brother Courtenay in 1843 arrived only "just in time to gild the nails of my Coffin".[1] Though professionally a mere country parson and part-time canon, he was everywhere accepted as a literary and political lion; he had been intimate at Holland House, headquarters of the aristocracy of Whig intellect, for twenty-five years. In London he gave evening parties once a week, and his time was passed in a stream of social engagements, in the course of which he met members of the Government almost every day, whichever party was in power, though they did not necessarily discuss politics.[2] Apart from his irrepressible wit and drollery, he was trusted for his judgement, being himself one of those whom he described as "real philosophers, no assertion admitted without reasoning and strict proof".[3] He had also a shrewd sense of the way in which commonplace people would react to public events. "I am astonished", he wrote in 1838,[4] "that these Ministers neglect the common precaution of a foolometer, with which no public man should be unprovided: I mean the acquaintance and society of three or four regular British fools as a test of public opinion. Every Cabinet

[1] *Letters* 397, 508, 911.
[2] Holland, 304; *Letter* 704.
[3] *Letter* 881.
[4] *Singleton*, II, 231.

Minister should judge of all his measures by his foolometer, as a navigator crowds or shortens sail by the barometer in his cabin." He claimed to possess a very valuable instrument of that kind himself; but, though as far as possible from being a fool, he was his own best foolometer.

There may be some impression in the minds of people imperfectly informed that Sydney Smith was worldly and irreligious. In the sense that he moved freely in the world, and understood how to influence it, and detested every kind of fanaticism, he may be called worldly: he used but did not abuse worldly things. Irreligious he certainly was not. His piety was practical but deep. He was surprised, as a young man in Edinburgh, to find that the Scots totally neglected all religious worship during Holy Week: there was nothing like the sound of prayer in their churches, even on Good Friday, nor the smell of buns in the open shops of their pastrycooks. He thought that politics, meaning "questions of national existence", were "not to be despised, though they are not equal in importance to questions respecting the existence of another world". Unless the *Edinburgh Review* were careful not to profess or encourage infidel principles, he declined to continue any association with it. To a firm of publishers who sent him as a gift a novel in defence of Deists, he wrote protestingly that though he hated the insolence, persecution, and intolerance which often passed for religion, he had "an unaffected horror of irreligion and impiety", and entertained nothing but suspicion for any man who professed himself an infidel.[1]

The character of his religious views is well displayed in the sermon which he preached in St Paul's on the accession of Queen Victoria. He praised first the late King for his sincerity. "Our late Monarch had the good nature of Christianity; he loved the happiness of all the individuals about him, and never lost an opportunity of promoting it." His primary appeal to the young Queen was that she should foster

[1] *Letters* 34, 121, 298, 505.

Christian education, through which the fine morality of the sacred Scriptures might be engraved on the minds of the young. He expressed a rooted horror of war and begged Victoria to "worship God by loving peace". He pleaded for religious toleration, and maintained that a love for the Church of England and the protection of its establishment, to which he exhorted her, were fully compatible with the concession of civil rights to all who dissented from its doctrines, in particular the Roman Catholics: "The Church of England is now a rational object of love and admiration . . . it is an institution for worshipping God and not a cover for gratifying secular insolence." A patriot Queen, such as he attempted to depict, "reverences the National Church—frequents its worship, and regulates her faith by its precepts". Profoundly but wisely religious, she "casts herself upon God, and seeks from the gospel of his blessed Son, a path for her steps, and a comfort for her soul". Sydney was honestly religious.[1]

Of such a kind was the intellect now brought to address itself to the problems of the Cathedral; and it is astonishing to find, with his many preoccupations, how honestly and assiduously Sydney Smith gave himself to Cathedral affairs. He kept his residences regularly; he preached his plain and practical twenty-minute sermons to the accompaniment of much vigorous action of the limbs and beating of the cushion (he could not see why orthodox clergymen, unlike "every semi-delirious sectary", should "call in the aid of paralysis to piety" and preach like "holy lumps of ice");[2] and he took over the oversight of Cathedral business and conducted it with an efficiency to which it was entirely strange. His old friend Milman, who succeeded Copleston as Dean, subsequently wrote an impressive testimony to Sydney's work: "I find traces of him in every particular of Chapter affairs;

[1] *The New Reign* (1837), 10, 12, 15, 18 f., 23 (reprinted in *Works*, III, 279–88).

[2] Reid, 356; Holland, 84 f., 369; cf. *Letter* 784.

and on every occasion where his hand appears, I find stronger reason for respecting his sound judgment, knowledge of business, and activity of mind; above all the perfect fidelity of his stewardship. . . . His management of the affairs of St Paul's (for at one time he seems to have been *the* manager) only commenced too late, and terminated too soon." [1] This verdict is borne out by an inspection of the minutes of Chapter proceedings. "Mr Smith" was the canon repeatedly deputed to examine details of business or to exercise his discretion in their execution, whether the matter in hand related to the care of property, leases, sales, legal proceedings, or to the repair and maintenance of the Cathedral fabric, or to schemes for the division of parishes in Cathedral patronage, or to the attendance of minor canons and the provision of prayer books for the choir, or even (though he was no musician) to reporting on the musical attainments of the choirboys.

His report on the efficiency of the choir was made in 1835 [2] and is worth quoting: "I represent in the first place that the insufficiency of the choir proceeds from the boys being retained after their voices have failed. Secondly, from the mode of selecting the music adopted by the Succentor, who chooses difficult music, will never accommodate that music to the capabilities, accidents and wishes of the choir, and does not give sufficient notice to those who are to execute the music. As a remedy for these defects I advise that the singing boys should be pensioned off as soon as it is reported that they are no longer serviceable; and that the Succentor be admonished to give longer notice of the music he selects, to consult the capabilities of boys and men in selecting the music, not to be too various and abstruse in his selection, to change the music selected as often as the accidents of the choir may require it; and that Mr Smith be requested to converse with the Succentor and to make arrangements according to these suggestions."

The tenor of such criticisms has been heard to echo in

[1] Holland, 302. [2] *Acta*, 17.

more modern times. The Succentor in question was Minor Canon E. G. A. Beckwith, who had recently succeeded his father in that office.[1] He was at loggerheads with Hawes, the Almoner and Master of the Choristers, in 1838,[2] and threatening legal proceedings; whereupon Chapter directed Goss, who had been appointed organist in succession to Attwood two months earlier, to play only such music as was enjoined by two other of the minor canons whose judgement was apparently trusted, and to observe "the strictest secrecy" about the whole matter. It seems probable that the Succentorship remained in virtual abeyance for some time after this dispute. In 1845, after difficulties with the vicars-choral, Canon Hale (of whom more will be heard later) considered that "we are much to blame unless we support the authority of the Succentor"; if that officer were thought to have acted injudiciously he must be given advice, but his reasonable directions ought to be enforced by Chapter.[3] In 1847, after further trouble with vicars-choral and minor canons, and after some research among the statutes of the Cathedral, steps were taken "for restoration of Succentor at St Paul's", and Beckwith, as Succentor, was charged with the voice trials of candidates for a vacancy in the choir.[4] The active presence of a Succentor is implied in the new statute concerning vicars-choral enacted in 1848. Beckwith died in 1856. But there remained endemic difficulties between an ineffectual Chapter and a recalcitrant body of vicars-choral until the vigorous administration of the '70s and '80s.

Unhappily the behaviour of the vicars-choral had been getting slack, and their attendance irregular, during Attwood's later years, as young Mr Hale, not yet a canon, was prompt to note;[5] and Goss, though a working musician of diverse talents and prolific accomplishments, was too amiable a man to pull things together. (Not that it was his duty to

[1] *Muniments*, VII, 73, 24 Jan. 1833.
[2] *Acta*, 76 f.
[3] Russell, 88; *Acta*, 106 ff.
[4] Russell, 98; *Acta*, 148.
[5] Russell, 33, 36.

maintain discipline among the choirmen but, nominally at any rate, that of the two Cardinals.)[1] Immediately after Goss's appointment the order had to be issued that "one bass voice at the least, one tenor, and one contra-tenor of the vicars-choral or their deputies" should always be present at service, and the minor canon on duty was requested to report "any great deficiency".[2] In 1843, on the occasion of an organ recital in the neighbouring church of Christ Church, Newgate Street, not one vicar-choral attended at Evensong in St Paul's; but it was a day of "tempestuous" weather.[3] Owing to disputes, to the organist's incapacity for administration, and to other causes, the services became a byword for slovenliness.[4] Once, the story runs, of men's voices there was none save a single tenor and a single bass, and the Hallelujah Chorus had to be sung. They sent a message up to Goss in the organ-loft. "Do your best", he replied, "and I will do the rest with the organ." [5]

Goss lived to see great changes in the character and capacities of that instrument, changes to which his early request to Sydney Smith for some new stops to be added made an insignificant prelude. His petition elicited a characteristic grumble from the Canon. "Mr Goss, what a strange set of creatures you organists are. First you want the bull stop, then you want the tom-tit stop; in fact, you are like a jaded cab-horse, always longing for another stop." [6] Goss survived three Deans and resigned in 1872. Throughout his tenure of office he had as sub-organist a remarkable and ill-remunerated assistant in George Cooper, junior. Cooper was the son of Attwood's assistant and had actually been allowed to accompany services in St Paul's as a boy of 12, under Attwood, in addition to extemporizing at the organ for the benefit of Mendelssohn. His playing of Bach is said to have been "simply unsurpassed". He was made organist of the Chapel Royal

[1] *Statt.*, 282, 305. [2] *Acta*, 75, 76. [3] Russell, 79.
[4] Bumpus, 173. [5] Sinclair, 309. [6] Bumpus, 160.

in 1867, and applied unsuccessfully for the post of organist at St Paul's on Goss's retirement.[1]

However slack the vicars-choral were, and however combative the minor canons, the choirboys suffered no serious neglect in the Almoner's school-house. In consequence of attacks levelled against Hawes in 1836 by somebody unnamed (was it Miss Hackett?), a very long and detailed report [2] on the choir-school was presented to Chapter on behalf of the Cardinals, of whom Barham was Senior. Hawes was completely exonerated by the investigators and complimented by Chapter. The report records some interesting details. The boys rose at 7.30 a.m. (at 8 in winter), ran over the psalms for the day before their breakfast, which consisted of milk, bread, and butter, and so to Cathedral at 9.45. From 11 to 2 they practised music and singing; but on one morning a week the six senior boys had an hour's Italian from a master supplied by Miss Hackett. Dinner was at 2, a good square meal, including meat every day, with vegetables and trimmings: half a pint of beer was served, and second glasses if desired. Evensong was at 3.15, then recreation. From 5.30 till 8 p.m. on four weekdays they had a master in to teach reading, writing, arithmetic, and the Church Catechism; but on Wednesdays their time was free, and at the week-end they were allowed to go home between Saturday Evensong and Monday Mattins, at liberty except for attendance at the Sunday services in Cathedral. Supper was at 8 (bread, butter, and beer); bed at 9. If they were engaged to sing at public dinners or in oratorios they were always accompanied, and usually back in school by 9 p.m., oratorios keeping them longer out of bed, but "seldom" after midnight.

On Lord Mayor's Day they were parcelled out in pairs among different City Companies; they arrived after dinner but were permitted to take fruit or wine; they never sang in theatres or any other place of public entertainment except

[1] *Acta B.*, 214 f.; Bumpus, 184; Frost, 24. [2] *Acta*, 44–53.

on oratorio nights. They changed their linen at least twice a week. Their beds were clean and warm, and they slept two in a bed; their room had been redecorated, and was fully as comfortable as a dormitory in a public school. They had holidays from school, but not from Cathedral, for three weeks after Christmas, two weeks after Easter, and a month in midsummer. (The choristers still had to attend Cathedral twice every day of the year, except for a few weeks during the annual closure for erecting and dismantling the scaffolds for the charity schools' service.[1]) A maid was kept to wash and comb the younger boys under the supervision of Miss Hawes; Miss Hawes also usually carved the joint at dinner. An isolated scandal had to be admitted: one boy was liable to become verminous, being "constitutionally subject to the complaint" and frequently relapsing in spite of having his head "constantly washed with a strong decoction of larkspur seed and brandy" (oh, happy vermin!). Some consolation was perhaps drawn from the fact that the boy in question was not one of the St Paul's choir, but of the Chapel Royal boys who were boarded with them.

In Sydney Smith's time a clear distinction still obtained between the common fund of the Chapter, which supplied minor running expenses and the "dividends" of the residentiaries, and the Fabric Fund, on which the Chapter relied for maintaining the fabric. This Fabric Fund [2] consisted of the invested residue of the money raised by Parliament after the Great Fire "for building and preserving the Church of St Paul", of which stock to the nominal value of some £7000 remains to this day; its Trustees were (and are) the Archbishop of Canterbury, the Bishop of London, and the Lord Mayor. For some years the Trustees (or "Commissioners") were in the habit of paying out of the Fund for such things as "coals and candles, for Bibles and books, braziery ware, tin ware, turnery ware and upholstery ware" for Cathedral

[1] Russell, 58; cf. *infra*, pp. 102–4. [2] *Acta*, 155 ff.

purposes, to say nothing of wages for watchmen and "the servants called labourers" (whose status seems to have been more or less that of cleaning and maintenance staff), and for bell-ringers. But in 1753 the situation was reviewed and the Trustees declined to be responsible for more than the upkeep of the fabric; this obligation was generously defined, including repair of organ, clock, and bells; the question who should pay for winding the clock was remitted for further consideration, but other accessory expenses were left to be met from the common fund, "as they were when the Old Church was standing, and as they are provided for in all other Cathedrals". It has to be remembered that the more the Chapter had to expend out of the common fund, the less was left to be distributed in dividends to the residentiaries at the annual audit.

For the future, the Trustees decided to appoint "one skilful architect to take care of the building, who shall be called Surveyor of the Fabric"; he was directed to inspect the whole building every six months; to report on the work which he considered should be undertaken; and with the approval of the Dean and Chapter to arrange for its execution and to check the contractors' accounts. He was also to have a deputy nominated by the Dean and Chapter, to make inspections inside and out every week and see to running repairs. (It is somewhat shattering to find that the deputy appointed in 1766 was the then Dean's Virger; that he was succeeded in both offices by John Lingard in 1798; and that Lingard's successor, Edward Cummings, again took over both posts in 1845 and held them till his death in 1871.) At a later period the Surveyor's report was made annual instead of half-yearly; and it was laid down that Chapter should not spend in any one year more than was covered by the income actually arising from the trust fund, without the consent of the Trustees.[1] In practice the Chapter sometimes spent more than this amount on maintenance, and the Trustees sold out

[1] *Acta*, 159.

part of the capital of the Fund to meet the cost. This happened in 1832. Thereupon the Trustees demanded [1] that the Chapter should replace by instalments the sum of £674 15*s*. thus realized; part of the money had been spent on the Chapter House, which had been built out of the Fabric money and had always been regarded as forming a charge on the Fabric Fund. The Chapter rejected this attempt "to fling the burthen upon individuals" (in plain English, to diminish the amount available for canons' dividends), but promised to continue, from time to time, what they had already undertaken for the year 1833, by making substantial voluntary contributions from their common fund for repairs to the Chapter House. As a further act of grace they volunteered to "take upon themselves the salary of the chandelier-cleaner and the repairs of the clock". Chapter's letter to the Trustees, which embodied these terms, was framed under the direction of the Dean and Mr Smith.[2]

It is quite clear that the Dean and Chapter entrusted to Sydney Smith the general oversight of administrative operations, both those that were assigned to the Surveyor's "department" and were financed from the Fabric Fund, and those which fell within the "departments" of other officers and imposed a liability on the common fund. It is equally clear that immediately upon his admission to the Chapter a vast improvement ensued in the manner of conducting business. It was ordained, early in 1833, that the annual bills should not be paid at the Audit unless they had been sent in to the Receiver in advance, examined and signed by the officer to whose department the matter belonged, and countersigned by the Dean or one other residentiary.[3] Such precaution was unheard of. Mr Cockerell, the Surveyor, an architect of high standing, found the new canon's new methods "extremely unpleasant", and other officers of the Cathedral entirely concurred with him. Sydney Smith began by suspecting everybody's honesty on principle; but if, after strict investigation

[1] *Acta*, 9 f. [2] *Acta*, 5. [3] *Acta*, 5.

and what he called a "little collision", he was satisfied that all was well, he behaved with the utmost consideration and won both the confidence and the affection of the staff.[1]

The Canon was indefatigable. He disputed about contracts, materials, and prices. He would permit no new work to be put in hand without his approval, nor without previous submission of estimates; often he demanded competitive tenders to be procured; once he got a piece of work executed for exactly half the cost estimated by the regular contractor.[2] He clambered about roofs and towers and squeezed through openings insufficient to his portly figure: "If there are six inches of space," quoth he optimistically, "there will be room enough for me." He banished damp from the neglected library by installing an American stove, and instituted repairs to the books. He paid new and systematic attention to cleansing the monuments.[3] He insisted on insuring the Cathedral against fire, introduced mains water into the lower parts of the church and placed cisterns and portable engines in the upper parts: if fire broke out after that, he declared, he was in a position to "reproduce the Deluge". Surveyor and Chapter Clerk, who in their long years of service had never seen industry like his, were astonished at the spectacle of a canon mastering his, and their, business. What amazed the Surveyor as much as anything was the fact that so much bother was being undertaken to effect savings in the Fabric Fund, which had no bearing whatever on the common fund or on canonical incomes. The Chapter Clerk, experienced lawyer that he was, said that Mr Sydney Smith was one of the most strictly honest men he ever met in business.[4] Beside this estimate may be set the judgement of Sydney's elder brother, "that Sydney's life was the only instance of undeviating honesty that he had ever known to answer".[5]

To Sydney Smith's energy the Cathedral largely owes the

[1] Holland, 298 ff.; cf. *Letters* 615–22, 766–8, 781, 809–11.
[2] *Letter* 781.
[3] Cf. *S.C.N.M.*, qu. 367, 416, 458.
[4] Holland, 301.
[5] Holland, 290.

fact that it still enjoys possession of the estate at Tillingham which is said to have formed its original endowment, given by King Ethelbert of Kent. Its preservation was the result of a strange series of circumstances. According to the practice commonly followed in managing the Cathedral's properties, Tillingham Manor [1] was let on a long lease which could be extended indefinitely by the periodic payment of substantial "fines" or premiums. The "reserved" annual rents were very small, and the fines formed the principal source of revenue to the owners, who on granting a renewal of the leases, after seven or more years, struck a fresh bargain with their tenants for a lump sum fixed on the estimated annual value of the property. In 1679 Dr Clarke, Dean of Winchester, who then held the lease of Tillingham, left his interest in the estate (that is, the profits of working it) on trust: a first charge was to provide sufficient money to pay the periodic fines needed to renew the lease in perpetuity, a second was to augment the value of ten specified livings by £30 a year each, and the residue was to go towards the rebuilding and repairing of St Paul's, then rising from its ashes.

For some years Dr Clarke's trustees had been dispensing their surplus in further augmentation of the livings, instead of paying it over to St Paul's, and early in Sydney Smith's administration the Chapter Clerk called attention to what was happening.[2] Chapter therefore brought a suit in Chancery to establish the Cathedral's rights under the charity. Sydney Smith displayed his customary energy and acumen in the conduct of the legal business, with the result that from 1837 the residue of the income was again secured to the Fabric Fund; in 1853 it was estimated at £800 a year.[3] Since the profits under the lease accrued not to the common fund (like the fines) but to the Fabric Fund, special arrangements were made in 1872, when the Ecclesiastical Commissioners

[1] *Suppl.*, 130 ff.; Gregory, 187 f.
[2] *Acta*, 13, 22, 44; Holland, 300.
[3] *Acta*, 252.

took over the other Cathedral properties, by which the Tillingham estate reverted to the Dean and Chapter to endow the repair of the fabric. In 1878 a fund was established by the Charity Commissioners from invested surpluses of the charity, with some help from Chapter, to secure the permanent payment of the ten benefice augmentations; and Tillingham became once more the unencumbered property of the Cathedral.

In 1837 Sydney Smith, acting on behalf of the Dean and Chapter, had a triumphant brush with the Home Office.[1] The Government wished the Cathedral to be opened to the public free of charge like any other "national building or establishment containing works of art, historical or literary monuments, or objects of natural history"; the words quoted are from the Home Secretary, Lord John Russell. But for more than a hundred years past a fee of 2d. had been levied on all who entered the Cathedral at other times than those of divine service, when naturally no charge was made. The twopences formed the main item in the remuneration of the four virgers who had to admit the public and maintain order.[2] Returns (dependent on the virgers' statements) have been preserved of the amounts they received for the fourteen years from 1837 to 1850.[3] These show that in each of the first six years a virger received on the average over £100 from this source; from 1843 to 1847 over £130; from 1848 to 1850 about £112. A simple calculation reveals that in the worst year (1840) at least 48,000 persons must have paid the 2d. in the course of the twelvemonth, in the best (1845) about 71,000. The monthly figures vary from year to year but, as might be expected, are two, three, or four times higher between April and September than during the winter.

The Chapter's initial response to Lord John was signed by the Dean. He stated that new St Paul's, though rebuilt chiefly through a parliamentary grant, was no more subject to

[1] *Acta*, 59, 61–74; cf. *Letters* 1023–26.

[2] *Acta*, 118.

[3] *Acta*, 100, 125, 204, 345.

Government control than Old St Paul's had been, and had not "acquired more the character of a national building on that account"; the Chapter judged that the admission fee was necessary in order to set some limit on the number of casual sightseers and so to preserve decency and quiet "in the House of God", and no further charge was made for viewing the monuments; "a church ought not to be regarded in the light of a gallery of art or of a place of public exhibition". A few days later Sydney Smith wrote to point out that anybody attending service in St Paul's had entire liberty to stay and view the monuments for the rest of the day, without fee or molestation. Two months later the Home Secretary wrote again to inquire whether Chapter had done anything further, and to suggest employing the services of additional members of the City police inside the Cathedral; it will be recalled that Peel had organized the new London police force in 1829, and in fact two constables had been stationed inside St Paul's, at the expense of Chapter, every Sunday for several years past.[1] Letters flew to and fro; long and exquisitely ironical epistles from Sydney Smith, brief notes from the Home Office. Sydney Smith threw open the entire floor outside the choir during service on Sunday afternoons; the crowd made so much noise with feet and voice that the concession had to be revoked after two or three Sundays, and the normal barriers were replaced, leaving merely a broad pathway open between the door in the north transept and the corresponding door in the south transept.[2] The Home Office asked for an extra hour of free opening on weekdays. Sydney Smith replied that Chapter would admit the public gratuitously on weekdays between 9 and 11 a.m. (Mattins was then sung at 9.45).

The Home Office retired from the unequal contest with an acid expression of dissatisfaction. In the course of the correspondence a frightful picture is disclosed of the gross irreverence and physical indecency with which some members of

[1] *S.C.N.M.*, qu. 358, 385. [2] Ibid., qu. 6.

the public behaved in the Cathedral. Nevertheless, the Chapter had again to resist Government pressure for free admission in 1842,[1] after the report of a Select Committee of the House of Commons on National Monuments before which evidence was given by Sydney Smith, the Surveyor, a minor canon, and two virgers; Milman gave evidence on similar lines on behalf of Westminster Abbey. The admission fee was finally abolished, at the solicitation of the Government, from the end of April 1851, in view of the forthcoming opening of the Great Exhibition; the virgers were compensated from the Cathedral revenues by arrangement with the Ecclesiastical Commissioners.[2]

But the finest efforts of the witty Canon were reserved for his epic conflict with Government and the leading bishops over the establishment of the Ecclesiastical Commission. During the agitations over the Reform Bill in 1831 the Church had attracted profound unpopularity: the clergy were mainly Tories and the bishops had voted almost solid against the Bill. In 1832 the Bill was passed, and everybody was waiting to see what "the first revolutionary Parliament" (as Mr Keble pre-named it in October) would do to the Church which (Dr Arnold had remarked in June) "as it now stands no human power can save".[3] The bishops were so frightened that not one of them dared to run the gauntlet of the streets in order to attend St Paul's in May 1832 for the annual service of the Sons of the Clergy, and the dinner which was the usual sequel to the service had to be put off.[4] An Ecclesiastical Revenues Commission was appointed in June, chiefly through Peel's efforts, to inquire into pluralities, sinecures, and financial inequalities. It reported statistically in 1835, furnishing abundant material for study by the Ecclesiastical Commission, appointed by Peel earlier in the same year and heartily adopted by the Whigs who came into power in April.

[1] *Acta*, 93. [2] *Acta*, 189 f., 212 f.; *Acta B.*, 5.
[3] Liddon, *Life of Pusey*, I, 266; ibid., 225. [4] Russell, 39.

The latter Commission produced four reports in less than eighteen months. The third (May 1836) proposed the creation of a permanent executive body of Ecclesiastical Commissioners for England, a plan which was promptly passed into law. The fourth recommended a sweeping reorganization of the cathedrals and the appropriation of their surplus revenues (this specially hit St Paul's and Durham) in order to augment the number and resources of the parochial clergy. Canonries were to be suppressed all over the country to bring the establishment in each cathedral down to four; for minor canonries a maximum of six was set. Non-residentiary dignities and prebends were to be extinguished. The separate estates belonging to particular cathedral offices, and the entire property of minor canons (subject to provision for the future performance of choral services), were to be confiscated. The patronage of benefices in the gift of individual members of cathedral bodies was to be transferred to the bishops. All sorts of constitutional changes in the organization of cathedrals were bulldozed into the scheme. Though St Paul's and Lincoln had previously managed with only three canons (other than the Dean), a fourth canonry was to be created in each of these churches, and annexed to an archdeaconry, and placed in the gift of the Bishop: as both the Bishops concerned were members of the Commission, Sydney Smith had a perfect opening to exercise his wit on this diversion of large sums by the shepherds from the hungry sheep in order to magnify two of the Bishops' own officials.[1] Finally, when the Bill came out, it contained the provision that future deans and canons were to be limited to maximum stipends of £2000 and £1000 respectively.

The chief broom of all the lustral operations thus directed at the Augean ecclesiastical abuses of the time was Charles James Blomfield, Bishop of London since 1828, who had himself waded through pluralities to that throne. Once there, however, he laboured to reform others, though he himself

[1] *Singleton*, II, 232; III, 245.

retained in his own hands the entire income of the bishopric as it was before 1840, a fact that Sydney duly noted.[1] He was an incessantly active bishop, built nearly two hundred new churches in London, and took sufficient interest in his cathedral to hold his ordinations there each Trinitytide, instead of at Fulham Palace chapel.[2] His cathedral did not agree at all with his besom of reformation; in March 1840, when the Cathedrals Bill was before Parliament, Chapter formally resolved that in its opinion "the wisest plan would be to leave the Church as it is"; but if that could not be, the most that was desirable was a scheme for taxing "the various dignified preferments" on a variable scale "so as to raise an effective fund for the improvement of small livings".[3] Meantime Sydney Smith had expressed his own views in three inimitable open *Letters to Archdeacon Singleton*, published in 1837–9.

Sydney Smith was fully conscious that reforms were needed.[4] But he objected most strongly to the particularly destructive methods of reform proposed by the politicians under Blomfield's inspiration, methods conceived in a panic over the events of 1831 and 1832, all grounds for which had by now entirely disappeared. The Whig ministry was behaving "with the grossest injustice" to the Church, taking its cue from the "temporary delirium of archbishops and bishops", and delighted thus to score off "these eminent Conservatives".[5] The Ecclesiastical Commissioners, unreasonably frightened by the mob, had "allowed themselves to be hurried on by the constitutional impetuosity of one man" (Blomfield) "who cannot be brought to believe that wisdom often consists in leaving alone, standing still, and doing nothing".[6] No representative either of cathedral

[1] *D.E.C.H.*, "Blomfield"; Blomfield, *Memoir of Charles James Blomfield* (2nd ed. 1864), 15, 37, 49, 71, 274; cf. *Letter* 814 (p. 708).

[2] Russell, 31, 36, 39, 67.

[3] *Acta*, 85.

[4] E.g., *Letters* 751, 760, 780.

[5] *Singleton*, I, 206.

[6] Ibid., I, 204.

dignitaries or of the parochial clergy was included on the Commission.[1] The bishops were acting on the principle that "*Bishops can do no wrong, and cannot have too much power*";[2] though they were roughly equalizing their own incomes they were sacrificing nothing in the aggregate;[3] they were taking to themselves a lot of patronage belonging to the cathedrals, which there was no reason to infer, from experience, that they would exercise with better judgement, since "episcopal nepotism" was "notorious"[4] (the case of Belli illustrates the charge); in fact, as in the glorious (and spurious) history of the Synod of Dordrecht,[5] the Bishop Commissioners had cast their own dinner to the mob and were sitting down with great content to consume that of the deans and canons instead.

But, Sydney Smith inquired,[6] "is it necessary that the Archbishop of Canterbury should give feasts to Aristocratic London; and that the domestics of the Prelacy should stand with swords and bag-wigs round pig, and turkey, and venison, to defend, as it were, the Orthodox gastronome from the fierce Unitarian, the fell Baptist, and all the famished children of Dissent?" The picture of the opulence of Lambeth, based on an annual income of £15,000 which the see was to retain, presents a true sketch of the régime which ended with Howley; and The First Report of the Ecclesiastical Commissioners themselves bears out the basic idea that the Church was being made permanently safe for prelacy. "In considering the Incomes of the Archbishops and Bishops," states that Report,[7] "it is proper to advert . . . to the Expenses necessarily incurred in Journies for the Purposes of Confirmation, Consecration, and other Official Duties; in maintaining ancient and extensive Houses of Residence; in keeping Hospitality; and in contributing to all Objects connected with Religion and Charity, in a Manner suitable to their Station."

[1] Ibid., 169. [2] Ibid., 199. [3] Ibid., II, 226; III, 244 f.
[4] Ibid., 179, 194. [5] Ibid., I, 195 ff. [6] Ibid., II, 226.
[7] *E.C. First Report*, p. 10.

Moreover, there existed "a Burthen which presses heavily on newly-promoted Bishops, who are seldom Men of Wealth," in the "unavoidable Expenses attending their Appointment", calculated at a whole year's income at the least; nor does it seem to have occurred to the reforming Commissioners either that domestic fixtures should be purchased for the sees or that regal and legal blood-suckers should have their profits restricted in order to relieve the working Church from extortion.

Sydney Smith was strongly opposed to the principle of "centralization" embodied in the Commissioners' schemes, their disregard for local claims and feeling, and their taste for enforcing a "regulation pattern" on the cathedrals.[1] If the entire endowments of the Church were equally divided the money available would not nearly suffice to secure tolerable conditions for all the clergy,[2] he honestly believed (and there is substance in his argument) that it was better for some to be comfortable than, after a process of levelling out, for all to be left in equal and only slightly modified discomfort. Life in civilized and Christian England was something of a lottery. If a reasonable number of prizes were left, educated men would be tempted to bring their private capital into the ministry and thus endow the Church with their personal resources.[3] But he would not leave the prizes to be enjoyed without corresponding services rendered. The sinecure prebends should be attached to poor parishes in the neighbourhood of the estates from which their income was derived.[4] The stalls of residentiaries might similarly have annexed to them some large and populous parish near their cathedral. Alternatively, members of the Chapter might be given diocesan responsibilities, either individually, to superintend separate divisions of the diocese under the general control of the bishop, or collegiately, to take oversight of

[1] *Singleton*, I, 171, 177, 197 f.; II, 232. [2] Ibid., I., 172 f.; III, 249.
[3] Ibid., I., 173; III, 246 f.; cf. *Letter* 658. [4] Ibid., I, 171.

education throughout the diocese and for "a thousand useful purposes".[1]

So deep was Sydney Smith's conviction of the faults and dangers inherent in the official scheme of reform that in 1840 he presented a petition against the Bill to the House of Lords, and got it read to them,[2] reiterating at some length the arguments which he had previously addressed to the public. But his opponent was too tough a nut to be cracked by any practicable opposition. Milman, writing in 1841 [3] about "my worthy diocesan Charles James" and "the onslaught of Sydney", relates a most revealing incident. Blomfield had been having difficulty with a refractory Puseyite who quoted to him the authority of St Ambrose. "Sir," ran Blomfield's reply, "St Ambrose was not Bishop of London, and I am. Yours etc." Like some other great men, he was ruthless. So in spite of all Sydney's efforts and his serious attempts to suggest alternative remedies, he failed to get anything more than minor adjustments conceded, and the plans of the Commissioners passed into law in the Cathedrals Act, 1840. Sydney thought, as always, in terms of men and women, not, as the leading reformers thought, in terms of administration and moral government.[4] He had a passionate sympathy for the parochial clergy and their families. He prophesied that in the outcome the clergy would become "a collection of Beggars and Bishops—the Right Reverend Dives in the palace, and Lazarus in orders at the gate, doctored by dogs and comforted with crumbs".[5] He might have added that the spaniels were as likely to lick the hand of their episcopal patron as the sores of Lazarus. What the reformers wanted, and what in considerable measure they obtained, was a system of successful careerists in the dioceses, with £5000 a year, and extra for the princely bishoprics; climbers and pensioners in the cathedrals at a maximum of £1000, with

[1] Ibid., II, 222 f. [2] Holland, 325 ff. [3] Milman, 153 f.
[4] Cf. *Singleton*, II, 198; III, 248–50 and *passim*; *Letters* 945, 947, 965.
[5] *Singleton*, I, 180 f.

double for deans (in very few cathedrals was the maximum ever reached and in most it was nowhere near approached)[1] and pliable dependants in the parishes at anything from £130.[2]

To conclude his controversy with Blomfield Sydney delivered a delicately annihilating moral broadside in *The Times*, comparing his adversary's professions with his acquisitions. Blomfield had published a speech made in the House of Lords, in which he contrasted the number and endowments of the Cathedral clergy with the "most wretched state of destitution and neglect" of the population, numbering at least 300,000, whom he met while traversing the streets of London in an easterly and north-easterly direction from St Paul's. Suppose, said Sydney, that Blomfield in his "stroll in the metropolis" had turned about and crossed London Bridge, proceeding thence in a south-westerly direction, "to make your walk as impartial as possible". He would soon have perceived a vast palace at Lambeth, containing not a Chapter and prebendaries but one attenuated prelate, with an annual income for himself alone of £30,000, and £15,000 a year secured to his successors, though one-third of that sum would be ample provision for effectual discharge of the duties of the office. Restored by contemplation of this beautiful and consistent scene from the horror of spiritual destitution occasioned by the sight of St Paul's, he might then continue his religious promenade along the Thames, pausing for a few minutes' rest at his own palace in St James's Square, "no scene certainly of carnal and secular destitution". Resuming thence, he could reach his other palace of Fulham and refresh his animal spirits by reflecting on his own income of £20,000, "not a shilling legally given up during life to 'the masses who are living without God', and £10,000 per annum secured to the successor". Both Howley and Blomfield were generous and munificent men; but £2000 or £3000 given in subscriptions, though much more noticeable, was also much

[1] Cf. *Singleton*, III, 248. [2] Cf. *Whitaker's Almanacks*.

more economical than a fixed and legal diminution of income. Blomfield's feelings on the subject of spiritual destitution, added Sydney, "seem to be under the most perfect control when bishops are to be provided for, and of irresistible plenitude and power when prebends are to be destroyed".[1]

[1] *Letter* 814; *The Times,* 5 Sept. 1840.

3

THE ENERGY OF MR HALE

THE FIRST impact of the cathedral reformation on St Paul's came with the appointment by Blomfield of Archdeacon Hale to the newly created canonry. Hale was a typical "bishop's man" and a miniature of his master. He had been ordained in 1818 to a City parish and used to frequent the Cathedral. In 1821 he became Blomfield's assistant curate at St Botolph's, Bishopsgate. Two years later he was appointed Preacher of the Charterhouse; in the following year Blomfield became Bishop of Chester and made Hale his domestic and examining chaplain. Blomfield was translated to London in 1828; he was enthroned in January 1829, and appointed Hale a prebendary of St Paul's shortly afterwards.[1] It was a modest prebend that Hale acquired; but he still had his preachership at the Charterhouse, which included a house of residence, so he spent a whole day studying the Cathedral statutes, did quite a bit of preaching for absent residentiaries, fretted over the behaviour of the choir, and bided his time.[2] 1839 saw him Archdeacon of St Alban's, then part of the diocese of London; 1840 advanced him to the Archdeaconry of Middlesex and the new canonry; 1842 brought him the Archdeaconry of London and the Mastership of the Charterhouse, a comfortable supplement to his canonry. In 1847 he caused some surprise by claiming in addition the Cathedral living of St Giles', Cripplegate (canons could still hold one parochial benefice in plurality); he had to sustain a lawsuit in order to make good his right against the rival claims of the Sub-Dean, who was, as always at St Paul's, a minor canon. The benefice

[1] Russell, 20–9. [2] Russell, 31, 33 f., 36.

was worth £1700 a year (less cost of assistant curates) and he held it till 1857.[1] He died in 1870.

This indefatigable reformer continued to live at the Charterhouse; but for nine years his activities in the Cathedral were minute and unremitting, and his head was full of ideas. From his first appearance in Chapter, in December 1840, Hale made his personality felt in its affairs, as the now ageing Sydney Smith (afflicted with asthma and gout)[2] had done before him. He was deputed, alone or with some other residentiary, to correspond with the Ecclesiastical Commissioners and to draft a statement of the Cathedral revenues and establishments for submission to them,[3] to wrestle with the attendances and technical qualifications of choirmen, to index the records, to provide new matting for the floor of the choir, and to pull down the canons' coach-houses and stables in Amen Corner which were, after the fire in August 1848, reckoned to be "now totally useless".[4] Nothing was too small or too great for his attention. Before he had been three years a canon he was writing to the Dean that "during the period of your necessary absence from London you are pleased to look upon me, in a certain manner and degree, as supplying your place", and hinting not obscurely that he might perhaps usefully receive a formal appointment as Locum Tenens. Again and again Sydney Smith had to beg him to go slow and to exercise discretion in his interferences.[5]

But Hale was a good practical man of business and, living at the Charterhouse, lay within easy reach of the Cathedral. Sydney Smith therefore promptly turned over to him the whole care of the Fabric Fund, retaining in his own hands the management of the general Chapter fund: the one was

[1] Russell, 97; *Acta*, 256; Green, 11; cf. *Acta*, 370.
[2] E.g., *Letter* 813.
[3] *Acta*, 87, 113 *ad fin*. and ff.; cf. Russell, 87.
[4] *Acta*, 109, 122, 160, 167 and *passim*.
[5] Russell, 81 and *passim*; *Letters* 1027–30, 1036, 1037.

henceforth "your department", the other "my department".[1] Hale was in his element. He instantly proposed important developments in the system of gas-lighting.[2] That form of illumination had first been introduced into St Paul's experimentally in May 1822, and was continued through the following winter; the supply of gas was obtained from the City of London Gas Light and Coke Company. Pipes were laid from the crypt to "eight elegant pillars of gilt brass" in the choir, each furnished with three burners, with larger and yet more brilliant clusters attached to the altar rails. In 1834 Chapter agreed to an estimate of £34 "for fitting up the Gas apparatus". It seems that in the early days of gas-lighting private consumers grumbled about the price and quality of gas purveyed by the companies, and it was common for them to install their own apparatus in the basements of their houses; they usually returned to the companies' service after an interval, as their private mechanisms often ended with an explosion. St Paul's was thus only following common practice when it set up an indigenous and self-supporting supply: but no explosion, apparently, followed until 1859, when the Cathedral was back on company's mains.[3]

Sydney Smith had been enthusiastic over gas-lighting as early as 1820. But what Hale now wanted was something elaborate, involving mains and meters, such as he had had introduced at the Charterhouse. Sydney objected to such precipitate and costly improvements, though it is possible that a more modest request, to supersede candles with gas in the organ loft, may have been granted. It is worth noticing that gas was first installed in the dome area for the Duke of Wellington's funeral in 1852; and that, until his burial brought new hordes of visitors to the Cathedral underworld, the tomb of Nelson was shown by the ghostly light of a

[1] *Letter* 1028 *ad fin.*; Russell, 62; cf. 78. [2] Russell, 52, 56.

[3] *The Times*, 7 and 29 May 1822, 15 Oct. 1822; *Acta*, 12; Green, 15; private communication from Stirling Everard, Esq., author of *History of the Gas Light and Coke Company 1812–1949*; cf. *infra*, pp. 76–8.

lantern, which was handed down *ex officio* from virger to virger in a sort of demonic succession.[1]

Hale also laid plans at once for warming the Cathedral. Sydney Smith replied that "the only real way of doing it is to warm the County of Middlesex": but for once Sydney was wrong. Hale enclosed or glazed all the openings through which the atmosphere of Middlesex blew violently into St Paul's, and the first half of the battle was won.[2] He attacked the residual problem from a number of angles. There were two stoves under the choir, which Barham in 1839 induced a friendly expert to come and inspect, and on which Hale tried to improve. At one stage Hale is said to have caused a kind of wagon to be drawn about the floor, filled with red-hot coke.[3] The prosaic method finally prevailed over the spectacular, and Chapter discovered (apparently in 1858) that an adequate distribution of stoves throughout the crypt would secure the circulation of warm air, through gratings set in the floor, to all parts of the building. Improvements were effected in 1867, and again in 1871, since it was found that, in the process of refuelling, the stoves projected dust and smoke, as well as warmth, into the church. The temporary cast-iron gratings in the floor were replaced with bronze in 1881. A system of hot-water heating was introduced about 1909.[4]

Turning to homelier matters, we find Hale waging a relentless war on dirt. In 1841 he lime-washed the staircases and replaced the rusty iron rails which tore the ladies' shawls, and made the Morning Chapel "as clean as when Sir C. Wren built it".[5] In 1842 he closed the church for more than two months (in summer) in order to dust and paint choir and

[1] *Letters* 383, 1033; Russell, 70; *Acta*, 279; *Acta B.*, 35; Green, 5.

[2] Russell, 51, 60 (cf. *Hale MSS.*), 86, 93; *Letter* 1027.

[3] Barham, I, 90 f.; *Acta*, 124; Green, 14.

[4] Green, 14; *The Times*, 24 Nov. 1858, p. 8, col. 6; 27 Nov. 1858, p. 6, col. 6; *Acta*, 396; *Acta B.*, 72, 163, 189; *Acta C.*, 69; *Acta D.*, 226.

[5] Russell, 60, 70, 71.

transepts, walls and monuments. He closed it again in 1844, in spite of editorial protest in *The Times*, to clean the nave and dome below the Whispering Gallery;[1] perhaps we may also ascribe to his more austere sense of religious propriety the Chapter edict which went forth earlier in this year that "the clapping of doors in the Whispering Gallery for the purpose of shewing the effect of the Echo be discontinued".[2] In 1845 the western portico, with its pillars and frieze, was cleaned and painted on the orders of the Dean; Hale grudged the second coat of oil which the Surveyor applied to the stone-work.[3] But the effect was largely transient, because the Cathedral still possessed no adequate staff of regular cleaners. In 1868 the monuments were described as thick with grime: "black angels are conveying Ethiopian heroes to their long rest".[4]

The struggle of Chapter with the vicars-choral, in which Hale took a vigorous part, came to a head in 1844. According to traditional usage each new vicar had been admitted to his probationary year with the proviso that the appointment would not be made absolute if in the meantime he should "behave himself unworthy of the said office". At the end of his probation he took oaths of allegiance and canonical obedience and faithful execution of his office and was thereupon admitted to the office or place of vicar-choral "according to the statutes and laudable customs" of the Cathedral; and the Succentor was instructed to have him installed. But in 1832 a change had been introduced. In July of that year a probationary vicar was admitted to full status by a revised form, of which a draft has been preserved in the actual hand of Sydney Smith, who was in residence for the month.[5] The reference to admission according to the statutes and customs was omitted, and instead a phrase was inserted specifying admission to the office "and to the execution of the same according to the rules laid down, or hereafter to be laid down,

[1] Ibid., 77, 86. [2] *Acta*, 106; cf. *Plan*, 5. [3] Russell, 90.
[4] Sinclair, 307–8. [5] Cf. *supra*, p. 15.

by us the Dean and Chapter". Chapter was obviously trying to reduce the independence of the vicars and subject them to the rule of law, and that not merely a law already in being but one liable to future development. Moreover, a clause was added stating that Chapter reserved to itself the full right of removing the vicar from his post "if you shall prove yourself to be unworthy of holding the same". In fact the good-conduct clause appropriate to probationers was transferred to substantive vicars, who were thus put under perpetual probation.[1]

It is highly significant that in the year following this attempt to find means of enforcing discipline on the vicars a corresponding alteration was made in the form of admitting virgers. Both in 1833 and in 1839 new virgers were required to sign an undertaking to resign their office if called upon to do so by the Dean and Chapter.[2] This extension of authority over virgers forms part of a long and complicated story, of which it is convenient to postpone the detailed discussion.[3] It is sufficient for the moment to note that during Sydney Smith's early years as canon a serious effort was made to establish the right of Chapter to dismiss unsatisfactory subordinates, whether vicars or virgers, by a simple administrative act instead of a protracted and difficult legal process of deprivation. It is also both interesting and unexpected to find that no protest is recorded against Chapter's action, although, whatever may have been its real rights as against virgers, such limitations on the statutory position of the vicars would seem to have been of very doubtful legality. Nevertheless, for ten years successive vicars were admitted according to the form drafted by Sydney Smith.[4]

Chapter must have thought its *coup* completely successful, and ventured to take a step further. In February and March

[1] *Muniments*, VII, 62 (13 June 1831), 70 (9 July 1832); for the ancient form of admission cf. 46 and 70 (1829).

[2] *Muniments*, VII, 77 f., 129.

[3] See pp. 174 ff.

[4] *Muniments*, VII, 113 f. (28 May 1839), 145 (10 Feb. 1842).

Sydney Smith, Canon 1831–45

Charles James Blomfield, Bishop of London 1828–56

1843, two fresh probationary vicars were to be admitted, and in each case the appointment was made conditional upon the candidate's "consent to the terms which shall be proposed to him, which terms Mr Canon Hale will draw up".[1] The terms were stringent, and referred not to the probationary year but to the vicar's future status in the event of his being admitted to permanent office. The first rule made his employment subject to the pleasure of the Dean and Chapter and no longer. The second laid him under obligation to any statutes and regulations hereafter to be laid down. The third set him an age limit of 55, or earlier if Chapter considered him incapacitated for full and regular attendance. The fourth deprived him of that part of his emoluments which was paid by Chapter, amounting to £20 a year, and assigned it to a fund for providing a pension on his retirement. The fifth enacted that his post would be *ipso facto* vacated by his acceptance of any appointment, whether as principal or deputy, in any other church or choir. Both men were made to sign agreements to the above effect before they were admitted to their year of probation.[2]

The object of this new assault on the vested interests of vicars-choral was no longer, as in the previous decade, simply to render them amenable to due authority but to introduce a systematic reform of their status and obligations. It is important to observe that one of the new conditions of employment directly, and others indirectly, touched on the matter of their emoluments. As will shortly be described, the attempt on the liberties of vicars was part of a more general plan, largely if not wholly inspired by Hale, for effecting far-reaching reforms in the finance and administration of the Cathedral.[3] It was therefore not to be expected that the virgers should be exempt from the shears. Nor were they. When it fell to appoint a new virger, a few months after the new vicars, he not only had to promise to resign if called

[1] *Acta*, 96, 98. [2] *Muniments*, VII, 156 f. (16 and 29 March 1843).
[3] *Infra*, pp. 53 ff.

upon, as on previous occasions since 1833, but was admitted merely to such portion of the customary profits of his office as Chapter might from time to time determine.[1]

But in trying to apply a combination of reformer's logic and the big stick to vicars-choral, Hale had overreached himself. Both the new probationary vicars were indeed admitted to permanent office a year later in a form revised to accord with the agreements which they had signed. But the body of vicars-choral raised legal objections and Chapter was forced to give way. The agreements were set aside, the new regulations were suspended, and the new vicars were placed on the same footing as their older companions. A capitular olive branch was waved aside: when Chapter invited the vicars to frame regulations for their own good conduct and submit them for approval, as Hale had previously suggested in 1843,[2] the vicars "advisedly and most respectfully" declined to become parties to restricting their own freedom. Thereupon Hale and another canon were charged to inquire into the whole subject of vicars-choral and to report. The outcome appeared in 1847, when Chapter announced that future entrants would not be given a freehold of their office. In fact, this determination was not carried out, because the vicars threatened to refuse recognition to any newcomer accepting appointment on Chapter's proposed terms, and to withhold from him all payment of a dividend from their corporate funds.[3]

Chapter took Counsel's opinion, as a result of which Hale enjoyed the doubtful pleasure of admitting a new vicar according to the ancient forms, both to his probation and to full office: even the advance won in 1832 was lost. The only way left open for the regulation of the vicars-choral was by framing a new statute. Accordingly a statute was prepared, and formally confirmed by the Visitor in February 1848. It

[1] *Infra*, p. 179. [2] Russell, 79.

[3] *Muniments*, VII, 189 f. (9 April 1844); *Acta*, 106 f., 110 f., 140 f., 142–4.

laid down detailed conditions about attendance and deputies, and ordained that a weekly report on the vicars' compliance with the regulations should be presented to the Dean or the canon in residence. But nothing more was heard of abolishing the freehold; the only allusion to removal from office was in the warning that disobedience might be followed by suspension or deprivation—a constitutional rather than an arbitrary mode of dismissal.[1] Hale had long contended that the choir could be reduced to order only if continuity of administration were established; otherwise any gain made by an active canon in residence would be thrown away by the slackness of his successor. A Chapter meeting, formal and efficient, should be held every week, as required by the ancient statutes. Hale had indeed already succeeded in persuading Chapter to meet more frequently than had of late been customary.[2] But it was not until 1870 that a regular weekly meeting was restored.[3]

Another subject of incessant contention was the choir-school. The choristers were still in the care of Hawes at Adelphi Terrace; four probationers had by now been added, but were not boarded.[4] Apparently it was being alleged that their general education, on which they would depend for a future livelihood, was neglected. The Dean was anxious to take some action, and was with difficulty restrained until a full Chapter could be assembled; meantime, as early as December 1840, he talked the problem over with Hale.[5] Hale thought the real difficulties were that the boys had to spend so much time in Cathedral and that they wasted so much more in walking to and from Adelphi Terrace. He therefore proposed [6] in the first place that the number of the choristers should be doubled, twelve to sing at Mattins and twelve at Evensong; an arrangement could be made for the Chapel

[1] *Acta*, 145, 163 ff.; *Statt.*, 317 f.; *Muniments*, VII, 226 (19 July 1847), 230 (28 July 1848).

[2] Russell, 80 f., 88, 95.

[3] *Suppl.*, 3.

[4] Russell, 58, 65.

[5] Ibid., 52, 55, 57, 58.

[6] Ibid., 58 f.

Royal boys, who were only required on Sundays and festivals, to form the second choir for St Paul's: and in the second place, that the Almoner and his charges should be given domicile in the Chapter House; "it would be a pleasing sight to see the little fellows playing at taw and hoops in the great Western Court", which was at that period a cat-run considerably larger in extent than the present paved forecourt, enclosed with high railings, and in Hale's words "the most dreary and forbidding area in all London". Sydney Smith objected strongly to these suggestions: "pay them for their singing as is done in Westminster", and "pay to each parent a sum for the educating his own child".[1] At this point (March 1841) Hawes tendered his resignation; Chapter asked him to continue until Midsummer. On 4 May Mr Hale and Mr Smith (who was in London) were deputed to investigate means of boarding and educating the boys; six days later Hale had made several inquiries and was bursting with confidence; by the 17th it had become plain that Hawes must be asked to remain in office for another quarter; on the 24th Sydney Smith announced to Hale that Hawes wished to withdraw his resignation and that Chapter ought certainly to consent.[2] Hale had to content himself with improving the choristers' seats in choir, so that they could sit and kneel in a devout attitude.[3]

In 1845 Hawes was still Master of the Choristers.[4] But in that year Hale accomplished his dream and at Michaelmas the boys were transferred from Hawes' house to the Chapter House, where they were installed with a singing master, a grammar master, and a matron.[5] It seems that Hawes remained in remote control as Almoner; but in February 1846 he died. At once Hale was appointed Almoner, with instructions to devote the entire income of the office to "the

[1] Russell, 62; *Letter* 1029.

[2] *Acta*, 87, 90; Russell, 65, 68, cf. *Hale MSS.*; *Letter* 1031; Russell, 69; *Letter* 1032.

[3] Russell, 78. [4] *Acta*, 119. [5] Russell, 90.

maintenance and education of the choristers". All this implies that the boys were boarded.[1] However, the arrangement does not seem to have worked, since in 1848 the boarding scheme was abandoned. Instead Minor Canon Coward, a young man recently appointed, was given Hale's residentiary house at 1 Amen Corner for his own accommodation and the instruction of the choristers, but the boys were sent home to their parents to sleep.[2] The next thing that happened was a fire at No. 2 Amen Corner which caused considerable damage to all three of Wren's canonical houses, and probably accounted for the "uselessness" of the stables and coach-houses.[3] But with that, stability was achieved. Hale resigned the Almonership in 1853 and Coward succeeded him,[4] retaining office and duties till 1872, when the office was abolished and new provision was made for carrying out the duties. In 1859 the parents petitioned Chapter to provide their sons with a daily meal. Their request was granted in 1873, as a preliminary to the receipt of full board in the new Choir House then about to be erected.[5]

Hale as Almoner drew up a prospectus for the school dated 1849. Candidates for admission had to exhibit certificates of birth and baptism, and testimonials to the respectability and good conduct of their parents. The school consisted of eight choristers and four probationers. Annual allowances were made of £15 to the four senior choristers, £12 to the four juniors, and £5 4s. to the probationers. Each boy was paid 1d. a day pocket money and was provided with two surplices and all necessary school books. (A return made in 1853 shows that at that date each boy on leaving the school received also an apprenticing fee of £30 to provide training for future

[1] *Acta*, 130; Frost, 95; cf. *Suppl.*, 172 (the account there given is inaccurate in some details, and the statement that the boys went to the Charterhouse for lessons is erroneous, arising from confusion between Charterhouse and Chapter House).

[2] *Acta*, 167; Russell, 92; Frost, 95.

[3] *Acta*, 167; Russell, 100 f.

[4] *Acta*, 282.

[5] *Acta*, 402; *Acta B.*, 257.

employment.)[1] Attendance was required daily from 9.30 a.m. till 6 p.m., after which the boys returned home. They were to sing the services in Cathedral twice daily, spent three hours a day under the hand of the grammar master learning "the rudiments of Latin besides the usual Education in Arithmetic, &c.", and were taught music for an average of one and a half hours by the singing master. A total cessation from study was conceded during the four periods of vacation, at Christmas, Easter, Midsummer, and Michaelmas, but they still had to attend to sing in Cathedral "unless during a suspension of the Choral Service". Their allowances might be stopped if they arrived at school otherwise than clean and properly dressed; they would be dismissed if "from defect in natural ability or from want of industry" they failed to satisfy the music master that they were likely to be effective in choir, or if, however great their musical gift, the grammar master reported them as "of an evil disposition, disobedient, idle, using bad language, or incorrigible". Their faults would be punished, whether committed in or out of Cathedral, in such manner as their grammar master might find convenient, and according to the usual practice of schools. They were forbidden to sing anywhere else than in Cathedral without permission, and were finally reminded how valuable was their privilege of attendance on the service and praise of God in his house.[2] One of the children advanced from probationer to chorister in 1849 was John Stainer. Hale just failed to live long enough to see him organist of the Cathedral.

The care of the Cathedral fabric and the working of its various institutions did not, however, afford the only worries with which Hale had to grapple. There was also the problem of his own stipend. He was indeed a residentiary, being assigned two periods of residence of thirty-six days each (eighteen days from each of his fellow canons);[3] but except for the small sums which it was customary for absent canons to pay to their deputies and with which Chapter now agreed

[1] *Acta*, 249. [2] *Scrap Book*, 362 ff. [3] *Acta*, 89.

that its members should remunerate Hale, he was not paid. The reason is simple. Existing residentiaries had all their old rights of income assured them, and the most important part of their income came from the receipt of their several dividends or shares of the annual surplus in the common fund. So stringent was the right to a full dividend that in 1848, when Chapter paid for damage done to the canons' houses by the fire in Amen Corner, it also paid compensation to the Dean (the only pre-1840 canon then surviving) for the consequent diminution of his dividend, though actually Copleston returned the money.[1] If the new "fifth canon" had been paid out of the common fund, the statutable dividends of his brethren would have been diminished in proportion: and there was no other source of stipend available for him until a vacancy should occur in Chapter and the limitation of the new canon's stipend to £1000 should leave an unappropriated balance in the fund. Accordingly, on Blomfield's somewhat rueful advice, Hale retained his prebend until he should have profit of his canonry.[2]

Nevertheless, there was compensation. In February 1842 he was elevated from Preacher to Master of the Charterhouse, with a consequent increase in salary from £300 to £800 (with perquisites and allowances in both cases).[3] In the following August Sydney Smith, in sending him a cheque for residentiary duty done during July, took occasion to make certain observations on the propriety of a canon, who was also Master of the Charterhouse, accepting fees from his brother canons for duty which he was in any case bound to perform, paid or unpaid. Hale, whose sense of humour must be entered as a debit balance, returned the cheque with a note both pompous and curt, followed by a long and equally stuffy epistle devoted to searching his own soul and the Cathedral statutes. Sydney sent him back a fresh cheque, and by a combination of bluntness, high spirits, and adroit flattery induced him to accept it: "you can't have long to wait till the death

[1] *Acta*, 168, 181. [2] Russell, 50. [3] *Charterhouse Report*, 22 f.

of some of us old fools gives you those emoluments which you knew, upon accepting the preferment, were only contingent upon such an event"; "I have said my say, and am silent, and have done with the subject."[1]

In the following November Hale succeeded to the Archdeaconry of London: this helped to clear up part of the complications attendant upon his position in the Cathedral, since the emoluments of the new canonry were meant to be shared, unequally in the proportion of two-thirds to one-third, between the Archdeacons of London and Middlesex, but the seat in Chapter was really intended for the Archdeacon of London.[2] In February 1843 Chapter voted him a "voluntary payment" of £40 a year as residentiary.[3] Later in the year Canon Tate died, a surplus arose in the common fund, and Hale received his "first ecclesiastical revenues",[4] though he seems not to have resigned his prebend until 1846. An interesting contingency ensued. Hale and the newly appointed canon were each assigned their full three months of residence, leaving only six months to be divided between the three seniors. On the next death of a canon the process was repeated, leaving the two seniors only six weeks each to fill.[5] Presumably when the third of the pre-1840 canons died, in 1847, the Dean was entirely relieved of any further duties as residentiary; but history seems not to have recorded what arrangement was actually reached.

Meantime the finances of St Paul's were involved in preternatural complexity. The simple way of dealing with cathedral estates after the reform would have been for the Ecclesiastical Commissioners to take them all over, and pay out to the holders of life interests an agreed average of their

[1] *Hale MSS.*; *Letters* 1034, 1035.

[2] Order in Council, 25 Jan. 1841, referred to in Preamble of Archdeaconry of London (Additional Endowment) Act, 1897.

[3] *Acta*, 96.

[4] Russell, 84 (Russell himself fails to understand the allusion).

[5] *Acta*, 108, 113.

previous profits, while newly appointed residentiaries received stipends in accordance with the Cathedrals Act. This was not done nor, at the beginning, even intended. Instead, the cathedrals continued to manage their own properties while accounting to the Commissioners for the profits, and the Commissioners became a kind of sleeping partner in the several cathedral establishments. Thus at St Paul's the old canons paid themselves in the old manner; canons appointed after the passage of the Act were subject to the statutory limitations; and the surplus was due to the Commissioners. To sort matters out, in some degree, the Commissioners prepared a scheme, by which a proportion of the net revenues should be transferred to themselves.

The Cathedral had its own answer to the situation thus confronting it, and early in 1845 Hale prepared for Chapter a long memorandum on the establishments and expenditure of the Cathedral, for submission to the Commissioners; he himself appeared personally before them to expound it. The gist of this communication was that Chapter strongly wished to place the emoluments of the minor canons, vicars-choral, and virgers (hitherto derived from variable and haphazard sources) on a secure and regular footing, and to double the number of the choirmen, since the existing six could not possibly be expected to attend twice daily throughout the year. These projects, in their judgement, would more than absorb all the surplus income arising through the recent demise of two pre-1840 residentiaries. They therefore prayed the Commissioners to let them devote the surplus of their income to these pressing reforms, rather than pay it over to the Commission.[1] Manifestly the hopes now entertained by Chapter of putting stipends and salaries on a rational basis were associated with its efforts during the previous two years to introduce a revision of the terms of employment both of virgers and of vicars-choral.[2] The parties concerned were to be subjected to limitations and conditions of various kinds

[1] *Acta*, 113–21; Russell, 87. [2] *Supra*, pp. 43 ff.

simply in order to prepare the way for a comprehensive scheme, which would both make them stipendiaries in the same way as members of Chapter had been made stipendiaries by Blomfield and the Church reformers of 1840, and would also put them more directly under Chapter's command. Chapter was now asking the Commissioners to grant it the use of what had been its own money in order to bring its scheme into operation.

The principal author of the whole project clearly was that ingenious physician of other people's ailments, Archdeacon Hale. No less clearly, Sydney Smith had disliked and opposed the proposals in detail. The earlier measures of control, imposed on prospective vicars and virgers in 1832 and 1833, had only been aimed at simplifying the procedure for dismissing unsatisfactory subordinates; they had not touched the profits of the offices. But Hale, from the first moment of his entry into Chapter, had been agitating plans involving interference with finance. In December 1840 he had proposed to double the number of the choristers, and had shortly afterwards fallen foul of the Almoner who had charge of the boys.[1] He had asked, in February 1841, that Chapter should "grapple boldly" with the distribution of the profits derived from showing visitors the cupola, and Sydney had replied with a warning against raising "insurrection" from the minor canons, who drew much of their income from that source.[2]

Early in 1843 he had drafted a stiff set of regulations for new vicars-choral, and imposed indefinite restrictions on the emoluments of new virgers,[3] thrown out in the course of a letter to Copleston, that the existing minor canons and the vicars-choral "should themselves be brought to suggest regulations for their own government, and only require the Chapter to give authority to such regulations".[4] The last proposal certainly did not bear upon their salaries directly, but illustrates Hale's anxiety to introduce systematic reforms

[1] *Supra*, pp. 47 f.
[2] Russell, 60, 62; *Letter* 1029.
[3] *Supra*, p. 45.
[4] Russell, 79.

which in current circumstances were bound to involve finance before they were completed. Tate died in September 1843. By November Hale was bringing forward a plan to enlarge the choir—presumably the singing men—and a note in his diary for the early part of 1844 reveals that he hoped to pay for doubling the existing number out of the surplus revenue of Tate's stall: the idea does not seem to have occurred to him that the surplus might belong in law to the Ecclesiastical Commissioners. Sydney Smith told Hale that he would resist, if necessary in the law-courts, any increase of the choir that might be attempted at the expense of canonical dividends, and that in any case the plan could not be realized without dragging into public controversy the extremely disagreeable question of the cupola money. Hale commented grimly in his diary that "Sydney Smith is quite impracticable".[1] Nevertheless, Sydney was old and sick, and it was Hale's ideas that prevailed in Chapter's memorandum to the Commissioners.

Incidentally, that document discloses that the Dean's Virger received £13 14s. 6d. a year from capitular funds and the three junior virgers £7 14s. 2¾d. each. Chapter wished to give them fixed salaries of £130 and £100 respectively, and at the same time, no doubt, to abolish their pecuniary interest in the fees for showing the cupola. In addition to the four virgers the staff at this date consisted of two "labourers", of whom one was organ-blower at £40 19s. (to be raised to £50), the other bell-ringer at £33 (also to be raised to £50); one "library-keeper", who on £8 a year, which Chapter suggested augmenting to £20, was presumably a part-time worker; and three "Sunday attendants", paid £11 a year, which Chapter proposed to double. Some further facts can be added from other sources. Visitors to the crypt and also to the ball were conducted by the virgers, whose perquisite it was to retain the fees charged, or by an assistant provided and paid by themselves; one such assistant served his

[1] Russell, 83, 85; *Letter* 1036.

employers from 1809 to 1856 and was buried in the crypt. Visitors to the "cupola" (including the library, the geometrical staircase, the model-room, the whispering gallery, and the two outside galleries above and below the dome but, strangely, not the ball) were conducted by four attendants appointed and paid by the minor canons and vicars-choral acting jointly. Members of the two bodies concerned in the management had been in the habit of dividing the proceeds monthly among themselves (with a share to the virgers for showing the upper regions) in proportion to their recorded attendances in choir; this fact explains why Hale found in 1841 that the attendances in the summer months were exemplary and the choir was virtually deserted in winter, when sightseers were few. It must be reckoned to the credit of the minor canons that in 1842 they had decided to make the distribution every six months, in January and July.[1]

The Chapter's plea for means to finance a substantial reformation of these astonishing arrangements fell, unhappily, on deaf ears: it is more than doubtful whether the Commissioners possessed legal power to consent. The reform should have come earlier. Hale had wanted it, even at some expense to the dividends; but Sydney Smith had opposed him vigorously, and his resolute defence of full canonical rights to dividend in defiance of capitular duties towards the Cathedral establishment argues a singularly blind spot in his mental outlook. An Order in Council was made in August 1845 which fixed temporarily what proportion of the profits of each of the old canonries (as they fell vacant) should be paid over to the Commission; when all the old residentiaries were extinct seven twenty-seconds of the net divisible revenues were to be transferred to the Commissioners, and of the remainder one-third became payable to the Dean and one-sixth to the holders of each canonry. It was reckoned that this arrangement would leave about £2000 to the Dean

[1] *Acta*, 115, 404; Russell, 60, 83; *S.C.N.M.*, qu. 174, 301, 309–16, 336; Green, 8; *minor canons' minutes*, 15 April 1842.

and £1000 to a canon. In practice the amount available for distribution sometimes slightly exceeded the estimated sums, though on occasion it fell somewhat short.[1]

The old Chapter was dissolving rapidly. Sydney Smith, to whom St Paul's owed so great strength and inspiration, died in February 1845. Blomberg, who is not recorded as present at any Chapter meeting after the end of 1844, died in March 1847. Last of all died Copleston, who also deserved well of St Paul's, in October 1849. And with him died the *ancien régime*.

[1] *Acta*, 284, 386; *Acta B.*, 52.

4

PROBLEMS OF ADMINISTRATION

THE APPOINTMENT of the new Dean, Henry Hart Milman, intimated an extraordinarily happy choice of man for the post. He linked the immediate past of the Cathedral to its imminent future with a felicity to which few others, if indeed any, could have approached. While yet at Oxford he had graduated as poet by taking the Newdigate in 1812, and writing a tragedy, *Fazio*, which held the boards for years; he was still able to enjoy the satisfaction of attending a distinguished revival of it in 1856 after he had become Dean.[1] Ordained in 1816, he was almost immediately given the living of St Mary, Reading, then a country town of fewer than ten thousand inhabitants; he owed this preferment to the fact that his father was physician to the King and a trusted adviser of Queen Charlotte.[2] Here he made fame and money (so strange was the taste of his day) by a series of long poems; was elected Professor of Poetry at Oxford and held the chair from 1821 to 1831, John Keble postponing his own candidature in order to avoid a contest; attached himself to the staff of the *Quarterly Review*; published a striking sermon on the office of a Christian teacher; and wrote *The History of the Jews* (1829), which created nation-wide scandal by making the Old Testament interesting and referring to the patriarch Abraham as a "sheikh". One result of this theological indiscretion was that when Melbourne was considering him for a bishopric the serious-minded Blomfield put a rigid spoke in Milman's wheel.[3]

Nevertheless, in 1835, when an able priest was needed to take charge of the enormous and unspeakably degraded

[1] Milman, 33 ff. [2] Ibid., 52, 54. [3] Ibid., 56 ff., 83 ff., 167.

parish of St Margaret, Westminster (which then extended into Kensington Gardens),[1] Peel selected Milman. The rectory of St Margaret's had previously been the joint responsibility of the Dean and Chapter of Westminster, who had usually discharged their responsibility by delegating the cure to one of their own number. The Church Commissioners had just recommended that the rectory should be permanently annexed to one particular stall in the Abbey, which happened to be vacant;[2] and apparently by arrangement with the Dean and Chapter the chance was taken to bring the proposal into force at once, without waiting for legislation. So after eighteen years in Reading Milman came to Westminster, where he threw himself into the work of slum clearance [3] and parochial reorganization, while yet finding time to maintain his literary output (happily in vivid and entertaining prose), and to indulge his gift for social life and fashionable friends. In early manhood he had enjoyed the friendship of John Keble and of Mrs Siddons. Now he revelled in the society of Sydney Smith and his circle, and was intimate with people like Arnold and Macaulay, Lyell the geologist, Motley and Prescott the American historians, A. P. Stanley and J. A. Froude. Milman's was not a very subtle or theologically profound mind; but his intuition was acute, his breadth of vision exceptional, and his intellectual honesty complete. In many ways he recalls Sydney Smith, presenting some correspondence alike in profile and career, sharing his character of literary parson with a strong bent for practical reform, exhibiting that worldly realism which strangely elevates fervour above fanaticism, and displaying a great capacity for business.

Milman was appointed Dean on 13 November 1849, a month after Copleston's death. He was reluctant to prolong even this interregnum; but as he had "a kind of fancy to close the ecclesiastical year as canon of Westminster", he

[1] Milman, 138. [2] *E.C. First Report*, 11.
[3] *R.C.I.M.*, qu. 92–143; Milman, 139 ff.

postponed his installation until 30 November,[1] and presided at his first Chapter on 3 December. He had been selected for St Paul's, as he was informed by Lord John Russell, expressly with a view to "the measures of reform and improvement which are needed in that cathedral", in particular to the problem of regulating the admission of the public in a more satisfactory manner.[2] His first utterance on receiving the offer had been "Thank goodness! No more vestries!" Now he would be able to devote himself with less interruption to completing the great work on the *History of Latin Christianity*, on which he was engaged.[3] Nevertheless, his experience as Treasurer of the Abbey, with charge of the fabric, was to prove invaluable to the Cathedral over which he was now called to preside. In sober fact, he conceived the design and roughed in the outlines of all that was to be accomplished later by the efforts of Gregory and Church.

The immediate effect of Milman's advent as working and resident Dean was to end the informal system by which first Sydney Smith and then Hale had taken virtual charge of Cathedral business: Milman himself assumed the controls. Hale continued to be useful on occasions, especially in dealing with big questions of finance and administration; but in the conduct of day-to-day affairs he suffered inevitable eclipse.[4] In his relegation he gave signal proofs of medieval scholarship, publishing a very thorough study of the manorial property of St Paul's in the twelfth and thirteenth centuries, and other fruits of research. Moreover, the larger sphere of London public life remained open to him. In October 1852 it was proposed to open the Crystal Palace (on its removal from Hyde Park to Sydenham) on Sunday afternoons, and *The Times* made merry with a meeting of protest in which Hale evidently bore a large part: "it was confidently asserted . . . that even if the practice of Sunday morning service continued, the few worshippers would be outraged on coming

[1] Russell, 102.
[2] Milman, 232.
[3] Milman, 168.
[4] Cf. Russell, 103.

out of church by seeing streams of cabs rush by to the station; that the Crystal Palace . . . would be surrounded by an *enceinte* of gin palaces, in which the thirsty multitude, after a short visit to the Palace, would spend the remainder of the day; late at night 50,000 intoxicated wretches would return shouting and quarrelling to the metropolis, the aspect of which would be anything rather than what a Christian metropolis ought to wear on a Sunday." It was decided to dispatch an address on the subject to the Prime Minister by the hands of "a numerous and influential deputation, consisting of the Archdeacon of London, a Canon of St Paul's, the Master of the Charterhouse, the Vicar of St Giles', Cripplegate, and several other dignitaries".[1] As readers of *The Times* were doubtless well aware, names and persons of all the dignitaries specified were united in the individuality of Hale.

Apart from Hale, almost all the other canons who served under Milman were primarily parish priests, and far better known as such than for the fame of their Cathedral activities. J. E. Tyler had been Fellow of Oriel for sixteen years and thus well known to Copleston, and had then held the large London parish of St Giles-in-the-Fields from 1826; he was canon from 1845 to 1851, when death removed him both from St Paul's and from the parish, which he had continued to hold together with his canonry. H. M. Villiers, an extreme Evangelical, was Rector of St George's, Bloomsbury, from 1841. He worked his big parish ably and energetically; from 1847 he also combined it with a canonry of St Paul's; in 1856 he was made Bishop of Carlisle. Another parish priest who, when appointed to St Paul's in 1851, retained his parish in plurality was W. W. Champneys, a notable pioneer in educational and social work, a pious pamphleteer, and pastor of over 30,000 souls in Whitechapel. He exchanged Whitechapel for St Pancras, a Chapter living, in 1860, and became Dean of Lichfield in 1868.

[1] *The Times*, 30 Oct. 1852.

Thomas Dale (1845–70) was Vicar of St Bride's, Fleet Street, which he exchanged for St Pancras in 1846; in 1860, when he left St Pancras for another well-endowed but less exacting Chapter living at Therfield in Hertfordshire, the ancient parish was subdivided into no fewer than twenty districts, a significant (though posthumous) fruit of the forward policy of Bishop Blomfield. Dale was nominated to the deanery of Rochester in 1870, but died before he had time to settle in. He had published some seventy works, mainly of a homiletic character. Henry Melvill (1856–71), unlike his colleagues, was always pre-eminently a preacher rather than a pastor; for many years he enjoyed the reputation of being the most popular pulpit orator in London, thus ranking on either hand with Sydney Smith and Liddon. He is described as a master of ornate rhetoric. His sermons usually lasted for forty-five minutes, but were so rapidly delivered that they would have lasted for a whole hour on any less mobile lips. He was Rector of Barnes from 1863 onwards.[1] It was the recognized procedure for canons of St Paul's to occupy large (and well-paid) parishes in London and to reside regularly on their benefices;[2] their residentiary houses in Amen Corner were either bestowed on minor canons and others, or reserved for the emergency of Cathedral duty.

Not much anxiety was occasioned by the general state of the Cathedral fabric. Cockerell, the Surveyor, who had held office since 1819, resigned some time after making his annual report in March 1852. He was succeeded by F. C. Penrose, an exceptionally gifted architect who had rowed three years for Cambridge, invented the system of charting bumps in College races, was a distinguished amateur astronomer, and in 1847 had proved once and for all that the Parthenon was built, not in straight lines, but in delicately modulated geometrical curves: the results of this investigation were

[1] *D.N.B.* for all the above canons.

[2] *Acta*, 261 (answers to the Cathedral Commission, 1853).

published in 1851.[1] Cracks had been noticed in the exterior masonry of St Paul's in 1852, and again in the southern supports of the dome in 1859; these were filled with "a peculiar cement", and showed no evidence of further movement. Additional precautions were taken against the risk of fire in the dome: more water tanks and apparatus were installed in the galleries, and in order to secure rapid access the seventy different keys previously required to open communicating doors throughout the Cathedral were replaced by some twenty subordinate and three master keys.[2]

In December 1867 Irish sympathizers tried to rescue two Fenians confined in Clerkenwell Prison, by blowing up the wall with gunpowder. The explosion caused great alarm at St Paul's, and fresh measures were put in hand to minimize the dangers of incendiarism: the old wooden staircase inside the dome was taken out and an iron staircase was substituted; the bellows of the organ, situated in the crypt, were also covered with wire-netting as a protection against possible inflammatory missiles.[3] For the rest, repairs were executed on the lead-work of roofs and dome, and to the glazing; it was acknowledged that funds did not permit of doing as much as was desirable for the stone-work.[4] It is pleasant to record that on the occasion of the marriage of the Prince of Wales, in 1863, the cupola was illuminated, in some manner that involved the use of outside scaffolding and so enabled the ball and cross to be regilded.[5]

Unlike most other bodies associated with the Cathedral, the old prebendaries had followed pretty much the advice given by St John Baptist to the military—they attempted no violent exertion and were content with their wages. But their wages had now been taken away and were being paid to the Ecclesiastical Commissioners; and their successors showed signs of unrest. Twelve prebendaries, supported by the

[1] *Penrose.*
[2] *Acta*, 329, 367, 394, 407, 416.
[3] *Acta B.*, 72, 84.
[4] *Acta*, 368; *Acta B.*, 85, 164.
[5] *Acta B.*, 45.

Treasurer and the Chancellor, claimed in 1853 that they should have a voice in the deliberations of Chapter, and in particular that they should be summoned to the election of proctors to represent Chapter in Convocation. They appealed for justice to the Bishop as Visitor. Chapter, after taking Counsel's opinion, replied that the Great Officers had never possessed such rights, and that any such membership of Chapter as had been enjoyed by former prebendaries had been extinguished by the Cathedrals Act of 1840. The Visitor apparently decided against the claimants. In 1856 Bishop Blomfield brought his long, far-sighted, and energetic administration to a close and resigned the see; Chapter took elaborate legal advice as to the right of prebendaries to assist in the election of a new Bishop, with results again apparently adverse to the prebendaries. By 1867 legal proceedings had been instituted by the prebendaries in order to enforce their claims, and on appeal they obtained a decision in their favour from the Court of Exchequer Chamber. Accordingly, at the next election of a proctor, in 1868, they were summoned to Chapter—and solemnly protested that according to ancient right the four residentiary canons, no longer being prebendaries, were ineligible to vote. They repeated their protest at the election of a new Bishop in the following January; on both occasions they submitted to being overruled, though without prejudice to future claims.[1]

Another tremendous controversy, involving appeal to the Visitor and the assistance of learned Counsel, was raised by the minor canons in 1850 and lingered on for more than four years. The old procedure was that when a vacancy occurred in the College the minor canons themselves should select two candidates for the post, and Chapter should appoint one of those two. They now claimed to exercise that privilege; but the Dean and Chapter maintained that the Cathedrals Act of 1840 (which was so wantonly destructive of ancient

[1] *Acta*, 266 ff., 366; *Acta B.*, 70, 75 f., 77 f.

constitutional procedure) had transferred unfettered right of choice to themselves. The minor canons appear to have forgotten a fact recorded in their own minutes: in 1841 they had formally recognized that the Act deprived them of the right of nominating new members of the College and transferred it to Chapter. Chapter now disregarded their claim. Nevertheless, by the merest accident, "without regard to the nomination of the minor canons", Chapter appointed one of their candidates.[1] Thereupon two of the senior members of College launched an appeal to the Visitor, asserting that for long years past the residentiaries had been feathering their own nests while continuing to pay the minor canons virtually at the same rate as had obtained under Henry VIII, that they took the best Cathedral livings for themselves and had latterly shown both meanness and partiality in providing benefices for minor canons, and that since 1840 they had illegally maintained the number of minor canons at twelve, so making College unwilling partners in their illegalities.

These unkind cuts penetrated uncomfortably near the bone. Chapter, however, was able to reply that the Cathedral Act had been so drafted as to make it impossible to interfere with the constitution of the College, a royal foundation incorporated under charter, without further legislation. The complainants seemed to have wanted to secure two principal objects: a reduction in the numbers of the minor canons, which would leave fewer members to divide the common fund, and a fair apportionment of Cathedral livings. On the other hand, Chapter repeatedly expressed the view that twelve part-time minor canons were none too many to maintain an adequate performance of the Cathedral services. In 1854 the Visitor gave sentence. He dismissed the rest of the appeal, but directed Chapter to prepare a scheme for the fair disposal of Cathedral benefices. A plan was therefore drawn up and embodied in a new draft statute, the Bishop

[1] *Acta*, 202, 207 f., 209, 296 f.; *minor canons' minutes*, 11 June 1841.

signified his consent, and the statute was confirmed by Order in Council in February 1855.[1]

In the very next year another minor canonry fell vacant. Milman wrote a letter to the College, explaining that, though Chapter was bound to exercise the right of appointment imposed on it by Act of Parliament, it had not the slightest wish to nominate a person unacceptable to the body of minor canons, and would therefore value the assistance they could give by recommending someone qualified by character, conduct, and musical attainments for the post. College conducted voice trials of the applicants, and again presented two candidates in the ancient form for Chapter to select one. Again, with the magnanimity of victors, Chapter appointed one of those thus nominated, "without regard to the nomination of the minor canons". On the next vacancy, in 1859, Milman asked the College to select the two most eligible names from the list of candidates, without prejudice to the right of Chapter to appoint at its discretion. College readily complied with the request by nominating in the ancient form. A working agreement had now been reached. When another vacancy occurred, in 1860, Chapter merely invited the College "to take the usual steps for filling up the vacant minor canonry"; and at the only other election that took place before the constitution of the College was remodelled by the St Paul's Cathedral, London, Minor Canonries Act of 1875, the same procedure was observed.[2] The hatchet was buried; the pipe of peace was smoked. When a scheme for reorganization and union of City parishes was undertaken in 1861, Chapter gave its support to objections raised by College and secured the amendment of the scheme in the interests of the minor canons.[3]

The only solution to the interminable scandal of minor

[1] *Acta*, 231–40, 285–302, 326 f., 331–9; cf. 248, 261 f.; *Statt.*, 371 ff.

[2] *Minor canons' minutes*, 23 Oct. 1856, 11 Nov. 1856, 11 Jan. 1859, 10 Feb. 1859, 7 Dec. 1860, 17 Jan. 1862; *Acta*, 369 f.

[3] *Acta B.*, 20–5.

canons' stipends, as of the payment of virgers and vicars-choral, lay in the reform of the Cupola Fund; moreover Chapter was well aware that without reasonable stipends it was hopeless to expect loyalty and discipline. Accordingly, one of Milman's first acts, in February 1850, was to approach the Ecclesiastical Commissioners with a renewal of the appeal for help which had been made in 1845.[1] Congregations were large, and Chapter was already considering means of extending the accommodation provided for them. But nothing effective could be done to encourage worshippers unless Chapter could secure and pay more choirmen. If the Commissioners would render at least temporary aid, the vicars-choral were willing to surrender their corporate estates; and these, under new management, should be capable of such improvement as to produce ultimately sufficient revenue to provide an adequate choir of men. Secondly, Chapter thought nothing could be more objectionable than the long-standing system of paying virgers, guides, vicars-choral, and minor canons by letting them control and enjoy the receipts from visitors' fees. But Chapter could neither abolish the twopenny entrance fee to the Cathedral nor assume responsibility for the Cupola Fund unless it could obtain means of compensating all those sections of the Cathedral staff whose incomes depended mainly on such fees. The Commissioners were reminded that they had recently come into possession of all the separate estates of the deanery; and "the Dean and Chapter are strongly of opinion that there is a prior and undoubted claim on all the revenues of the church for the celebration of divine service in a manner befitting the metropolitan cathedral, and for the decent maintenance of the servants of the church".[2]

Nothing was done about the Cupola Fund. But with the Great Exhibition drawing near, pressure was being exerted "in high quarters" to get the entrance fee to the church remitted; and in April 1851 the Commissioners proposed terms.

[1] *Supra*, p. 53. [2] *Acta*, 188 ff.

They offered no restitution of the plunder of the prebends, which indeed they had no legal power to restore; but they were ready to permit that £400 for the four virgers and not more than £200 for an increase of choirmen should be deducted from the Commissioners' share of the net revenues of the Cathedral. In return they made two conditions: the twopenny entrance fee must be abolished, and Chapter must agree to measures for improving the estates of the vicars-choral, or alternatively to vesting them in the Commissioners in consideration of an annual cash payment. To all this Chapter assented. The charge for admission was immediately cancelled, and in the following year the choir was doubled, on Sundays only, by the engagement of six assistant choirmen. Another of Hale's dreams had come true.[1] But nothing whatever appears to have been done by Cathedral or Commissioners to initiate improvements in the estates of the choir.

By 1859 the Commissioners were doing very well out of the endowments of St Paul's, and untold benefit was being conferred on the whole Church of England as a consequence of their enrichment. The separate estates of the Dean, the Chancellor and twenty-seven of the thirty prebendaries had already fallen into their hands, and a few of these estates were extremely valuable: the richest prebend, that of Finsbury, alone had been so much improved as to be producing £7000 a year at that date, and was expected to produce ten times that income when the existing lease expired; it was said to be bringing in £67,000 annually in 1872:[2] Chapter, on the other hand, was involved in fresh expense for the popular Sunday evening services which had recently been inaugurated, and was as anxious as ever to take the Cupola Fund under its own direct control and to get rid of the abuses associated with it. It therefore appealed once more to the Commissioners, inviting them to pay the cost of the special

[1] *Acta*, 212 f., 263; Russell, 85.

[2] Gregory (quoted in *Cathedral Decoration*, p. 13).

services, and adding for their consideration a composite and ingenious proposal which bears evident traces of Milman's mind and plans. Would the Commissioners charge their own share of the net cathedral revenues with the cost of compensating minor canons, vicars-choral, and virgers for the loss of their several rights in the Cupola Fund, in the same way as they had already granted £600 to extinguish entrance fees and to enlarge the choir? If so, Chapter would take over the administration of that fund, employ more numerous and responsible guides (as was in the highest degree desirable), pay for the special services out of the profits, and employ any balance, under the superintendence of the Trustees of the Fabric Fund, "in the much wanted ornamentation of the sacred edifice".[1]

The generosity of the Commissioners could not, unhappily, be stretched so far. They replied that they had no legal power to finance the special services. Thereupon Chapter withdrew its request; and it was agreed that the expenses should be met from the corporate funds before division of the surplus, so that, in effect, the Commissioners would bear seven twenty-seconds of the cost and the rest would be deducted from the personal incomes of the Dean and canons.[2] And in May 1860 a heavier blow fell. On receiving Chapter's appeal for the special services, the Commissioners had been led to examine the extent of their legal powers and to consult the recently appointed Government auditor, who proceeded to disallow the agreed payment of £600 which had now been made for nine years.

The terms of the concession granted in 1851 really implied that a fresh valuation should be made of the Cathedral's resources and a new proportion of the divisible surplus should be defined as between Chapter and the Commissioners: but this, like so many other things which ought to have been done, never had been done. Chapter now therefore had to take its choice between revaluation and agreement to share

[1] *Acta*, 402–6. [2] *Acta*, 414 f.

the payments with the Commissioners in the existing proportion. In deep disappointment and indignation it chose the latter course.[1] The motive probably was that the revenues were rising somewhat,[2] and it was hoped that canonical incomes could bear the necessary reduction without bringing them down in fact to their theoretical level of £1000. Deans and canons of St Paul's appointed after 1853 had, by an Order in Council of that year, had their incomes fixed at £2000 and £1000 precisely, the Commissioners undertaking to make up the full stipend if a deficiency occurred in the dividend, and themselves appropriating any excess; and there was already one canon in that category, bringing additional confusion into the intricate capitular accounts. But the senior members of the Chapter still drew their dividends under the financial settlement of 1845; though offered the choice of voluntary adhesion to the terms of 1853, they rather significantly declined the option.[3]

The objection to the system of paying wages and stipends out of fees was not merely that the management was out of Chapter control, but that the amount accruing from the fees varied largely from season to season and from one year to another. Thus, in 1851, the year of the Great Exhibition in Hyde Park, the Cupola Fund probably derived large sums from tourists. In 1852 receipts certainly slumped. The fashion set in International Exhibitions was followed in 1855 by one staged at Paris, and in 1862 by another, at South Kensington: in that year receipts from exhibiting the cupola and the crypt (with Wellington's tomb on show in the crypt since 1858 and his funeral car since 1861) were large, and led to bitter recrimination on the part of the vicars-choral against the virgers.

A twenty-second share of the Cupola Fund for the six months from May to October, 1862, was said to be worth £120; twelve such shares were divided among the minor

[1] *Acta B.*, 2–11.

[2] Cf. *Acta B.*, 49–52, with *Acta*, 283 f.

[3] *Acta B.*, 7–8, cf. 52.

canons, six among the vicars-choral (in each case proportionately to their attendances), and one share went to each of the four virgers. But in addition, each virger received for the same period £50 as his regular allowance in compensation for the twopenny entrance fees, and also a fourth part of the fees for showing the crypt, estimated by the indignant vicars-choral at £750 per man, and admitted by Chapter to be large, though "very much below" £750. (The virgers returned them at less than £300 net per man for the whole year.) The fixed salary of a vicar-choral, on the other hand, was £21 for a whole year (together with a further £15 in lieu of Sunday dinner), and the fluctuating supplement which he derived from his common fund only averaged about £65. But the sole redress obtained by the vicars for the unfair consequence of the new attractions in "the vaults" was an order that in future a weekly return should be made of takings in the crypt, Chapter reserving the right to dispose of them on such objects as it thought fit. So the virgers' fleeces were clipped but the vicars-choral derived no warmth from the wool; and in the following year the average share of each vicar from the Cupola Fund dropped from about £150 to little more than £30.[1]

The Cathedral was involved in another practical difficulty in the management of its finances. Its property was largely let on leases for twenty-one or forty years, at a very small annual "reserved rent"; most of the income derived from it came in the form of "fines" paid once in seven or once in fourteen years on granting an extension of the leases. Much of the property was ripe for development, which would greatly increase the income. But development could not be undertaken until the leases had been allowed to run out; and if the leases were not extended no fines would be payable for renewal and the Cathedral would be deprived, for the time being, of the revenue required to pay the stipends to its staff.

[1] *Acta B.*, 33–6, 59–65; cf. Green, 23.

Out of this labyrinth of coagulated financial and administrative quagmire only one path now seemed to open. For some years a number of Deans and Chapters, beginning with York in 1852, had agreed with the Commissioners to vest their property in the Commissioners in return for a fixed annual payment of equivalent value in money. In 1858 the long-lived Treasurer of St Paul's had commuted certain estates included in the endowment of his office for a cash payment from the Commissioners of £4500.[1] Accordingly, in 1863, Hale and the Chapter Clerk were given the task of drawing up a preliminary statement of "items of charge" on the Cathedral resources, "with the view ultimately of proposing to the Ecclesiastical Commissioners the relinquishment to them of the Chapter estates and revenues". Some progress had been made with this work when it was discovered that doubts existed (but not in the minds of the Commissioners) whether they had legal power to enter into such arrangements. The plan was therefore postponed, and nothing came of it at the moment.[2] By 1868, however, the doubts had stretched to the minds of the Commissioners, and they procured two Acts of Parliament. The first, passed in May, was a short measure validating a large number of agreements into which they had already entered. The second, the Ecclesiastical Commission Act of July 1868, was a more comprehensive measure, which included provisions for the commutation of cathedral property, by agreement, for a consideration in money, and also for the payment, as part of such consideration, of capital sums for repairs, restoration, and improvements. A road was thus compacted for decisive progress under new auspices.

[1] Order in Council, 11 June 1858.
[2] *Acta B.*, 44, 46 f.

5

THE INVENTION OF DR MILMAN

DURING a period of domestic reconstruction it was unavoidable that problems of a business character should occupy uncommon attention from the authorities of the Cathedral. Meantime St Paul's was also playing its part in the life of the nation. In November 1849 it observed the Day of Thanksgiving (Thursday) for the cessation of the cholera epidemic; the collections, taken partly at the offertory and partly at the doors, exceeded £37.[1] In 1854 the first Sunday in October was observed with a Thanksgiving Service for the plentiful harvest. There followed in March 1855 the Day of Humiliation (Wednesday) for the Crimean War with Russia, declared a year before, and the Day of Thanksgiving (Sunday) in May 1856 to celebrate the ensuing peace, succeeded in June by a display of fireworks in the parks which the Dean and Charles Dickens watched from the Golden Gallery at 11 p.m. Next year saw the outbreak of the Indian Mutiny and a Day of Humiliation on Wednesday 7 October; the corresponding Thanksgiving took place (under the dome) on Sunday 1 May 1859. In the following month the remains of Sir Thomas Picton, who forty-four years earlier had been wounded at Quatre Bras and killed two days afterwards at Waterloo, were brought to St Paul's on a gun carriage from the cemetery at Bayswater and deposited in the crypt. The Sunday after the death of the Prince Consort, in December 1861, brought vast crowds to hear funeral sermons, Milman preaching himself in the morning; the choir of the church was draped for the occasion with black cloth, edged with white. Another Day of Humiliation,

[1] *Acta,* 180.

this time for the cattle plague, was kept on Tuesday 20 March 1866: the Bishop of London (Tait) drew a crowded congregation to St Paul's in the afternoon. It is regrettable to have to record that the special service previously held each autumn on September 2, to commemorate the Fire of London, was discontinued after 1858.[1]

The most colossal religious spectacle, however, that was staged in St Paul's at this or any other period of its existence was the funeral of the Duke of Wellington, on 18 November 1852. The Duke died on 14 September. In due course it was determined that his funeral should be held in St Paul's, and Milman, who as a schoolboy had witnessed the funeral of Nelson, was summoned to a Council at Windsor to discuss with the Prince Consort and the Prime Minister the manner of burying Wellington. At Milman's suggestion it was decided that the obsequies should centre, not in the choir, like Nelson's, but under the dome.[2] Rather late in the day, on 18 October, workmen were sent by the Office of Woods and Forests to start preparations in the Cathedral; during the last week in October and throughout November all services were discontinued.[3]

Immense works had to be completed in a short time. In the end the job was scarcely done. Virger Green and his colleagues "were in the Cathedral all night previous, and in the morning the workers had to be driven out; some of the fittings were scarcely finished when the doors were opened to admit the people at 8 a.m., and many of those had been waiting in their carriages outside from 6 a.m." The clergy and choir prepared to go in procession to the west doors shortly after 11; there was nearly an hour's delay in removing the coffin from the funeral car to the bier; the weather was raw and cold, the wind blowing frigidly through the open doors; and Bishop Blomfield caught an inflammation in his eyes which seriously affected his sight for the next four

[1] Green, 4, 7 f., 12, 15, 21, 29.
[2] *Acta*, 274. [3] *Preachers Book.*

months.[1] Milman had had a fearful time for the final three days in the general scramble to beat the clock, having "to settle and balance affairs with the Woods and Forests, the Lord Chamberlain, Garter King-at-Arms, the Lord Mayor, and City Police".[2]

Tiers of temporary galleries had been erected in the nave, transepts, and even against the choir-screen. Seats were thus provided for 13,000 people; the Government disposed of 10,000 sittings, 3000 being reserved for the Dean and Chapter, who had to find accommodation, among others, for all the officers and representatives of the City. The peers and Oxford University sat to the south; members of the Commons and Cambridge University to the north. Vocal music was supplied by eighty men and forty boys drawn from the choirs of St Paul's, the Abbey, the Chapel Royal, and other cathedrals; they all wore mourning scarves and were supported by another forty professional singers, together with instrumental performers, stationed in the organ gallery. The service was the Prayer Book burial office; Milman read the lesson. The whole church was lined in every part with heavy black cloth, which, incidentally, explains why the Dean's voice could be heard everywhere, since the galleries and hangings stifled the Cathedral's normal twelve-second reverberation. The black cloth was the locus of a mare's nest. On such occasions the authorities of a church were wont to claim as their perquisite all the cloth provided for funeral decoration. Gentlemen signing themselves "Laicus" wrote to *The Times* some weeks before the funeral and accused the Chapter of profiteering on the accessories of the burial. But the Dean and Chapter had already agreed to forgo any possible claim on the timber, black cloth, or fittings brought into the Cathedral; they were able to state that neither they nor any member of the Cathedral body would reap pecuniary gain from the proceedings.

It had been intended to exclude all natural light from the

[1] Green, 1 ff. [2] Milman, 179.

church. Although, owing to the haste with which the preparations were concluded, this design was only imperfectly realized, the effect was profoundly impressive: lines of artificial lights traced out the main features of the architecture, and a corona of gas-jets running under the Whispering Gallery encircled and illuminated the dome area. After all was over, the Government issued tickets for the public to inspect the arrangements and the lighting at certain hours of the day, but showed no sympathy towards a request forwarded by the minor canons and the vicars-choral that they should be compensated for loss of cupola money during the weeks that the Cathedral had been closed. The two bodies represented to the Chief Commissioner of Works that the fees for showing the cupola provided a very substantial part of the income with which their services to the Cathedral were remunerated. But they got a very dusty answer. The Chief Commissioner observed in reply that Her Majesty's Government could not be expected to take upon itself the costs of maintaining the daily service, "for which *the Cathedral was originally endowed*", and added that in view of recent efforts to have the cathedrals thrown open freely to all classes he felt "specially bound not to recognise *the objectionable system* upon which the Memorialists have based their claim to compensation". Since entrance fees to the Cathedral had been abolished more than a year before, and most of its endowments had been confiscated, this attack was magnificently unfair.[1] The Government did, however, make a generous offer to the Cathedral to leave the whole of the gas fittings in place. After consulting the fire insurance offices Chapter decided that it would not be safe to retain for permanent use more than the fittings of the corona round the dome.

The subject of the lighting of St Paul's is wrapped in general obscurity, but some few details emerge. The Cathedral was once more taking its supply of gas from the City

[1] *Acta*, 241, 274 ff., 279, 295 f.; Milman, 234 ff.

St Paul's Cathedral from the South, c. 1842

Richard Harris Barham, Minor Canon 1822–45

Robert Russell Green, Dean's Virger 1871–99

Gas Company by 1852; the Company's Committee of Management rested on that fact an unsuccessful application for cards of admission "to be present in the Cathedral to witness the funeral solemnities of the interment of the remains of His Grace the late Duke of Wellington". During the year ending March 1859 the Surveyor notes "some additions to the gas standards in the choir and an improvement to the supply of the gas". Alas for scientific novelty! The next recorded fact is that on Saturday, 4 June 1859, in the words of Virger Green, "the large gasmeter in the crypt exploded; it was fixed in the carpenter's shop, poor old Stubbs had a narrow escape". A fuller account of the mishap was given in the *Journal of Gas Lighting*. Stubbs was occupied in doing something unspecified to the meter when, "from a cause which is unexplained, an explosion took place, by the force of which the thick metal plates of which the front of the meter was composed were rent in pieces, and some of them hurled to a considerable distance. A solid timber bench, used by the carpenters in the employ of the Cathedral authorities, was shivered to pieces." Fortunately for themselves, all the workmen who would normally have been employed about the scene, except Stubbs, were away at dinner when the explosion occurred; Stubbs was saved from death by the circumstance that the back of the meter, where he was working, withstood the force of the eruption with all its plates intact.[1]

Another certain fact is that the construction of the Wellington chamber, containing the actual tomb of the Duke, involved the importation of gaslight into the crypt. New burners were fitted in 1870 to the corona round the dome, which was giving delight to the great congregations at the special services on Sunday evenings. During the next year the experiment seems to have been tried of lighting the nave by means of two "corona candelabras" (*sic*): no record is preserved of the result, but gas standards were installed in

[1] Records of City Gas Company, November 1852; *Journal of Gas Lighting*, 21 June 1859; *Acta*, 408; Green, 15.

the nave during 1878.[1] Apparently until these improvements were introduced the nave was without any modern system of artificial lighting. After some previous and unsatisfactory experiments with electricity the whole Cathedral was fitted with electric light in 1902 by the munificent gift of Mr J. P. Morgan, the American financier.

When the funeral rites had been completed the Duke's coffin had been deposited on the tomb of Nelson, and there left. In the following May, 1853, Chapter wrote a strong letter to the Office of Woods and Forests, pressing that the work of interment should be promptly completed "so far at least as the immediate commission of the coffin to the ground". Chapter was having other troubles at the very same time over the presence of human remains in the crypt. Ever since 1757 the parishioners of St Augustine and St Faith had had the right of using the north-east aisle of the Cathedral crypt as a burying-place. Chapter complained to the church-wardens that the pavement needed repair, and asked that two large heaps of human bones and mould should be removed. As full satisfaction was not obtained, and dirt was being scattered over the whole crypt, Chapter secured the closure of the burying-place by Order in Council in the following October. In November the Duke's coffin was "removed from off Nelson" and presumably interred. But it was not until April 1858 that the sarcophagus of Cornish porphyry was ready and the remains were finally deposited therein. By August all the work was completed in the Wellington and Nelson chambers, and the public was readmitted to inspect them—for some time free of charge on Mondays, Thursdays, and Saturdays. Three years later the funeral car (which weighed twelve tons, took twelve horses to draw, and was entirely constructed in three weeks) was re-erected, complete with model horses, in the crypt, towards the eastern part of the nave. The state of the horses became so decayed that they were removed in 1871. In 1878 the whole nave of

[1] *Acta B.*, 35, 136, 161; *Acta C.*, 17; Sumner, 19.

the crypt was cleared of the lumber which had previously been stored there, and the car itself was moved to its western extremity.[1]

Yet even this was not the end. In 1856 Palmerston, then Prime Minister, had brought Prince Albert to St Paul's to consider sites for a monument to be erected to the Duke. Two years later, the entombment in the crypt being now accomplished, formal consent was asked and given for the appropriation of the south-west chapel, then used for the Bishop's Consistory Court, to the destined monument. The chosen sculptor, Alfred Stevens, wanted to place it under the middle arch in the north arcade of the nave (where it now stands), but Milman and others, not without weighty reasons, favoured the chapel. Stevens laboured with adoring procrastination at the monument; he was no man of business; storms blew up in Parliament and press over the delay. In 1870 he was deprived of his contract, but as nobody else could well have finished off his work he had to be re-engaged, under fresh conditions and controls. Next, in 1875 he died. But only the last touches remained to be given; at long last the fine monument stood complete, and in April 1878 the public was admitted to see it. In 1892, through the energy and liberality of Lord Leighton, P.R.A., the sum of £2000 was provided to move it into the nave.[2] The sculptor's full design was only perfected in 1912 when an equestrian statue of the Duke was placed on the summit of the monument.

Milman was extremely quick to perceive how usefully the empty spaces might be employed for popular services. On 4 February 1850, only two months after his installation, he secured the approval of Chapter to a memorandum which he himself had drafted, in which reference is made to enlarging

[1] Green, 3, 12; *Acta*, 265, 329, 395; *Acta B.*, 29, 181, 195; *Illustrated London News*, 27 Nov. 1852; Sinclair, 475.

[2] Green, 8, 141; *Acta*, 399 f.; Milman, 305 f.; Sinclair, 351; *Cathedral Decoration Min.*, 3 Feb. 1912.

the accommodation available for the numerous worshippers in the Cathedral. During the Great Exhibition of 1851 a two-manual organ was erected in the west gallery, and stood there for six months; *The Times* announced that on 22 June Evensong would be transferred to the nave, though the arrangement was "temporary and experimental". It seems to have been repeated only a few times. Consideration was still being given to the problem of increased congregations in 1853. In the following year some expenditure was incurred in making arrangements to hold divine service under the dome, but no details are given of the result. Then at the end of 1856 Tait became Bishop of London and immediately agitated the Chapters both of St Paul's and of Westminster to fill their ample vacancies with people.[1]

The Cathedral was not unwilling. The main difficulty was that the performance of additional services and the handling of large masses of people cost money which, in the state of its finances then obtaining, the Cathedral did not possess: the reformers of 1840 had not foreseen a situation of this kind when they were confiscating cathedral revenues as "surplus". However, Milman conferred with the Bishop, and Tait lent his support to the appeal opened in 1858 for the double object of decorating St Paul's and adapting it to the use of vast congregations. Virger Green had noted in January 1858 that Westminster had started Sunday evening services in the nave of the Abbey, thus testifying to the interest felt at the Cathedral in the experiment; and in November, on the first Sunday in Advent, was held the first of a similar series at St Paul's. Two thousand five hundred chairs were packed in for the service, which was held under the dome, and the floor was covered with matting (removed in 1877);[2] Tait preached; Ludgate Hill was blocked; and a sensational number of

[1] *Acta*, 183, 188, 264, 353; Gregory, 199; Sumner, 18 n.; *The Times*, 21 June 1851, 29 Nov. 1858 (leader).

[2] *The Times*, 27 Nov. 1858; Sinclair, 475.

persons, variously reckoned at anything from 10,000 to 100,000, failed to win an entrance. Already, earlier in the month, Tait had delivered his primary charge under the dome; it lasted for four hours and twenty minutes. The "special" services were discontinued at Easter; but thenceforward in every year a fresh series began each January and ran until Easter or after; while he lived and was in health Milman usually read the lessons himself, and by distinct enunciation made himself astonishingly well heard. It seems that alms-boxes made their first appearance in St Paul's in 1859, when they were provided in order to receive voluntary contributions towards the cost of these special services.[1]

Another consequence of the Sunday evening services was the institution of the small but valuable and eager society of the Wandsmen of St Paul's. The need for a body of responsible persons to control the crowds inside the church on those occasions was obvious; the situation lay far outside the capacities of the official virgers. Accordingly in 1861 the Wandsmen were called into existence, taking their title from the wands of office with which they were originally armed. The organization was at first informal. In 1879, however, the revived Saturday Chapter is found considering a proposed set of "rules for the gentlemen who act as Cathedral Wandsmen"; the rules were discussed with the Wandsmen themselves, and agreed to. Thereupon the Wandsmen met in formal session and elected a secretary. Two years later Chapter decided to supply members of the society with ribbons and bronze badges, to be worn on duty. Like most other officials of St Paul's, the Wandsmen were long lived; one of the original band, "whose service dated from the year 1861", continued to act until his death in 1913; another served from 1864 to 1923. From 1877 these voluntary workers, together with their colleagues of the special service choir, have been

[1] *Acta*, 385, 402; Green, 12 f. and *passim*; Elliott-Binns, *Religion in the Victorian Era*, 424 f., 432 f.; Milman, 236.

entertained to dinner by Chapter once a year after the patronal festival.[1]

At the same time as he had on his mind the reform of the administration, the problem of the finances, and the task of applying the church more fully to the purpose of worship, Milman was also cherishing the strange idea of beautifying it; he had had the intention already definitely in view when he secured the appointment of Penrose as Surveyor in 1852. The first-fruits of this design took the form of a restoration of Sir James Thornhill's frescoes on the underside of the dome, begun in 1853 and completed in 1856; the artist employed was E. T. Parris, a facile painter of panoramas and female portraits. During 1858 a committee was formed, in association with the Dean and Chapter, "for assisting them in the special evening services and in the embellishment of the interior of the Cathedral", and the "St Paul's Cathedral Fund" was established to carry out their plans. Curtains were hung at the entrance doors of both transepts; windows were renewed in the drum of the dome, and its interior wall and the great cornice below it were gilded; in 1861 the Corporation of London gave £750 to gild the roof of the choir; in 1864 and 1866 mosaics were inserted in two of the eight spandrels of the dome (Isaiah and St Matthew). Individual benefactions were attracted also: in 1867 an aged bookseller, Mr Brown, presented stained glass for the great west window, and during the next two years other windows were given by the Drapers' and the Goldsmiths' Companies. In its first four years, from 1858 to 1862, the Fund raised £12,000 and spent £13,000; a "National Guinea Subscription" was instituted in 1865; by October 1868 the totals had risen to £25,000.[2]

[1] *Min.*, 24 May 1879, 7 June 1879, 24 Dec. 1881, 2 Aug. 1913; records of the society.

[2] *Penrose*, 343; *Acta*, 329, 384, 408, 417; *Acta B.*, 31, 56, 85, 115 f.; Green, 8, 26, 30, 31; *D.N.B.*, "Parris"; *Scrap Book*, 26–8; summary of accounts 1858–68 in *Scrap Book*, 33.

This large sum, however, was by no means expended wholly on decoration and repairs. Embellishment and increased accommodation went inseparably together in all Milman's plans for the Cathedral. Oddly enough it was the organ which afforded the occasion for immense developments in both these directions. Modifications had been introduced into the instrument by the organ-builder, J. C. Bishop, both in 1826 and again in 1849. In 1852 some unspecified "contrivances" were added which proved both unsightly in appearance and inconvenient in action. In May 1859 it was decided to spend £1000 on enlarging and improving the organ, and the Chapter obtained a grant from the Trustees of the Fabric Fund to cover half the cost. Work was begun, in September, on taking down the organ. Everybody concerned was thrilled by the "central vista" thus partly opened to view, and vaster schemes were soon afoot. By November discussions were in progress, in collaboration with the Committee of the St Paul's Cathedral Fund, for transferring the organ permanently to the middle archway on the north side of the choir; a drawing by Sir Christopher Wren had been discovered which showed it in that position, though no proof was forthcoming to decide whether the drawing was evidence for Wren's preferring or discarding that arrangement. As corollaries to this design the existing very solid choir-screen was to be removed; a new and open screen was to be erected nearer the dome than the old (it will be remembered that the choir-stalls in their old position enclosed only two of the three bays of the structural choir); and the easternmost stalls were to be moved westwards into the newly enclosed bay, so providing space for more worshippers at the choir services. For the time being, the stalls of the dignitaries, which had faced east from beneath the organ-screen and were displaced by its removal, were laid by in storage.[1]

[1] Sumner, 17 f.; *Acta*, 408–10, 412–14, 417 f.; Green, 16; Sinclair, 419; cf. *infra*, p. 94.

All these changes had been adopted and formally approved by January 1860. Here was reconstruction of radical character and importance. But ideas were still expanding. On 1 June Hale was writing to Penrose to advocate "the erection of a splendid Baldachino [i.e., canopy] or other structure which might remedy the great defect of the Cathedral, the termination of the Vista in the present bald Apse"; that was what (he seems to suggest) Sir Charles Barry would have wished.[1] Unluckily Sir Charles, the brilliant architect of the Palace of Westminster, who served on the executive committee of the Cathedral Fund, had just died and could no longer speak for himself. This interesting proposal anticipated by nearly thirty years the erection of Bodley's reredos, and by about ninety the final decision to replace the reredos with a baldachino.

Other events moved more rapidly. The choir-screen had already been taken down in May, the daily services being suspended for five days.[2] From Monday 2 July until Saturday 1 December services were transferred entirely to Christ Church, Newgate Street, in the immediate neighbourhood of the Cathedral, while major alterations were effected.[3] In the first place the organ was shifted to its new site. But since space was strictly limited underneath the arch, little addition could be made to the instrument. Instead, a second and larger organ was purchased from the Panopticon of Science and Art in Leicester Square at the knock-down price of £1050. The Panopticon was a queer edifice in the "Moorish" style of architecture, opened some seven or eight years previously for the improvement of the British public, and resembling in aim and appearance a cross between a Polytechnic and the Albert Hall. It did not prove a success, and was turned into a theatre.[4] The organ was re-erected on a gallery at the far end of the south transept of St Paul's; its case was rejected as being somewhat secular in tone, and the case of the old choir organ was employed as a screen to veil its technical anatomy.

[1] *Hale MSS.* [2] Green, 17. [3] *Preachers Book*; Green, 17 f.
[4] Thornbury and Walford, *Old and New London*, III, 169.

This instrument was known as the "great organ" as distinct from the "choir organ". Its performance was inaugurated on St Paul's day, 25 January 1861, with a grand recital of the *Messiah*; Sims Reeves, the famous tenor, was one of the soloists in the augmented choir. Unhappily Milman himself was absent through serious illness.

Thereafter the "great organ" was employed to accompany the special services held under the dome, particularly on Sunday evenings, when a large voluntary choir (including both men and women) was recruited to lead the singing. Members of this choir sat in the transept on a semicircular platform and were conducted by a vicar-choral from an elevated "box", placed between transept and dome. If it may be assumed that the arrangements followed those of the inaugural service, the congregation under the dome faced not eastwards into the choir but southwards into the transept; they are plainly so depicted in the drawing with which the *Illustrated London News* accompanied its report of the proceedings on St Paul's day. The effect, according to a report made in 1871, was "rather that of a concert room than of a place of worship". The pulpit was set originally against the eastern pier of the arch between dome and transept, just inside the circle of the dome; the new marble pulpit promised in response to the embellishment appeal of 1858 backed on the next pier, between the Dean's aisle and the choir, and there remained. From January 1873, after Goss had been succeeded as organist by Stainer, the Sunday evening special services were made continuous throughout the year and the singers were transferred from the transept to the reconstructed choir of the church. The Sunday evening choir also was reorganized. Women were no longer included, the number of men was reduced, and no boys were retained except the Cathedral choristers. The "great organ" was sold as redundant.[1]

[1] Sumner, 19 f.; Green, 19, 36; *Acta B.*, 29, 45, 242; Sinclair, 316, 321; Frost, 12 f., 46, 81; *Scrap Book*, 8, 68, 128.

Certain consequential adjustments followed on the alterations made in 1860. Before that date the minor canons had sat in the sub-stalls in line with the vicars-choral. They were now placed in the upper stalls behind the other singers; and the vicars, who seem previously to have occupied the middle block of the choir (as shown in a plan preserved in the Cathedral library) now found themselves, since the drift of the stalls to westward, in the eastern section of the stalls. On the mechanical side, Chapter introduced a hydraulic apparatus for blowing the choir organ; its motive power was derived from a cistern in the roof of the south choir-aisle containing 3000 gallons of water. The changes in and about the choir organ were unlucky. First of all, the position of the key-board was most awkward and the mechanism worked too stiffly; in 1863, therefore, the organ was transferred to the charge of "Father" Henry Willis, who spent four months in reconstructing it, daily service being held meantime in the north-west chapel. Then the hydraulic machinery was found inadequate to the task of supplying air to the reconstructed organ, and in 1866 a new and improved engine was obtained, the old having proved, according to Penrose's exasperated report, "a source of perpetual trouble, annoyance and expence". Readjustments were still in progress during 1868, and left the engine still unsatisfactory; but in the end Willis and the hydraulic engineer between them made it work with less irregularity, until in 1879 it was replaced with a gas-engine, which was itself supplanted by electricity in 1920. Between 1866 and 1868 a good deal of money was also spent on the substructure and casing of the great organ in the transept; six monolith marble columns, nearly 17 feet long, were procured to support the burden of the instrument. These enterprising experiments, which were all superseded within a very few years, were costly, and constant appeal had to be made to the Trustees of the Fabric Fund to help defray the expense.[1]

[1] *Acta*, 416–18; *Acta B.*, 45, 53 f., 67, 68, 72 f., 84, 114 *et al.*; *Acta C.*, 19, 30; Sumner, 19, 20; Green, 18, 24 f., 154.

Nevertheless, under Milman the Cathedral was able to display some generosity towards others. Chapter minutes show that a favourable response was frequently forthcoming to appeals for financial assistance in restoring or enlarging churches in which the Cathedral had an interest; in 1857 a definite policy was instituted for contributing such sums as could be spared to aid in the erection and maintenance of Church schools in parishes where St Paul's owned property. Renewed attention was also paid once more to the neglected library. In 1853 the library was believed to contain about 8000 volumes, many of which bore evident signs of incipient disintegration when they came to be examined nine years later. In 1862 reform began with the appointment of William Sparrow Simpson as Librarian, with an annual grant of £20 to spend on the books.

Simpson was a most devout priest and a meticulous student of antiquities, who had become minor canon twelve months earlier. He remained Librarian till his death in 1897. In the interval he had had some 3400 volumes bound and had increased the number of items to 21,000, not by indiscriminate purchase of publications which were equally accessible elsewhere, but by concentrating mainly upon the history of the Cathedral and the diocese; though not till 1872 was the library grant increased to £100 a year. Like Barham before him, Simpson spent long days of personal application in the library itself; he both catalogued its contents, and studied them. In 1869 he received additional responsibility as honorary librarian of Lambeth Palace Library, and started a new catalogue of its printed books. In 1872 he was the obvious scholar to choose for the task of collecting and editing the statutes of St Paul's; till then much of the statutes had been preserved only in a single manuscript, and the rest lay scattered in detached documents or buried in different books belonging to various great libraries. The results of his admirable research were embodied in an immense volume, erudite and indispensable, which was privately printed and appeared in 1873, to be followed by a supplement of later material in 1897; he lived just long enough to revise the proofs of the supplement.[1]

On the same level as the library but on the opposite side of the church was the Model Room, now known as the Trophy Room, containing the model, equally enormous and exquisite, which Wren made of his own favourite design for the new Cathedral in the form of a Greek cross. The right of exhibiting this beautiful specimen of craftsmanship belonged to the managers of the Cupola Fund, the minor canons, and vicars-choral, who claimed in 1862 to have spent £100 "some years back" in repairing it; but it was in so bad a state of repair in 1857 that Chapter accepted a proposal made by the South Kensington Museum for dealing with it. The Museum engaged itself to restore the model without charge and to return it to St Paul's at the end of three years, if so required. Meantime Chapter seems to have regarded the loan as permanent, since it promptly agreed to lend the Model Room to the Government for storing the wills filed in the Prerogative Court of Canterbury, which had just been abolished by statute. The wills were hurriedly removed in 1871 when, in order to regain possession of the Trophy Room, Chapter threatened to charge the Government a rent of not less than £500 per annum.

Nothing more is heard of the model until 1870, when the Museum, being pressed for space, suggested its deposit in the new East London Museum. Chapter requested its immediate return to the Cathedral. The Museum, which in thirteen years had only effected partial reparations, then offered to complete the repairs on condition of keeping it on exhibition for another ten years at South Kensington; and to this solution Chapter consented.[2] About the same time another model by Wren, of the upper portico of the west front of St

[1] *Acta*, 255; *Acta B.*, 30, 32, 231, 239, 264; Simpson, 39 ff., 48, 62 ff.
[2] *Acta*, 396 (cf. 391 f.); *Acta B.*, 35, 145–8, 198, 207 f.; *D.E.C.H.* 157, 160 (*sub* "Courts").

Paul's, came back into the possession of the Cathedral. It had apparently been acquired by the clerk of the works when the Cathedral was finished, and by him been carried off to his native Shiplake; it subsequently came into the hands of the vicar and churchwardens of the place, who now presented it to the Dean and Chapter. The incident affords an interesting illustration of the ease with which important properties could be alienated, though in this instance with an exceptionally fortunate outcome.[1]

In the immediate vicinity of St Paul's great improvements were taking place. In 1860 and 1861 the City Corporation was engaged in obtaining powers to close Newgate Market (between Newgate Street and Paternoster Row) and so relieve the neighbourhood of the manifold obstructions and nuisances associated with its existence. In exchange a new Meat Market was planned in Smithfield, though it was not completed until 1888; beside the spot where London used to burn its martyrs it now distributes frozen meat. The Cathedral was interested to the extent of securing adequate compensation for loss of its own and its tenants' rights, while glad enough to be rid of the slaughterhouses. It was perhaps in connection with plans for the redevelopment of the neighbourhood that Chapter decided in 1862 to decline a proposal that it should sell the residentiary houses in Amen Corner.

Nuisances seem to have weighed heavy on the Chapter at this period. Complaint was made in the same year of a nuisance arising from the melting of tallow at a candle factory in Paternoster Row; improvements were effected, with Cathedral assistance, in order to abate the danger of fire to contiguous Cathedral property; a serious fire had broken out among the tallow melters in the previous autumn.[2] Then there were demands for draining and fencing at Barnes Common. The Dean and Chapter, though lords of the manor, saw no reason why they should pay for work which they considered to be the obligation of the commoners; besides,

[1] *Acta B.*, 115.   [2] *Acta B.*, 13–19, 27, 29, 32; Green, 21.

encroachments were persistent, and the local gipsies used "the most blasphemous and immoral language". In 1867 Chapter agreed to co-operate with "the respectable inhabitants" in suppressing the races held on Royston Heath, near Therfield, another Cathedral manor; gipsies are not mentioned, but one may suspect their part in the proceedings. Nearer home, it was twice necessary during 1864, on the occasion of the execution at Newgate of five pirates and of the North London Railway murderer, to admit the sheriffs to the prison through Amen Corner, owing to the density of the crowd in Old Bailey. The same concession had to be made in 1868 at the hanging of the Fenian guilty of the Clerkenwell explosion; for a month between sentence and execution the inhabitants of the Corner were provided with an armed guard of police day and night. "This", observes Virger Green, "was the last public execution, a great relief to most people living in the neighbourhood." [1]

Mortality was laying its hand on the Cathedral also. In September 1868 Milman ended his great career; his last service to his cathedral was to complete his *Annals of St Paul's*. Within three years of his decease, the entire membership of the Chapter, including Milman's successor as Dean, had been changed; two accepted preferment, three died in office. Champneys went to Lichfield in October 1868; his stall was filled in December by the momentous figure of Robert Gregory. Dale was appointed Dean of Rochester in 1870, but he too died in May of the same year; his successor was Liddon. Hale died in the following November. Melvill died in February 1871, and was succeeded by Lightfoot. Dean Mansel (December 1868–July 1871) was a witty and eminent philosopher but was given little scope for originating new policies; his only task at St Paul's was to carry forward the work inaugurated by Milman.

There had been changes also in the see. Blomfield had resigned in 1856 and died (still at Fulham) in the following

[1] *Acta B.*, 13–19, 27, 29, 32, 38 ff., 69; Green, 21, 26 f., 33 f.

summer. His successor was Tait, the promoter of popular services. But within a few weeks of Milman's death Tait was translated to Canterbury, being succeeded by John Jackson, a pious and tolerant Evangelical who started the East London Church Fund. Two remarkable careers on the Cathedral staff ended in 1869. In January Christopher Hodgson resigned his offices of Registrar, Chapter Clerk, and Bailiff of the Manors and Bailiwicks after serving the Cathedral for no less a period than sixty-two years; his successor as Chapter Clerk and Bailiff was J. B. Lee. August witnessed the death of William Sellon, Receiver and also Steward of the Manors; he had held the latter post since 1835. Lee took over the Stewardship; Sellon's clerk, Hall, was promoted to become Receiver.[1] The stage was cleared of all its principal characters and a new scene was being set for the next act of the play.

[1] *Acta B.*, 78–80, 93–5, 110 f.

6

THE RESOLUTION OF MR GREGORY

THE TWO great needs of the Cathedral at this crucial moment were for the consolidation and development of the plans laid down by Milman, and for the enforcement of a bracing efficiency in its slack administration. When Robert Gregory received his canonry in December 1868, a few weeks short of his fiftieth birthday, the man and the occasion met. How great a proportion came from him of the elemental power destined to re-shape St Paul's and to establish its fame, may be proved by an examination of his activities in the Cathedral during his earliest years, while Mansel presided and abetted at the Deanery and old canons still survived and obstructed in Amen Corner.

Gregory was an archetypal High Church Tory of the school of John Keble, under whose brother Tom he served his first assistant curacy. Brought up as a spiritually unsatisfied Wesleyan, he had been converted through reading the *Tracts for the Times*; he happened to be present when Newman preached his farewell sermon at Littlemore in 1843, but had never been one of the preacher's fans; to the end his interests remained doctrinal and moral, not speculative, ceremonial, or emotional. Though tenderhearted under a gruff exterior, he was a man who "never tampered with his conscience". Uncompromising, dominating, hard as nails towards himself no less than towards others, to him black was black and white was white. Unlike Milman, who possessed so vivid an appreciation of history, he was no scholar and clung to old-fashioned views in theology; but his literalism and his single-mindedness were offset by his grasp of practical realities and his fund of common sense. From early manhood he had expressed his forceful personality in building model cottages for labourers, in fighting against clerical pluralities, in methodical parish visiting, in teaching both children and adults, and in punctual attendance at the daily services in church: he claimed that Tom Keble's was the first parish to revive the public recitation of the regular daily service both morning and evening. In the course of fifteen years as Vicar of St Mary-the-Less, Lambeth, he had utterly transformed a large and derelict area into a pattern of parochial organization, had won the hearts of his people, and had built up for himself a great reputation in the field of popular education—all upon a stipend which for ten years amounted to £90 per annum, or less than that of an assistant curate. Milman's first thought on his preferment had been of his consequent deliverance from vestry meetings: Gregory's was of relief from hard poverty for his family—"Now we can get a rocking-horse for the little children." [1]

It was his character and social work, perhaps also his extreme political conservatism, rather than his High Churchmanship which presumably recommended him to Disraeli for nomination to St Paul's. There was nothing at all to recommend him to his future colleagues, who marked their disapproval, according to Gregory's own account, by the manner of his installation. After Evensong on 21 December, the evening being specially dark even for the shortest day of the year, every light in the Cathedral was turned out, and the church was cleared of people, including some of Gregory's own friends from Lambeth who had come to see him installed; his wife and children alone were suffered to remain. A procession was then formed, consisting of the Dean's Virger carrying a wax taper in a tin kitchen candlestick (still preserved in the Cathedral as a relic of the occasion), Gregory himself, and Hale, who had been deputed to install him. They walked to the high altar, Hale read the usual prayers, the new

[1] Gregory, *passim*, cf. 155.

canon was "placed in a chair instead of a stall", and they returned to the vestry. Since Virger Green, who also records the event, notes that the "stalls" of the residentiaries were at that time situated at the east end of the choir (which had been rearranged in 1860), and it is on record that the dignitaries' proper stalls, formerly under the organ screen, had been stored away ever since that date, it would seem that the chair in which Gregory was installed was in fact one of a set then appointed and provided in choir for members of the Chapter. If so, the fact did nothing to mitigate his contempt for the slovenliness of the ceremony, and he entered on his office with a resolute determination to clean up the whole place at the earliest opportunity.[1]

Gregory was careful to put his own house in order. He had strenuously opposed the practice of clerical pluralities, and rejected Disraeli's suggestion, supported though it was by his predecessor at St Paul's and by other opinion in the Chapter, that he should hold the living of St Pancras together with his canonry. But he did not resign his benefice in Lambeth until he was assured of the appointment of a new vicar who would carry on the work as he himself had started it. For five years, therefore, he was technically a pluralist. In fact, however, he gave away in charity the whole of the benefice income, and devoted himself heart and soul to the work of the Cathedral.

He started his crusade immediately by "speaking very plainly" to his fellow canons on the need to develop the opportunities afforded in the central church of the diocese. Hale was the only member of Chapter who betrayed much interest, and the result was to increase their suspicion of Gregory's views. They were confirmed in their attitude when, on the second day of his November residence in 1869, he followed the vicars-choral to their vesting-place after Mattins and delivered a vigorous rebuke for the irregularity of their attendance and the consequent slovenliness of the services. His comments were promptly reproduced in the press of the whole

[1] Gregory, 157 f.; Green, 35 f.; Sinclair, 419.

country, to his own surprise and the dismay of his colleagues, who vastly and reasonably preferred to proceed by the method of private remonstrance rather than by that of public controversy. But in the following month (17 December 1869) it was resolved to restore, as from the first week in 1870, the ancient practice enjoined in the statutes of holding a Chapter meeting every Saturday in order to take note of lapses in duty; this measure was proposed by Hale, who thus brought to fruition, after a quarter of a century, a plan that he had first advocated under Copleston. So Hale remained to the end, as he had begun, a keen corrector of the faults of his subordinates.[1]

Gregory's primary aim was the improvement of the Cathedral services, and therefore in the first instance of the amenities and behaviour of the choir. Accordingly, even before his quarrel with the vicars, plans were being laid to provide better accommodation for the singers, which had always been deficient. Chapter now decided to construct a first-floor practice room in the north-west tower, or bell tower; long afterwards, at the end of the first world war, the floor was removed and the base of the tower was converted into the chapel of All Souls in memory of Lord Kitchener. The new apartment is described by Chapter as a vestry, by the Surveyor as a singing chamber, and by Virger Green as a music room; the work was completed in the spring of 1870 at a cost of £250, provided by the Trustees of the Fabric Fund. Vicars and choristers alike continued to put on their surplices (hitherto not even the clergy had worn cassocks in St Paul's) in the north choir aisle. But shortly afterwards the vicars were given the use of the Lord Mayor's vestry to robe in, and a closet included in the screen of the north aisle, which had previously been in their occupation, was handed over to the sub-sacrist. In 1880 the vicars were transferred to "a temporary vestry erected in the north

[1] Gregory, 166–72; *Acta B.*, 100; *Statt.*, 285; cf. *supra*, p. 47.

aisle", and in 1889 they descended thence to a new vestry in the crypt.[1]

At the same time attention was paid to the manner of their exits and their entrances. Gregory states in his autobiography (published after his death) that in 1868 "there was little or no order in entering the Cathedral at service time; the Canon came from his vestry, and the Minor Canons and singing men and boys from theirs, and met at the mouth of the choir, stragglers taking their seats afterwards." A regulation which was confirmed after six months' experiment in May 1871 denounced the penalties of absenteeism against singing men "who come late or leave before the end of the service"; vicars were no longer to be suffered to drift in or out of choir at their pleasure. A single procession was formed for the entry and departure of all those officiating, Virger Green recording that on Sunday 17 October 1869 the singers and clergy "came out of the Choir in Procession, 1st time". Six weeks later further dignity was added to the procession both before and after service by the institution of a voluntary on the organ. The piety of the age remained unfed with vestry prayers until 1872.[2]

Before Gregory delivered his complaints and rebukes he was careful to furnish himself with a complete statement of the relevant facts. From the time of his installation as canon until his promotion to the deanery he kept a detailed record of the choir attendance at every morning and evening service on weekdays during his own periods of residence. The note-book in which he entered his statistics is still extant, and shows a slight improvement in the average attendance from the middle of 1870, and a marked advance in regularity after the appointment of additional vicars-choral in 1873. At the other end of the book he records from day to day his

[1] *Acta B.*, 94, 100 f., 115, 163; *Acta C.*, 189; Green, 42, 46, 162, 209; Gregory, 164, 168 (in the latter passage "south aisle" is clearly a mistake for "north aisle"); Frost, 17; personal recollections.

[2] Gregory, 164; Green, 39 f.; *Acta B.*, 182a, 235; Frost, 32.

observations on the conduct of the services and the failures of those responsible for them. From 1873 the entries chiefly consist of reasons for his own occasional absence on important business, and of memoranda of the parties from clubs and schools and parishes whom he personally conducted round St Paul's: he notes at the end of 1877 that he had taken 1335 person in 19 parties over the Cathedral in the course of the year. But for the first few years the comments are ominous and grim. Here are some of them:

1868. 24 December, morning. "No organ for 'Venite' & the psalms. Sent for Organist directly after service, but he was gone. Virger says that the man who turns on water supply for organ was late, & that the fault was his."

1869. 2 April, morning. "Two choristers late, rushed past choir men, & joined procession at entrance of choir. No choirmen on south side, only two on north side. Minor Canon (Mr Calvert) knelt whilst pronouncing absolution."

7 April, evening. "Procession very disorderly. First one Vicar Choral, then five Vicars Choral in the middle of the Minor Canons, & one after the procession. One Minor Canon (Dr Vivian) went round the other way."

10 April, morning. "Vicars Choral late in procession; left vestry after Minor Canons & struggling all the way into the Cathedral to get into their places."

21 April and again 22 April, morning. "No vicars choral on south side."

3 August, morning. "Two Vicars Choral on north side: none on south side. Sent for Mr Lacy & warned him that I should certainly lay a formal complaint before the Bp, as Visitor, if the same occurred again, & that I might possibly do so now."

6 August, morning. "Mr Francis came into the vestry to request that I wd read the Com^{n} service & not attempt to intone, as I did it so execrably that it produced a harsh discord & gave him exquisite pain. Called his attention to the

manner in wch the Vicars Choral fail to discharge their duty."

21 August, morning. "Procession disorderly. One of the choir men (Barrett) late, started behind the Minor Canons, & had to struggle into his place. 'Te Deum' commenced with different chants by choir & organ: some verses sung through before all was right."

24 August, morning. "Procession very irregular. One of choir men stayed to talk with a friend at gate of north choir aisle, breaking the order, & then made a rush: all straggling & irregular."

26 August, morning. "Procession very irregular. Two choir men, then Minor Canons, then five choir men getting into their surplices & hurrying along. Procession stopped to get into something like decent order."

1 November, evening. "Six choristers came in after the service had begun."

1870. 7 December, morning. "R.G. late: but the service had not commenced when he entered the choir." R.G., like his friend Frederick Temple, was a just beast, and faithfully recorded his own misconduct.

It will be recalled that in 1852 six assistants had been annexed to the vicars-choral, for Sunday duty only;[1] by now they had become known as "supernumeraries" and reduced in number to four. In February 1870 a fifth was added to the company and the salaries of the other four were substantially increased; perhaps the increase in number and remuneration may have coincided with an extension of their work to week-days, as they are found, shortly after, to be singing regularly both at Sunday and weekday services. Detailed rules to govern their attendance and discipline, exhibiting much care and considerable firmness of demeanour on the part of Chapter, were drawn up and, "having been found to work satisfactorily", were confirmed. At the same time (May 1871) it

[1] *Supra*, p. 68.

was observed that the statute so hardly won in 1848 for the regulation of the vicars-choral was not in practice being enforced: but instead of deciding to enforce it for the future, Chapter commissioned the Dean and Gregory to prepare a fresh "code of regulations" which might ultimately be sanctioned as a statute of the Cathedral. The consequence appeared at the end of 1874, when a new and far more stringent statute was imposed upon future vicars.

The iron hand of Gregory was doubtless operative in framing the rules for supernumeraries no less than in drafting the new statute for vicars. In 1873 he had quashed a choirman's excuse for lateness, punishable under the statutes by a fine, with the promise that were the delinquent to fall down dead on the steps of the Cathedral on his way to service, his widow should be fined for his non-attendance. "Remember", he once said rather solemnly to H. S. Holland, "when I am gone, that the secret of a place like this lies in punctuality."[1]

Other evidences, small and great, testify to the infusion of a new spirit into the activities of the Cathedral during the first year of Gregory's presence within its walls. In May 1869 a grant of £20 was made towards the expenses of the voluntary Sunday evening choir, and in November its members were provided with fifty surplices at a cost of 15s. apiece. In the same month a small salary was assigned to George Cooper as sub-organist, for assisting the ageing Goss; and an unsatisfactory guide was dismissed. In May, on Gregory's recommendation, two women were appointed as cleaners, to act under the directions of the virgers. In October the Bishop approved a statute altering the times of service to hours more likely to suit the convenience of possible worshippers: on weekdays 10 a.m. and 4 p.m. were fixed; on Sundays Mattins was now to be sung at 10.30 instead of 9.45, Sunday Evensong alone retaining its traditional hour of 3.15. An event of even greater significance for Cathedral publicity had taken place

[1] *Acta B.*, 103, 181–3, 256; *Suppl.*, 112 ff.; Sinclair, 309; Russell *B.*, 21; Gregory, 259; Frost, 16, 57.

in the previous February. Gregory had been protesting to the Chapter that larger use should be made of St Paul's for special services, such as the festivals of Church societies. At that moment a request arrived from the British and Foreign Bible Society for a sermon to be preached by the newly appointed Archbishop of Canterbury (Tait) in commemoration of the completion of the Society's new premises at Blackfriars. Gregory welcomed the proposal, and the sermon was preached in the Cathedral on 3 May, from the text Ephesians 6. 17.[1] Of the most important move of all, that which led to the revival of Milman's plans for embellishing the Cathedral, it will be more convenient to write a little later on.

Though Gregory was clearly the force behind most of the developments of this period, he was not the sole inspirer of every change; some small details, regarded at the time as significant, had an altogether different source. At Christmas 1868, the Sacrist (one of the minor canons) had the choir decorated. At the following Epiphany a star in red cloth, worked in silver by Miss Hale, was placed on the altar. At Easter (1869) a semicircular "reredos", covered in crimson velvet and surmounted by a cross in the same material, was erected on the altar; Miss Hale embroidered it with the text "He is risen", and helped to decorate it with hot-house flowers, for which Hale himself paid £20; Hale had also personally designed the proportions of the cross. This was the first time that the Cathedral had been decorated for Easter, and the first time that any form of cross had been placed over the altar in St Paul's.[2]

Early in 1870 a vacancy was impending in the Chapter, and Liddon was nominated to fill it; he was installed in April, after the second lesson at Evensong, in the presence of the entire Chapter; the proceedings were in marked contrast to the installation of Gregory. Liddon was an ally after

[1] *Acta B.*, 83, 88 f., 96 f., 98 f.; Green, 39; Gregory, 167; Bible Society records.

[2] Green, 34 (inset).

Gregory's own heart. He was not merely an outstanding High Church leader in Oxford and the country at large, the first lieutenant of Dr Pusey and the mouthpiece through whom that hidden oracle was wont to speak, who could be relied on to maintain and defend with full conviction the traditional faith of the Church of England. He was a Student of Christ Church and a distinguished conservative theologian, who was no sooner installed in St Paul's than he was also elected (reluctantly) to the Ireland Professorship of Exegesis at Oxford. He had recently published a memoir of Bishop Hamilton of Salisbury, who as Canon, Precentor, and Bishop between 1841 and 1869 had done for that cathedral exactly what Gregory was trying to do for St Paul's, and had brought its dry bones to life. Liddon possessed great gifts, among which that of deep personal piety was conspicuous.

He was also one of the great preachers of his age, and not unknown to St Paul's, since he had preached quite recently for an hour and twenty minutes at a special service under the dome, on the evening of Good Friday 1868. At this period, and for years to come, sermons of about an hour were common custom at St Paul's. Such crowds came to hear Liddon in his first residence (May 1870) that he forsook the choir and delivered his sermons from the dome pulpit, normally used only for special services. In February 1871, when it was ordered that the doors be opened half an hour before the time of service on Sundays, the Dean directed the virgers to open them fifteen minutes earlier still on afternoons when Liddon was in residence. It may be worth mentioning, in order to correct a legend, not merely that his first sermon under the dome, delivered at a "special" Sunday evening service in 1863, was inaudible ("the Dean told me . . . that I exerted myself too much to be heard"), but that his audiences are stated by H. S. Holland to have filled only the dome area, the transepts, and the choir; witnesses with long memories recall that those who could not find seats in these parts of the Cathedral did not occupy the nave, but stood round the edge of the dome, and a person sitting in the eastern part of the choir "could only hear very imperfectly what he said".[1]

With Liddon to back him Gregory persevered in his course of reformation. At the end of June a petition was presented to Chapter, signed by about a hundred people engaged in business near the Cathedral, asking that a place should be set apart where they might say their prayers in comparative quiet. It was decided therefore to admit people to the choir for private devotion on weekdays between noon and 3 p.m. A more revolutionary decision took shape at the same meeting of Chapter, which led in the end to the discontinuance of the annual service for the Charity Schools of London. These schools dated back to the newly started activities of the Society for Promoting Christian Knowledge, in the earliest years of the eighteenth century.[2]

The children attending them were habituated from the first to being treated as a living advertisement for the good works of which they enjoyed the benefit. Queen Anne ordained a public thanksgiving in St Paul's for the Peace of Utrecht; it was held on 7 July 1713. Both Houses of Parliament attended the service: but before members reached the Cathedral they had already been regaled with the sound and sight of nearly 4000 children, collected from the charity schools in and about London and Westminster, and singing doggerel hymns in honour of the Queen and God from an erection in the Strand. The scaffold upon which the children were stationed was 620 feet long and contained eight banks of seats, one above another; and the innocent carollers were "new cloathed" for the occasion. For nearly three hours, as the procession passed, "they sung and repeated the Hymns which were prepared upon the expectation of her Majesty's Royal Presence". Repetition was certainly required, for it seems that only two brief texts had been provided to span

[1] Green, 33, 43, 49; Johnston, 55; H. S. Holland, *apud Gregory*, 251; Frost, 22; personal recollections.

[2] H. P. Thompson, *Thomas Bray*, 40; *D.E.C.H.*, *sub* "Education".

so long a period with sustained melody. A similar exhibition of the charity children was presented on the south side of St Paul's Churchyard on 20 September 1714, when King George made his public entry into the City of London.[1]

But for generation after generation the London Charity Schools had held a united annual service in St Paul's itself. It normally took place in June, and it occupied the nave and the entire space beneath the dome; the Cathedral closed down regularly for a month in order to allow of the erection of benches, tier above tier, for the children to occupy. They sat there in a vast horse-shoe of stands, built up on the north, east, and south sides of the dome area, blocking choir and transepts and reaching nearly half-way up the piers of the arches; they were cramped for space, unable to kneel, and looked like exhibits at a flower show. The spirit in which the celebration had sometimes been conducted may be illustrated by the fact that in 1837 the service concluded with three cheers for the Lord Mayor.[2] Gregory had already succeeded in getting the closure reduced from a month to about ten days for the service in 1870. But it was now ordained that in future the regular weekday services should suffer no interruption at all, and in December the vicars-choral were warned that they would be required to sing daily throughout the following June.

What actually happened in 1871 is not clear; presumably stands were erected as usual, in the intervals of divine service: in 1872 no Charity School service was held, as the Cathedral was being cleaned after the reconstruction of organ and choir-stalls which had recently been completed. In 1873 the service was not held until 9 October. Negotiations had been conducted between the Chapter and the Schools Committee, and on 14 June Chapter had laid down terms for the future: no carpenters' work was to be done in

[1] Information from a print dated 1715 and preserved in the offices of S.P.C.K.

[2] *Plan*, 33.

the Cathedral, but benches might be brought from outside between one Sunday and the next, without interrupting the daily services, and no scaffolding was to be erected which might cause discoloration of the walls or damage to floor and fabric. "Attendance very moderate." In March 1874 Chapter gave permission for the festival of the Charity Children to be held "on the same conditions as last year"; and Green notes: "1874. Thursday, June 4th. Anniversary service of the Charity Children, not so many children as formerly, no services suspended except on the morning at 10 a.m. the afternoon service as usual at 4 p.m." The service took place in each of the next three years, but after 1877 it ceased to be held. One gain was that the timber for the stands no longer had to be stored in the crypt, which was thus set free for more attractive uses.[1]

[1] Sinclair, 280; Russell, 35 f.; *Acta B.*, 117, 121, 144, 322 f., 376; Green, 44, 66, 85 f., 95, 109, 121, 132; Gregory, 200 ff.

7

ASSOCIATES IN REFORM

HALE died in November 1870. Melvill had been reported dead in September 1869 and the Dead March was played for him after service, but the report had been exaggerated, and he survived till February 1871. Meantime Gregory's ascendancy increased. At the end of 1870 he was charged with recommendations for a redistribution of surplus income among Cathedral benefices. It was also decided to celebrate the patronal festival of the Cathedral in a more becoming way than any living person could remember; accordingly on St Paul's Day, 25 January 1871, what was then the unusual number of fifty people made their Communion at the equally unusual hour of 8 o'clock, and the Dean preached at Evensong to a gathering which included the Bishop and seventeen of the prebendaries. The annual Chapter dinner was transferred to the evening of the same day, and in addition to the customary guests invitations were extended to the prebendaries, minor canons, and lay officials of the Cathedral: the dinner was made an annual Feast for the entire foundation a year later, when the vicars-choral were also invited. Thought was taken likewise (at Gregory's instance) for the provision of a musical service in Holy Week. For various reasons the attempt had to be delayed; but from 1873 the Tuesday in Holy Week has been appropriated to a performance of Bach's St Matthew Passion Music.[1]

Before summer ended in 1871 a mixed collection of straws indicates how the wind was blowing. The use of the Morning Chapel was granted to Gregory and Liddon to hold a weekly evening lecture through the ensuing winter, and steps were

[1] Green, 38, 48, 49, 79; *Acta B.*, 142, 144, 171, 230, 266; *Suppl.*, 3 f.

being taken to have the chapel itself refitted. Till then the chapel had contained no altar; seats were ranged all round it, and its most conspicuous feature was a great table in the centre, round which such worshippers as attended the early Mattins knelt. But by Advent 1871 it was altered and decorated and in use for early Eucharists; accessions in the form of marble and candelabra and mosaics came in the course of the next few years. Sparrow Simpson presented two sets of altar vessels, and further gifts of Communion plate for the Cathedral followed; Holy Communion was celebrated in the chapel on all Holy Days from 1871; and daily from 1 January 1877. It was also determined in October 1871 that all Sunday services with a sermon should be held under the dome, and that the service of Holy Communion in choir on Sunday morning should "be chorally rendered", though full effect was not given to the latter decision until Easter 1873. The previous custom had been to sing the Ante-Communion (with the Sanctus as an introit); the choir departed after the sermon and the rest of the service was said.[1]

In April 1871 the Dean's Virger died and was buried in the crypt. He was succeeded by the diarist, Robert Green. Till that time the silver wands or virges carried by the virgers had been the private property of those officials; the occasion was now seized to purchase them for the Cathedral, and to supply both virge and gown for each virger on his appointment. *Hymns Ancient and Modern* was introduced in May. From June worshippers at 8 o'clock were admitted by the north-west door, instead of the north transept, and in the next month the congregation at Sunday Evensong was allowed to depart by the great west doors. Gregory, Liddon, and the new canon Lightfoot spent many Saturday afternoons conducting vast parties of working-men and others over the Cathedral free of the normal fees. The weekly lectures planned earlier in the year actually started on 7 November. Gregory

[1] *Acta B.*, 166, 169, 170, 194, 199, 227, 250, 300, 374, 420a; Gregory, 181; Green, 58, 65, 80; *Suppl.*, 4, 7; Russell *B.*, 52; Frost, 21.

delivered the first course, at 8 p.m., but not in the Morning Chapel: the number of young men attending the opening lecture was about 1200. (Many City firms at that time followed the system of "living-in" for their employees, who found little rational occupation in the City for their evening leisure.) Gregory insisted that women should be excluded, for fear that the young men might be chaffed by their associates. Green presents a different aspect: "females refused admission by order of the Canon, which caused a good deal of grumbling." So many people were being drawn into active association that at an early Eucharist for the Lay Helpers, in June 1872, the communicants numbered 320. In one way or another the Cathedral was waking up to practical realities and learning the greatness of its opportunities.[1]

Still in 1871, Gregory and Liddon were involved in public controversy. They were neither of them what was called "Ritualists". But the revival of disused ceremonial, which the Ritualists believed to be ordered in the Prayer Book, had recently been spreading apace; its promoters had been prosecuted in the ecclesiastical courts, which had decided largely in their favour; but on appeal to the Judicial Committee of the Privy Council decisions had been given against them and an incumbent had been suspended by that court for disobeying its orders. In February 1871 another judgement was delivered by the Privy Council, condemning among other things the practice of the celebrating priest facing eastwards at the altar. This practice had been followed at St Paul's both by Gregory and by Liddon; and when a riot of prosecutions was threatened against those who followed it, they determined to protect the parochial clergy by demanding that they themselves should be the first to face a prosecution. To the dismay of the Bishop (Jackson) they therefore wrote him a formal letter denouncing their own illegality; nor could he, either by letter or by interview, dissuade them.

They said that the Privy Council had decided points of

[1] Green, 50 ff., 53 f., 57, 66; *Acta B.*, 184, 187 f.; Gregory, 197.

Church law on which the Church itself had reached no decision, in a way not only open to grave historical criticism, but suggestive of using judicial decision to impose what was in fact legislation—a procedure which "revolts consciences and creates anarchy"; that obedience to a civil court was only due in civil matters, and even there it could not claim unqualified submission without condemning the resistance offered under the Stuarts to the courts of high prerogative; and that the obedience which they had promised to the Crown was "canonical"—in order words, they felt themselves bound to obey in ecclesiastical affairs only an authority which was exercised constitutionally in accordance with the canon law of the Church. The dispute ranged into the press with the publication of Open Letters on both sides; the Bishop announced that he would prosecute his canons if called upon by the authorities of the Cathedral to take official cognizance of their offence; and nothing happened. They had won a moral victory, and incidentally had identified St Paul's with the opposition to secular regimentation of religion.

They sealed their advantage with a minor triumph. The same judgement against which they had protested enjoined that on high days a cope should be worn by the celebrant in cathedral churches: as the witty Mansel observed,

"Then Zion, in her anguish
With Babylon must cope."

It was therefore proposed in Chapter that a cope should be provided for the Bishop when he came on Trinity Sunday to hold his ordination. Gregory and Liddon maintained that to supply him with this vestment would be to recognize the judgement indirectly, and were successful in defeating the proposal. The Bishop had to bring his own cope. It was the first occasion on which modern eyes had seen such a garment worn in St Paul's, but perhaps the Bishop scored after all, for his cope was of a penitential violet hue.[1]

[1] Johnston, 144–51; Green, 51; Russell *B.*, 75; Gregory, 115.

On the side of religious teaching and worship there was manifest collaboration between Gregory and Liddon. But Gregory alone had been responsible for a scheme of administrative reform which, though it came to nothing at the time, was later carried into beneficial effect. Certain administrative duties belonged to the "great offices" of Treasurer (who controlled, or was supposed to control, the Sacrist and virgers), Precentor, and Chancellor. In order to abate the anarchy prevailing in the government of the Cathedral, Gregory proposed, in 1869, that the Bishop be requested to appoint residentiary canons to fill these offices when they fell vacant; that step was the more desirable since the stipends of these dignities had been confiscated by the cathedral reformers. Chapter agreed to the proposal and, when the Treasurer died in September 1869, unanimously asked that Gregory should be appointed Treasurer. But before anything could be done, one of his colleagues, discovering the powers assigned to the Treasurer by the statutes, and suspicious of Gregory's ascendancy, changed his mind; and although Gregory begged that some other canon should receive the post, it was given to a prebendary. However, in 1882, on another vacancy occurring, Gregory was at last appointed Treasurer; and in 1886, after the death of both the Precentor (Belli) and the Chancellor, their offices were conferred on Canons Holland and Liddon, and Gregory's plan was completed.[1]

It is no less clear that in other matters of great immediate concern to the Cathedral Gregory and Dean Mansel had blown the embers of capitular activity into an effective blaze before ever Liddon arrived upon the scene. In three directions practical policies had been initiated which heralded a vast alteration both in the appearance of the Cathedral and also in its capacity to execute its spiritual functions. Negotiations had been entered with the authorities of the City for throwing open the west front; Milman's old committee for the embellishment of the Cathedral had been recalled to

[1] Gregory, 170–4; *Suppl.*, 150 f.

action; and discussion had been started with the Ecclesiastical Commissioners for commuting the Cathedral estates on a mutually favourable basis.

The area of the Churchyard to the west of the Cathedral was enclosed with a low wall and a high railing; inside this precinct Queen Anne reigned in stone amid universal desolation and neglect. In 1834 the Commissioners of Sewers of the City of London and Liberties thereof, the authority responsible for the public highways, had sent a deputation to Chapter asking that the railings might be set back and sufficient land be sold to the City to effect an improvement of the street. Chapter considered the proposal and rejected it. Again in 1850, shortly after Milman's succession to the deanery, a letter had been received from the Commissioners of Sewers suggesting that the wall and railings should be removed so as to display the beauties of the west front, and that the space hitherto enclosed should be paved with flagstones for the convenience of the public; they also wanted to have the roadway widened on the south and east sides of the Churchyard. Chapter replied that they would gladly entertain any proper scheme for improvements to the Churchyard, but were not sympathetically drawn to that proposed: they would not cede Cathedral land to widen the roadway unless the City removed buildings at the upper end of Ludgate Hill so as to widen the approaches; the Churchyard road was already so far wider than the approach road as to allow an unsightly row of cabs to stand against the railings without creating any additional obstruction to the flow of traffic. They did, however, undertake to open (under police protection) the enclosed area to visitors on foot during the daytime, "so that an uninterrupted and leisurely view of the architectural elevation may be enjoyed by the public". The Commissioners twice returned to the attack, at intervals of a twelvemonth, but Chapter refused to budge.[1]

Early in 1869, however, the Commissioners of Sewers

[1] *Acta*, 19, 21 f., 198–203, 211, 227, 243.

made a fresh approach which found the Chapter more accommodating. The City proposed merely that the railings should be set back. Penrose, to whom the project was referred, brought forward a bolder and better scheme. Let Chapter sell to the City at a fair price the land required for widening the roadway at the top of Ludgate Hill (which amounted to nearly a fifth of an acre), and spend the proceeds on restoring and improving the west front of the Cathedral, paving the area remaining between the roadway and the portico, and enclosing it with a line of stone posts and chains, a course which would allow an imposing view of the church and permit free access to pedestrians on all normal occasions. Negotiations proceeded; but the situation was complicated by a demand in 1870 for opening the north side of the Churchyard to vehicular traffic. To this project Chapter fortunately declined to assent, and the business slowly resolved itself into a debate over prices and minor adjustments, with the Royal Institute of British Architects acting as consultants to the Chapter. Finally agreement was reached in 1872, the work was ordered, the sum of £15,000 was paid over, and by 1874 the great façade had assumed the aspect now familiar to everybody who frequents Ludgate Hill.[1] After forty years of alternating effort and paralysis, St Paul's had been made accessible from the west.

The committee constituted under Milman to assist in the embellishment of the interior of St Paul's had been quiescent since his death. It had abolished the western screen of the choir, shifted the organ to a thoroughly inconvenient position, bought another organ and planted it in another highly inconvenient position, and applied some sporadic and inconsequent decoration; this accomplished, it rested from its labours. Gregory was determined from the first to carry on the work. Since he could lay claim neither to artistic knowledge nor to any special aesthetic sensitivity he decided to

[1] *Acta B.*, 80, 90–2, 104–7, 118 f., 132–4, 137–40, 148–50, 173–80, 205 f., 231, 252, 345 f.; Green, 89; *Scrap Book*, 275 f.

inspect at first hand the style of decoration employed in other great Renaissance churches in Italy, particularly St Peter's, Rome, an unhappy choice. Accordingly in 1869 he made a tour abroad and studied to see how a view of St Peter's might educate his eye and save him from absurdities. On his return he held several acrimonious sessions with his colleagues and early in 1870 persuaded them to call together once again the surviving members of the Decoration Committee.[1]

The next step was to inaugurate the decorative policy at a public meeting at the Mansion House on 13 July 1870. The Lord Mayor took the chair, and the speakers included the Bishop of London, the Dean, and Mr Gladstone, now Prime Minister, whose son, the Reverend Stephen Gladstone, had taken his title as Gregory's assistant curate at Lambeth and was still working in the parish. Gladstone referred to the Cathedral's "cold, dark columns and its almost repulsive general condition" as a matter of "burning reproach to Englishmen", claimed that it was the noblest church of modern times, repeated the unfortunate comparison with St Peter's at Rome, described St Paul's as "unfinished and unseemly", indulged in some financial statistics relating to the wealth of the country, and appealed to the nation for £250,000. His eloquence, sustained by that of other influential laymen, resulted in immediate promises to a total of £25,000.

Unhappily, however, nobody quite knew precisely what it was that they wanted done with the money. The Chapter and the Committee had in fact inherited a legacy of indetermination from their predecessors. Milman and his friends had undertaken both to fill St Paul's and to decorate St Paul's, and in truth had done much under both heads. What they do not show much sign of having seriously considered was why —for what exact purposes or occasions—they should throw the choir open to the dome and nave, and how—on what scheme of art or decorative system—they planned to bring

[1] Gregory, 175 f. (N.B., dates on p. 176 are given incorrectly).

colour and splendour into the church. The ideas of Gregory and Gladstone do not seem to have been much clearer. Critics were quick to point out this defect, and in the outcome the Cathedral had to pay the price of its muddle-headedness in red-hot coin of controversy.[1]

In the matter of the Cathedral endowments, however, and of the objects for which provision ought to be secured in any bargain made with the Ecclesiastical Commissioners for the commutation of the estates, Gregory had not only formed a clear conception of the needs of St Paul's, but enjoyed the unanimous support of all who might claim expert knowledge of the management of active cathedral establishments. As has been already stated,[2] the Commissioners obtained full powers to commute cathedral endowments for money payments by the Act of 1868. In December of that year Mansel became dean and Gregory canon. Without delay, as early as March 1869, communications had been opened between Chapter and the Commissioners with a view to transference of the estates. Gregory knew that in order to make of the Cathedral the power-house of religious activity which he desired and intended, adequate staff and equipment would be required; and there was one obvious means by which the necessary funds could be secured. He had Mansel's active support, and it was doubtless under the pressure of their united determination that on 18 March Chapter laid down "the only terms on which the Chapter were willing to enter into a negotiation for transfer, viz. the determining what the future Establishment of the Cathedral should be and the making all needful provision for the maintenance of such Establishment". If the Commissioners were unwilling to accept this basis, "the negotiation for transfer must drop, and the Leases now renewable must be renewed".

The Chapter Clerk was therefore directed to start negotiations with the agents for the Commissioners; the Dean was

[1] Gregory, 176, 181; Green, 45; *Cathedral Decoration*, 5, 9 ff., 16.
[2] *Supra*, p. 72.

empowered to intervene personally on behalf of the Chapter whenever he thought it desirable; the scheme which it was hoped might result was to be submitted to Chapter in due course. The current sped swiftly but, unfortunately, towards rocks. The Commissioners thought that the older canons, whose income still fluctuated somewhat,[1] should have their financial position forcibly stabilized: Chapter insisted that Hale and Dale, the two canons concerned, should continue to be paid an income based on their average receipts for the seven years ending on 31 December 1867. This obstacle was removed by the death of both canons in the course of 1870, but only to be succeeded by another. In the summer of 1871 the Dean and Gregory held two interviews with Mr Yool, the Actuary and financial adviser to the Commissioners, at which Mansel spoke with unguarded volubility on the necessity for liberal treatment of the Cathedral. The only consequence was that Yool informed the Chapter Clerk: "Tell Canon Gregory that if he brings that Dean of his again I will not give St Paul's a penny more than I am obliged."[2]

Nevertheless, in spite of checks, preliminary arrangements for the New Deal continued to be set forward. In December 1870, on the Dean's initiative, Chapter agreed to purchase the lease of the Oxford Arms, a picturesque but dilapidated inn, then let out in tenements, on the site of which the minor canons' houses were later built. In the next month inquiries were begun for a property in the immediate neighbourhood of the Cathedral, suitable for conversion into a choir school or as providing a site for building one. In May 1871 an estimate was received of the cost of putting the fabric into good repair and of the sum likely to be required annually for its future maintenance. A plan prepared by Penrose was also approved for constructing a store room in the crypt and installing a hydraulic lift in the north-west corner of the north transept to give easy access for the material elements of restoration. In June definite proposals for the commutation

[1] Cf. p. 70. [2] *Acta B.*, 86 f.; Gregory, 179 ff., 189 f.

were received from the Commissioners and a committee of the whole Chapter was agreed on to examine them. In July Gregory reported a successful attempt to push up the price offered by the Commissioners.

Meanwhile efforts had been made to end the scandal of the Cupola Fund, of which the net average income for the previous seven years had amounted to £774.[1] In the same month it was announced that the college of minor canons had agreed to an annual grant in commutation of their interest in the Fund; this took effect from the end of the year. It was also decided to exclude newly appointed virgers from direct participation in the profits of the Fund, and to put them on fixed salaries. Chapter had worse fortune with the vicars-choral. A sum was offered; they demanded a larger share; Chapter proposed a slight increase; the vicars refused it, and negotiations broke down. A settlement was reached only in 1874, when the new statute to govern the affairs of vicars-choral was imminent.[2] But from January 1872 the Fund was controlled and administered by the Receiver, and the guides became the servants of the Dean and Chapter.[3]

Commutation now seemed to be drawing very near, and with its accomplishment a large and regular income would have to be administered. Gregory saw that executive responsibility for the finances of the Cathedral ought not to be deputed to a subordinate and could not be exercised efficiently by a corporation of five persons. He therefore proposed, in June 1871, that one member of Chapter should be appointed treasurer of Chapter funds, with the task of overseeing all receipts and expenditure, arranging, under the direction of Chapter, for the investment of surplus monies, and supervising everything concerned with the fees for showing the Cathedral to visitors; cheques would be drawn on the signatures of the Chapter Treasurer (as the new officer

[1] *Minor canons' minutes*, 19 July 1871. [2] Cf. p. 99.

[3] *Acta B.*, 147, 159, 181, 185, 188, 191, 193, 201 f., 218, 250, 267, 273, 384; Green, 60.

came to be called) and the Receiver jointly. A fortnight sufficed to see the plan enacted and Gregory himself elected Chapter Treasurer. How great a revolution had occurred in eighteen months! Gregory, the junior canon who could not safely be trusted with power over virgers, was now senior canon and entrusted by his colleagues with a controlling charge over their entire finances. They set only one limitation upon his authority: the office was to be held for a single year, subject to annual re-election. In fact, Gregory was re-appointed every year until, aged nearly 86, he sought relief himself at the end of 1904.[1]

The recent death of the Dean's Virger and the promotion of Green to succeed him enabled the institution of a Chapter Treasurership to be coupled with an important reform in the oversight of the fabric. For more than a century the office of Dean's Virger had been doubled with that of assistant to the Surveyor. Now the two posts were disjoined, and a professional Clerk of the Works was secured to superintend, with the aid of a greatly enlarged body of workmen, that vigilant care of the fabric for which the receipt of adequate funds was expected to provide. One small fruit of vigilance was duly gathered with the appointment of the first night-watchman, an ex-policeman, who assumed his patrol in November.[2] But the major harvest, which seemed almost within reach, had sustained another sudden check. The acute and vigorous Mansel, whose collaboration with Gregory had been so active and so fruitful, went on holiday in mid-July and died at the end of the same month. The foundations of future glory for St Paul's had been most truly laid by Milman; Mansel, during his brief tenure of the deanery, had assisted faithfully to raise the walls; but it was necessary to await the advent of yet another Dean before the keystone was placed in the vault.

[1] *Acta B.*, 189 f.; cf. 253; *Acta D.*, 199.
[2] *Acta B.*, 195; cf. *supra*, p. 25; Green, 58.

8

FINANCIAL RECONSTRUCTION

THE NEW Dean, nominated in August 1871 by Mr Gladstone after the post had been refused by Dr Hook, the Dean of Chichester, was a man of the highest distinction who had, characteristically, lived his life in obscurity, neither seeking nor desiring preferment. Richard William Church was born in 1815 at Lisbon, and spent most of his boyhood in Florence. Elected to a Fellowship at Oriel in 1838, he aimed at studiousness, acknowledged the influence of Butler, Coleridge, and Maurice, and formed close friendships with members of the Tractarian circle, above all with Newman; the breadth of his interests was displayed by his attendance at a course of lectures on human anatomy, but he kept carefully in the background of University politics, which then meant the great and bitter Tractarian controversy. He happened nevertheless to be Proctor in 1845, and thus enjoyed "the extreme satisfaction" and "unmixed pleasure" of assisting to veto the proposal of the Hebdomadal Board that the Convocation of the University should pronounce censure upon Newman's *Tract 90*.

Already suspect of sharing Newman's despair of the Church of England—quite unjustly, for as he wrote in 1843 he "never felt a temptation to move"—Church was given every opportunity to practise the retirement which he sought and to take refuge in books. He would smoke a cigar with his friend Johnson at the University Observatory and watch the planets through his telescopes; it was in Johnson's house at the Observatory that Newman spent his last night in Oxford in February 1846, and said goodbye to Church and other friends. Church spent the whole year 1847 in the

Mediterranean, chiefly in Greece and Italy. He was included in the University delegation to the funeral of Wellington at St Paul's in 1852: "it was, of course, as much of a triumph as a funeral; but . . . the burial service was not lost, as I half feared, in the spectacle." In the following January he exchanged Oxford for the rectory of Whatley, a Somersetshire village of 200 inhabitants situated three miles from Frome.[1]

He loved his rustic people and they loved him. He taught and preached with simplicity, brevity, and directness of purpose. He was indefatigable and authoritative as a pastor, gentle and interesting and delightful as a man. The academic side of his thought expressed itself in wide reading and frequent writing, particularly in the *Guardian*, founded by his friends in 1846; his reviews and essays went far to establish the reputation of the paper for enlightened critical information upon historical, literary, and scientific subjects. Church was formed by nature for a critic; he was unusually well equipped with fastidious taste, conscientious deliberation and balance, breadth of thought, independence and originality of judgement, humour, insight—all this, and with it a profound religious conviction, and a moral gravity which flamed into wrath only at the contact of insolence or injustice. For over eighteen years he had worked in secret, evading publicity by his own set choice, recognized only by his friends and by the elect few. He was most reluctant to abandon Elysium and come out into the great world; only under extreme pressure from Liddon was he induced to accede to the Prime Minister's desire. But having decided, Church went straight up to survey his new stage. "It is clear that what I am to come in for is very tough practical business. . . . It is to set St Paul's in order, as the great English Cathedral, before the eyes of the country." That was what Gladstone intended and what Liddon and Gregory expected from the new Dean. He was installed in October, half expecting that a breakdown in health might relieve him within a twelvemonth from the

[1] Gregory, 182; Church, 45, 57, 135 and *passim*.

"treadmill work" and "gloomy magnificence" of his decanal "prison".[1]

His colleagues in Chapter, in addition to Gregory and Liddon, were an Archdeacon of London who from the Cathedral point of view was insignificant,[2] and a Cambridge Professor, J. B. Lightfoot, engrafted on St Paul's earlier in 1871. Lightfoot was not only a Christian of sterling simplicity, and a delightfully genial companion; he was generally sympathetic towards the designs now being planned for the Cathedral (though he followed his own line during the quarrels over the new decorations in 1874).[3] But he also stood among the greatest in the succession of Anglican scholars, and his immense learning, bonded with a robust moderation in matters of current ecclesiastical controversy, brought into Chapter a solidity which no one suspected, even unjustly, of undue partiality for Ritualism. (He was, for instance, unlike Church and Gregory and Liddon, accustomed to celebrate Holy Communion from the north end of the altar.[4]) Lightfoot was far from being the only member of Chapter who was intellectually distinguished in a high degree; but as Church stood in the public mind for judgement, Liddon for preaching, and Gregory for practical organization, so Lightfoot was the pre-eminent representative of conscientious theological research. And when he was persuaded to become Bishop of Durham in 1879, he was succeeded at St Paul's for five years by another great scholar, the Oxford historian William Stubbs. Thus clearly was a high place in the life of the Cathedral marked out for religious learning.

With Lightfoot available for counsel and for lecturing, Liddon filling the church with the silver trumpet of his Scriptural eloquence and supervising an almost ceaseless round of devotional activities, and Gregory already half-way to the goal of financial and administrative reconstruction, Church occupied an enviable position. He had neither need nor wish

[1] Church, 200 ff. *et al.*, cf. *Preface*; Johnston, 152. [2] Russell *B.*, 26 f.
[3] *Acta B.*, 388 f. [4] Russell *B.*, 28.

to initiate new policy. His was the "judicial conscience" before which every proposal had to be brought and to which all bowed with loyal attachment. The first consequence of his disinterested goodness and authority, even before the confidence which they created in the public mind, was the creation of a practical unanimity in the working of Chapter. As H. S. Holland wrote, this was by no means a normal feature of cathedral chapters; yet "it was to this unity of purpose and mind that Dr Liddon continually attributed all that the Chapter succeeded in achieving at St Paul's; and this unity, as he was never tired of asserting, became a practical fact through the incomparable authority that resided in the character of the Dean".[1]

But it should never be forgotten how much the Cathedral owed to the statesmanship of Gladstone, who had picked most of the new capitular team, and to the virtual collusion in mortality among the old body, which had presented him with so exceptional an opportunity. On taking office at the end of 1868 he had found Gregory, towards whom he felt both confidence and affection, just established as a prospective canon; within less than three years, so providentially did the casualties fall, he had sent Liddon, Lightfoot, and Church to join him in carrying out a common policy so deliberate and consistent as St Paul's has scarcely ever been known to pursue before or since.

No longer was it thought tolerable that a canon should hold a cure of souls and share his energies between his parish and St Paul's. Strangely enough, pluralism was not on that account extinguished. In any case, each successive Archdeacon of London was a pluralist *ex officio*, and the greater the activity he showed as a diocesan official the less freedom he retained as canon to serve the Cathedral, out of the endowments of which his stipend was drawn. The anomaly was accentuated in 1897, when Chapter generously procured an Act of Parliament to authorize a further charge on its

[1] Church, 214–23; *Bundle*, 82–5.

resources in favour of this cuckoo in its nest, and assigned him a supplement from the general revenues of the Cathedral sufficient, with his two-thirds share in the income of the fourth canonry, to equalize his stipend with that of the other stalls. The acquisitiveness of the ecclesiastical bureaucracy reached its apex in 1935. The Ecclesiastical Commissioners were then induced to pay a stipend to the Archdeacon of Middlesex. The Archdeacon of London was relieved of the deduction hitherto charged upon his income, while at the same time he was allowed to retain the compensation charged upon the Cathedral revenues under the Act of 1897—a really pretty piece of work.[1]

Official pluralism was not new; but pluralities re-entered St Paul's in a fresh shape when members of Chapter began to hold, together with their canonries, professorial chairs at Oxford or Cambridge. Liddon had a part-time professorship at Oxford from 1870 till 1882, when he resigned immediately after Pusey's death in order to make time to write his *Life*; but he retained both his Studentship at Christ Church and the rooms to which it entitled him. Lightfoot retained his academic standing at Cambridge throughout his tenure of the canonry. Stubbs, who succeeded him at St Paul's, continued to serve as Regius Professor of Modern History at Oxford until he became Bishop of Chester in 1884. Thus from 1871 till 1884 (when H. S. Holland replaced Stubbs) only one, and from then till 1890 only two, of the canons of St Paul's were engaged predominantly in the service of the Cathedral. Indeed, until 1873 Gregory himself was technically a pluralist also. It is only fair to record that not only Liddon but all three of the distinguished professorial pluralists were active in Cathedral business and diligent in their attendance at Chapter meetings, even when these fell during University terms. But since the restoration of the Saturday disciplinary Chapter there was less need to hold frequent meetings for

[1] *Acta D.*, 94, 98; *Archdeaconry of London (Additional Endowment) Act, 1897; Min.*, 6 July 1935.

transacting formal business: routine matters were dealt with on Saturdays, and from time to time more important decisions were also taken then, subject in certain cases to later confirmation in the formal session.[1]

Gradually the Saturday Chapter came to supplant the true business meetings of the Dean and canons. Order was made in 1891 that the canon in residence should enter in the Saturday minute book any matter of importance which it was desired to record. It was no more than recognition of customary practice when in 1895 the Saturday Chapter was expressly authorized to determine questions needing rapid settlement, provided that every member of Chapter were given previous warning of the business proposed and that none objected. In 1903 it was resolved that the minutes of the Saturday Chapters should regularly be produced for confirmation at the now infrequent general Chapters; and from 1905, apart from a single Annual Meeting, the general business sessions fell into virtually complete abeyance.[2] One consequence, in some ways most unfortunate, was that the Chapter Clerk or his deputy ceased to be present at any but the single Annual Meeting of his Chapter, and business continuity as well as secretaryship rested in the less reliable hands of a perpetually changing canon-in-residence.

Academic pluralities in St Paul's did not long survive the death of Liddon in 1890. Church died before the end of the same year and was replaced in the deanery by Gregory. Gregory's canonry was filled, at the beginning of 1891, by Professor George Forrest Browne, an imaginative archaeologist and extremely able administrator from Cambridge, who tried for a time to do justice to his double responsibilities but abandoned the attempt as impracticable within a twelvemonth. By a neat irony of history Browne himself was chosen in 1895 to initiate another variety of pluralism as Bishop-suffragan of Stepney; the scheme originated with Frederick Temple, then Bishop of London, and Browne

[1] Cf., e.g., *supra*, p. 81. [2] *Acta D.*, 38, 88, 176; cf. *Min.*, *passim*.

himself felt some scruple and difficulty about the situation. On his translation to Bristol two years later the Prime Minister. Lord Salisbury, repeated the arrangement by immediately nominating Winnington-Ingram to the canonry, the man conspicuously marked out to succeed Browne at Stepney.[1] When Winnington-Ingram exchanged Stepney for the bishopric of London in 1901, his successor as Bishop of Stepney, Cosmo Lang, was again appointed to the vacant canonry. These last two bishop-canons were both preachers of extraordinary power and attraction; but it was fortunate indeed that on Lang's translation to York in 1909 St Paul's was given in S. A. Alexander a new canon who would devote himself entirely to the pressing needs of the Cathedral.

The Chapter which Gladstone had built up proved an effective instrument because, in the first place, it was composed of homogeneous or at least of compatible elements and, in the second place, it was inspired by one deliberate purpose, which embraced the finances, the choir, and the scheme of decoration. Everybody was agreed that the key to unlock the golden future now in prospect was a golden key: the Cathedral of good men's dreams could only be realized if money were forthcoming to pay for it: and that meant, in practical terms, a favourable commutation of the Cathedral estates by the Ecclesiastical Commissioners. Though the Commissioners held their resources in trust for the whole Church of England, they were making so enormous a fortune out of the confiscated prebends that they could well afford to be generous towards St Paul's in estimating the value of its remaining estates; what needed to be done in order to secure their generosity was to convince them that the cash endowment, which they were asked to provide in place of the estates, would be employed wisely and properly on the work of the Cathedral and not, as had largely happened in the old cathedral pattern, to foster individual interests. Here the character

[1] Browne, 303, 331 f., 335 f.; Green, 293.

of Church and the hard-headed realism of Gregory combined to bring about success.[1]

Before ever he was installed Church writes that "I am in the thick of papers left by Mansel about the arrangement with the Ecclesiastical Commissioners, which is the first thing I shall have to take part in". Accompanied by Gregory, he had his first interview with Yool, the Actuary to the Commissioners, on the day after his installation. In March 1872 Chapter consented to accept, with modifications mutually agreed on, the terms of commutation which the Commissioners had proposed in the previous June. Three weeks later Chapter apportioned the prospective annual revenue between the clergy and other officers of the foundation, organists, vicars-choral, virgers, choir school, fabric, maintenance, and sundry commitments, the total reaching £16,000. But by August, when an Order in Council was made enforcing the agreement, the total had been pushed up to £18,000. The Cathedral itself, together with the Chapter House and the residences of the canons, was excepted from the general transfer of capitular property to the Commissioners, as was also the ancient estate at Tillingham, the profits of which really belonged to the old Fabric Fund[2] and were now appropriated to the repair of the fabric.

In addition, an annual payment of £400 was granted, in the first instance as compensation to the existing Chapter Clerk; and a capital sum of £30,000 was provided for the repair, restoration, and improvement of the Cathedral and the buildings belonging to it.[3] One of the principal objects for which capital was needed was the erection of a choir school. But so much money was required for repairing deficiencies in the fabric and other projects that Chapter had to ask permission to finance the building of the school, at least in part, by borrowing from the purchase money given by the City for the western area of the Churchyard.[4] The corporate property

[1] Church, 200; Gregory, 190 f.
[2] Cf. *supra*, 24 ff., and 27 ff.
[3] Church, 200; *Acta B.*, 196, 234 f., 243.
[4] Cf. *Acta B.*, 164, 336.

of the vicars-choral was commuted at the same time as the capitular estates for the sum of £900 to be paid annually to Chapter on their behalf.[1] The property of the college of minor canons had to be left for independent treatment.

In the meantime, confident that the finances of the Cathedral would shortly be assured, Chapter saw no point in hoarding the balance still preserved in the Fabric Fund. In May 1871, before Mansel's death, they had already decided to apply to the Trustees of the Fund to sell out stock to pay for various works[2] estimated to cost over £1700. By December the estimate had risen to more than £2600, and a further claim for £4960 had been added for improvements to the organ and the heating. Chapter thereupon passed the following resolution: "That having regard to the pending negociation for the transfer of the Capitular Estates to the Ecclesiastical Commissioners and to the provision, contemplated by the scheme for transfer, for the present repair and the future maintenance of the Fabrick of the Cathedral, it is in the opinion of the Dean and Chapter expedient that the Fabrick Fund consisting of £16,000 2½ per cents standing in the names of the Fabrick trustees be at once expended in works in and about the Cathedral for which the Fabrick fund to be provided by the Ecclesiastical Commissioners will not be available . . .".

Apparently the current demands upon the Fabric Fund were met by the Trustees. But when, in May 1872, Chapter submitted further bills for £2650, the Trustees decided to call the procession to a halt. On receiving their refusal to co-operate in winding up the Trust fund Chapter expressed considerable embarrassment. Finally, after negotiations lasting from July to December, the Trustees consented to a compromise: they paid the bills outstanding, partly out of income but mainly by sale of stock, on condition that Chapter bound itself by formal resolution, to be recorded on the minutes of both parties, to apply in future for no larger sums

[1] *Suppl.*, 110 f. [2] Cf. p. 114.

than could be furnished out of the income of the Fund. The Trust was thus kept alive, with a balance in the Fund worth, in 1872, about £5000.[1]

The minor canons presented a more complex problem. The Cathedrals Act of 1840 had enacted that the number of minor canons in any cathedral should be limited to a maximum of six. Owing to the charter of incorporation of the College and to the absence of any specific provisions in the Act for reducing its numbers or dealing with its property, nothing had been done at St Paul's to carry out this intention, though in 1872, when one of the minor canons was promoted to a deanery, Chapter refrained from making a new appointment. At this period two minor canons still survived who had been appointed before 1820, two more dated from the reign of George IV (they died in 1874 and 1875 and were not replaced until a settlement had been effected), and another from 1833. Early in 1874 discussions were in progress with the Ecclesiastical Commissioners about the future of the body, and a draft Bill was approved by Chapter in April; the whole College had been invited formally to attend a conference on the proposals, but respectfully declined to go further than promise careful consideration to any suggestions submitted to it in writing; its members resented Chapter's policy of leaving vacancies unfilled, and reacted violently against the contemplated changes.[2]

At last, however, the Saint Paul's Cathedral, London, Minor Canonries Act, 1875, became law. Alternate vacancies only were to be filled until the number of minor canons was reduced to the legal figure; their freehold (or life-tenure) was abolished, always excepting existing holders, but a minimum rate of income was guaranteed for the future and provision was made for pensions. No future minor canon was to be permitted to hold a benefice with his minor canonry: it is

[1] *Acta B.*, 189, 218 f., 245, 279 f.

[2] *Minor canons' minutes*, 21 April 1874, 35 ff.; *Acta B.*, 306 f., 378 ff., 383 f.; *Suppl.*, 160; Russell *B.*, 39.

arguable whether this prohibition has brought unmixed advantage to the Cathedral. Following the pattern drawn for other of the ancient Cathedral endowments, the separate estates annexed to particular stalls were to vest in the Commissioners, but the corporate property of the College was left intact. Nor was the loss without compensation, for the Commissioners were required by the Act to build, as soon as conveniently might be, six suitable houses of residence to be at the disposal of the Dean and Chapter for the minor canons of the Cathedral: three were in actual occupation by 1879, and Amen Corner was thus expanded into Amen Court. Six weeks after the passing of the Act, Orders in Council were gazetted commuting by consent the separate estates left to the nine surviving minor canons during their lives, in return for equal cash annuities; and similarly commuting the corporate property of the College for an annual sum of £2000.[1]

One year later a scheme was gazetted (in accordance with the Act) for regulating the office and the duties of all minor canons to be appointed henceforward in St Paul's; the views of Chapter were glowingly reflected in the stipulation that they should be chosen not for musical excellence alone but also for fitness to teach, to lecture, and in general to assist in whatever ways Chapter might direct. And now the field was clear to bring in two new minor canons of the reformed type, for a fourth vacancy had recently occurred in College, Dr Vivian having died at the age of 91 after occupying a stall for sixty years and seventeen days. So in October 1876 two admirable priests were chosen, towards whom (as towards the Dean and Chapter) the old minor canons mostly behaved very unpleasantly, always excepting the gentle and loyal and sensible Sparrow Simpson. The last survivor of the old order, Mr J. H. Coward, who had been educating the choristers in Amen Corner from 1848 to 1872,[2] beat even Dr Vivian's record of service; he died in 1911, a minor canon of over sixty-five years' standing, having acted as Warden of the

[1] *Suppl.*, 94–103; Green, 154; Russell *B.*, 66 f. [2] Cf. *supra*, p. 49.

College continuously from 1858 to 1909. The number of minor canonries remained at six until 1920, when one was suspended in order to improve the stipends of the rest; the new statutes of 1936 imposed a maximum of five.[1]

The College lost its possessions and most of its ancient independence through the ordinances of 1875 and 1876. But it retained both its title and its character as a body corporate, and the new minor canons certainly wore a stronger complexion of co-operative responsibility than the old. All was not lost. The same years saw the completion of a unique act of restitution and re-endowment in St Paul's. Only one of the pre-1840 prebendaries still retained his stall and stipend, representing with Mr Belli, the Precentor, the last remainder of the age of Titans among the dignitaries of the foundation. Dr Randolph had been appointed in 1812 to the stall of Cantlers (probably so called from Roger Cantelupe or Cantlow, prebendary in 1249), otherwise known as Kentish Town, which then still formed part of the parish of St Pancras. The prebend was valued at £1079 a year in 1829–31, being one of the three or four rated at more than £1000; in 1861–3, when only two of the old prebendaries survived and the second (Ealdland) had derived for over forty years an average annual income of only £2 9s. 6d., Cantlers was worth a little over £2000. By the strangest of coincidences the prebendary of Ealdland also bore the name of Randolph; but his namesake of Cantlers outlived him, and in 1871, having enjoyed his good things for nearly sixty years, bethought him to repay somewhat to the Cathedral to which he owed their receipt. Accordingly, at Church's first chapter-meeting a proposal by Dr Randolph was gratefully approved, by the terms of which he undertook to pay over the sum of £200 every quarter "for the benefit of the prebendaries", and Chapter, in accepting the trust, stated its intention to form a fund of which the income should be attached to one or more of the

[1] *Suppl.*, 104–7, 160 f.; Russell *B.*, 39 f.; *Min.*, 3 June 1911; *minor canons' minutes*, 10 Dec. 1909, 27 Jan. 1920, 12 Oct. 1920.

existing prebendal stalls in return for duties to be determined thereafter as opportunity might occur.[1]

By the beginning of 1874 the annual income arising from Prebendary Randolph's gifts amounted to £25, and his quarterly contribution was still being continued. Lightfoot thereupon offered to add £500 to the fund, upon conditions which appear to have sprung from the fertile brain of Gregory, and recall the suggestion made by Sydney Smith in 1838 for giving to cathedral chapters the oversight of educational work within their dioceses:[2] the fund should be used to re-endow the stall of Cantlers, the Bishop of London should be asked to arrange for the stall of Cantlers to be annexed to the office of Diocesan Inspector of Schools, and means should be found from other sources to secure to the Inspector a sufficient total income. An offer on terms so practical and far-sighted, designed to associate an endowed diocesan official with the Cathedral instead of seeking to endow one out of Cathedral funds, could hardly fail to win acceptance. Randolph died in 1875. By the following March a scheme for carrying out the whole proposal had been formulated by Chapter, approved by the Ecclesiastical Commissioners, and ratified by Order in Council. Cantlers became an endowed non-residentiary canonry, and its first holder was immediately installed. The residue of Dr Randolph's fund was used, with his approval, to secure the payment of a small fee to each prebendary on fulfilling his obligation to preach a sermon in the Cathedral.[3]

Having successfully accomplished the commutation of the capitular estates, Chapter's next step was to build a schoolhouse for the choristers; their numbers could not be increased to the desired figure until a place had been prepared in which to board and educate them. Before final details had been settled with the Commissioners Gregory was charged,

[1] *Suppl.*, 151 f., 166; *E.R.C. Report*; *Acta B.*, 52, 57, 197.

[2] Cf. pp. 35 f.

[3] *Acta B.*, 348 f.; Gregory, 211; *Suppl.*, 137–40.

together with the Chapter Clerk, with an attempt to secure a site in Charterhouse Square; if that failed, then to select the most eligible site he could elsewhere. This occurred early in November 1871; and Mr Yool was to be informed of the result. Some weeks later negotiations were in progress for obtaining a site in Great Knight Rider Street, between St Paul's Churchyard and Queen Victoria Street; but there seem to have been difficulties in getting all the land that Chapter wanted, and also over the price. Then the lease fell in of some land in Carter Lane, adjoining the deanery, which had formerly been part of the separate deanery estate but had now passed to the Commissioners.[1]

Its history is too interesting to be omitted. The deanery did not always stand in a gloomy precinct, like the court-house in a county gaol. In the time of Charles I, before the Civil Wars, the deanery was set in a broad paddock. But during those wars the mansion was destroyed and the whole site was let on building leases and covered with shops and tenements. At the Restoration in 1660 the whole area, so covered, reverted to the ownership of the Dean, only to be overtaken by the Great Fire of 1666, which levelled all the buildings to the ground and left the area a waste. The Dean of that day was Sancroft, who was promoted from St Paul's to the archbishopric of Canterbury in 1678, put on trial as one of the Seven Bishops for refusing to be tyrannized by James II in 1688, and deprived by William III in 1690 for his still scrupulous honesty. In order to provide funds for rebuilding the deanery, Sancroft obtained an Act of Parliament enabling him to let off portions of the ground once more on building leases; and from that time the leases were regarded as forming part of the separate endowment of the Dean, and as such vested in the Ecclesiastical Commissioners on the death of Copleston. It was part of this estate which the Commissioners now granted as a site for the new choir-school, and so

[1] *Acta B.*, 202, 216; Gregory, 193.

a fragment of its alienated possessions came back to the Cathedral.[1]

The site was settled, but the house was yet to be planned; Penrose was given the task, with the Dean and Gregory and the newly chosen Headmaster to confer with him about details. Though designs were approved in June 1872 the final plans were not passed for another nine months; there was trouble about getting possession from the occupiers of the land, and about the estimated cost of the building. Penrose was authorized to proceed in October 1873; and as the patronal festival fell in 1874 on a Sunday its observance was transferred to the following day, when the Dean and Canons laid the corner-stone of the school at noon, in a snowstorm which soaked the surplices of the choir. A fresh annoyance ensued when the walls were actually rising. Chapter had been specifically advised that no claims for loss of light and air could possibly arise from neighbouring owners. But the advisers proved wrong, as experts sometimes do; and claims were suddenly presented which the same experts now stated to be irresistible. So with the house partly built the plans had to be revised in order to reduce the height originally intended, and instead of being ready for occupation by Christmas, as had been hoped, the choristers were not able to move into their new school till early in 1875.[2]

[1] *Memorial* addressed by Milman *to the Ecclesiastical Commissioners*, 1850, preserved in *Acta*, 184 ff.; *Suppl.*, 172.

[2] *Acta B.*, 249, 316, 329, 336, 377; Green, 90; Frost, 53 f., 58, 60, 95; Gregory, 194.

9

DOME AND DECORATION

MEANTIME Chapter and the Decoration Committee had to decide in collaboration how they meant to embellish and "complete" the Cathedral. The appeal to the public for a quarter of a million pounds had been launched in the summer of 1870.[1] In a sermon preached in January 1871 Liddon claimed that the erection of the great church had been the work not of the City or the diocese alone, but of the entire Church and country. He appealed to these interests, and to the whole Empire, not merely "to clothe in time this cold and dreary waste of walls", but to proclaim them thereby as a focus for "the moral power of a great work of adoring love". Money was coming in, and a great impetus was given to the flow by the Thanksgiving Service for the recovery of the Prince of Wales from typhoid fever, in February 1872. Chapter took advantage of the general enthusiasm by opening a General Thanksgiving Fund in association with the Decoration Appeal; a further public meeting was held at the Mansion House in March, at which support was invited from the boroughs and counties of England and Wales. The Queen gave £1000, and within a twelvemonth promises from a vast body of contributors had raised the total given since 1870 to almost £56,000.[2]

But what was intended to be done with it? The first task, on which all were agreed in principle, was to reconstruct the organ and replace it in a more suitable and more promisingly final situation than the archway where it had been put

[1] Cf. *supra*, pp. 111–12.

[2] *Cathedral Decoration*, 6 ff., 12 f.; Gregory, 204; *Scrap Book*, p. 103 (accounts of the appeal).

in 1860. This business was raised by Willis early in 1871. But its new station could not be determined without pre-judging the problem of the chancel as a whole; and on this subject controversy occupied the field. Nevertheless plans for the organ went ahead, nor were they checked even by Mansel's sudden death on 30 July; between his decease and his funeral Chapter approved a design prepared by Penrose for closing the choir and fitting up a temporary choir under the dome while the alterations were in progress. In fact the Decoration Committee had already announced, in April, its intention to divide the organ, and re-affirmed its policy in *The Times* of 17 July; the two works on which a decision had then actually been reached were: "1. The enlargement of Father Smith's beautiful old organ and its division into halves, to be placed opposite each other, north and south, against the piers of the dome, at the entrance to the choir. 2. The continuation to the verge of the dome area of the present finely-carved wood-work of the choir benches and stalls." [1]

These decisions were peculiarly unfortunate, from a controversial point of view, because Mansel, in a letter issued in the previous September, had defined the Committee's object as being "to render the interior of the Cathedral worthy of its unrivalled exterior, and to carry out the intentions of its great architect", and Milman, in inaugurating the original appeal in 1858, had thus proclaimed its policy: "Sir Christopher Wren's intentions, his mode of treatment, and, as far as they can be authenticated, his very designs, will be scrupulously kept sacred and followed." The Decoration Committee was bound by an explicit endorsement of that policy, given at the Mansion House meeting in 1870. But many still desired the old screen to be restored, in its original position, and with the organ resting on it as before 1860; among them was Sparrow Simpson, who had suggested the idea of dividing the organ, though in hope that it would

[1] *Acta B.*, 160, 162, 194; *Cathedral Decoration*, 18, 39; cf. Street in *Cathedral Decoration*, 21.

not be carried out. It was by no means universally taken for certain that Wren had had the choir-screen forced upon him, as frequently asserted, against his own judgement.[1] In any case, nobody could conceivably pretend that Wren had designed his stalls to match the position in which Chapter now proposed to fix them, far less that Wren had ever dreamed of cutting the organ in two halves. There was obvious ground for charging the Committee with a breach of faith.[2]

This was indeed the crux of the whole matter: was the church to be treated for practical purposes as containing one compartment or two? One plan aimed at using the choir for daily services and the dome and nave for the large congregations expected on Sundays and special occasions, as in a Gothic minster; the other proposed that the entire Cathedral should be thrown open, like the great Roman basilicas, from end to end, in spite of its very different topographical construction and the extreme depth of its choir, which removed the altar practically out of sight or hearing of the main body of worshippers. A great deal could have been said in favour of either method, since St Paul's is a classical building on a Gothic ground-plan. Most of what was in fact said was in favour of the two compartments. What Chapter clearly meant to do, in some fashion or other, and actually did, was to ignore the ground-plan and maintain a basilican indivisibility.

This was not the first time that proposals had been advanced for bringing the whole church into simultaneous use for divine service. It is true that Milman's experiments had all been made in nave or dome or transepts, in complete detachment from the choir, even after the removal of the organ-screen.[3] But in 1839, a dozen years before Milman put forth his first effort, an anonymous author, subscribing himself merely "A Clergyman", published an open letter to the Dean and prebendaries, advocating a scheme at once

[1] Cf. *supra*, p. 83. [2] *Cathedral Decoration*, 17, 22, 43; Sumner, 21.
[3] Cf. *supra*, pp. 79 ff.

devoutly chimerical and fantastically practicable for turning the entire Cathedral into a house of common prayer.[1] He pointed out that for many generations three-quarters of the area of any English cathedral had been treated merely as a disproportionately spacious vestibule to the choir. It was for this reason that visitors to Westminster Abbey customarily walked about the nave with their hats on, and that both the Abbey and St Paul's had come to be regarded, in recent Parliamentary debates, as national statue galleries.[2] He next quoted at length Dr Wiseman, then the Rector of the Venerable English College in Rome, who had written a most unfavourable comparison of St Paul's with the once heathen, but now converted Roman Pantheon. Our author frankly admitted the paganism of the sculptured "warriors and river-gods" in St Paul's, though he qualified the popish strictures by asserting at least the freedom of St Paul's from any practical idolatry; and he threw in a conjecture of his own, that any heathen stranger entering the Cathedral and trying to guess the purpose to which it might be dedicated would be struck chiefly by the inscription to Sir Christopher Wren, placarded upon the choir-screen,[3] and would naturally conclude that the entire edifice was but a mausoleum raised in memory of that most estimable citizen.

So far the anonymous Clergyman might have carried Sydney Smith along with him; his pamphlet affords timely evidence that others besides Copleston and Sydney were shocked by the suggestion that St Paul's was not, in its entirety, a house of God. But it would have been interesting to hear Sydney's comments on the detailed Plan presented for bringing the four quarters of the Cathedral into action in a Christian character. Obviously, the organ and screen would have to be removed, so that from a central position under the dome the four arms of the church would all be equally

[1] *Plan.* [2] Cf. *supra*, pp. 29–31.

[3] Cf. Green, 55: after the removal of the screen the inscription was re-erected in 1871 on the porch in the north transept.

accessible to sight and sound. The organ could be re-erected on a large gallery in the extreme west, which might also house a considerable number of charity school boys, trained to simple chants, to give a lead in the singing. Galleries should be built likewise at the extremities of both transepts for girl singers, similarly trained. There was method in this proposed distinction of the tuneful of either sex: in order to avoid all unseemliness of the kind of which complaint had recently been made, men and women had better be completely segregated, men being admitted solely by the west door, women only by the north and south transepts; the nave would be railed off in order to prevent their meeting. Places in the choir should be reserved exclusively "for clergy, nobility, magistrates, civic dignitaries, and any gentleman with tickets from the dean or chapter, but also, in a marked manner, for regular communicants in the Cathedral": no women to be tolerated here except out of sight behind the stalls.

These arrangements left the dome area to be utilized for the general benefit of all sections. Here a new liturgical choir should be constructed. Within a low barrier enclosing a vast central space, and raised above the floor by four steps, a double row of canons and choristers would sit in circular formation. Inside them, further elevated by a series of three circular and two square steps, would stand the altar with its attendant ministers, facing north and south, in plain view from each of the four cardinal points of the compass to every one in the body of the church; whether every one could hear distinctly or not, there would be no possible doubt of his being able to see, and with his Prayer Book to follow, the progress of the service. Something, however, could be done to promote mere audibility. The singing, swollen with the voices of charity children, would be fully congregational except in the anthems; these would be rendered by the choir alone, supported by a small organ to be concealed nearby in one of the choir aisles. Four minor canons, each facing one arm of the church, would chant in unison those parts of the service which are addressed to the congregation. The lessons presented a difficulty, which could be overcome if four readers, instead of merely one, were to issue from the choir enclosure and read the appointed scriptures, each from his own eagle, immediately facing the several sections of the people; the readers would be out of hearing of each other, separated by rather more than the whole diameter of the dome, "while at the same time a large body of the people would hear the Lessons"—an interesting commentary on the degree of audibility either expected or considered practicable at that date.

Our anonymous author conceded that parish churches and not cathedrals were the proper places for imparting religious instruction; cathedrals, built on a scale as vast as possible, existed for services of praise in choir or at the altar. But in order to make some provision for teaching, he recommended three pulpits, the first in the structural choir for the gentry, the second at the back of one of the transepts for the women, and the third at the west end for the lower orders of male worshippers. (May it be assumed that the hearers in nave and transept would be accommodated with backless benches on which they could turn about without awkwardness or clatter: or would they stand throughout?) He thought it desirable that the sermons to be delivered from these points of vantage should be postponed until the regular service had concluded. Finally, as a means of encouraging a full attendance on Sundays, he made two suggestions: first that people should be habituated to instruction by evening lectures in the nave and transepts during the week; secondly, that the minor canons should be strongly reinforced by a body of twelve unmarried clergymen, living in community like Fellows of a college at the universities (in 1839 dons still vacated their Fellowships on marriage), who would spend laborious days in pastoral visitation throughout the neighbourhood, under the supervision of the parochial clergy—at £50 salary and £30 board for each man the whole job could be done for £1000 a year.

Here was generous provision for worship and for missionary extension (though not for its living agents), based on a scheme designed to stretch the usefulness of the Cathedral to its utmost limit. Some of the proposals can hardly fail to raise a smile. What is much more significant, however, is the vision which inspired the coldly calculated project. It anticipated in a very remarkable way some of the aims and ideas which animated Milman and Gregory, Church and Liddon, in the reconstruction and reform which they were subsequently to effect. And though no notice seems to have been taken of the actual Plan produced by this anonymous, which dropped like a miscarrying birth before its time, a great deal more was to be heard in Church's day of the idea of a central altar either under or adjacent to the dome, to form the visual focus of worship for a great congregation, comparable to the dome pulpit from which rivers of exhortation now flowed across the breadth of the Cathedral. Nor can it be said that any such proposals arrived too late to be considered; they were put out by architects of eminence during February 1871, before the authorities of St Paul's had committed themselves to a decision.

Two main solutions of the problem were thus submitted. In either case the object aimed at was to draw down the principal activities of worship within easy range of the people; incidental to this purpose, but not without importance, was the wish to leave Wren's work as far as possible unspoilt and merely to add fresh equipment in the spaces which, for lack of occupants, he had left unfurnished. The first of these plans was sponsored by a pair of architects, of whom one, Somers Clarke, was destined to succeed the long-serving and long-suffering Penrose on his retirement from the post of Surveyor in 1897. Its basic principle was to replace the screen and organ exactly where they had been put by Wren, leaving a considerable area free under the barrel arch at the west end of the structural choir. In this space they proposed that a new altar should be erected, under a canopy of rich design. Immediately in front of it, under the eastern portion of the dome, they proposed to enclose a choir, on a platform raised slightly above floor level, for the clergy and singers. By this means the conduct of the service would be within full sight of all those present in the nave and dome area, and of very many in the transepts; and the eastern arm of the church, instead of becoming "a sort of magnified parochial chancel", would be retained as a distinct compartment for ordinary weekday use.[1]

The second plan, which differed little in principle from the foregoing, was embodied in a letter dated 29 February, addressed to George Richmond, R.A., a member of the Decoration Committee, and published in pamphlet form with a covering letter to Liddon in May. Its author was the distinguished architect, G. E. Street, whose Royal Courts of Justice (1874–82) were the least successful achievement of a brilliant designer of churches. Street also wished to see Wren's enclosed choir perfectly restored. He strongly deprecated waste of money in spreading coloured marble and polychromatic decoration over the surface of the church, as influential advocates were understood to be suggesting; let the walls rather be cleaned of dirt and whitewash, and be allowed to reveal "the honest and worthy materials of which they are built". The best use of the funds collected for decoration, in his judgement, would be obtained by following the analogy of Florence Cathedral. At Florence an immense octagonal choir opens under the dome, with large apses on the three sides not occupied by the nave; the high altar is set on the edge of the dome area adjoining the eastern apse. Street therefore recommended for St Paul's a noble altar under the dome raised on steps and covered by a magnificent baldachino, extremely rich. In front and on either side would be seats for the clergy

[1] *The Sacristy*, 1 Feb. 1871; Micklethwaite and Somers Clarke in *Cathedral Decoration*, 52.

and singers, surrounded by marble walls of modest height but of a costly delicacy.

Such a structure, attracting the eye of the most heathen visitor, would utterly redeem St Paul's from any possible charge either of chilliness or of paganism. Access would be easy to the choir through the ample area to be left vacant between the new altar and the deeply recessed organ-screen. Nothing of Wren's work would need to be altered; none of it would even be concealed, for the organ reinstated on its screen would over-top the new baldachino; and around and above his organ-case Wren himself had been careful to leave sufficient space to allow of suggestions, at least, of a distant view beyond, and thus to create a devotionally effective "mystery of things half seen".[1]

Street's proposals showed a splendid insight, both in a religious and an architectural sense, and might have provided a very glorious solution of the problems before the Decoration Committee. They won distinguished support among his professional colleagues. But on the other side of the controversy it has to be admitted that Chapter, with all its aesthetic deficiencies, was better acquainted than Street with the perplexities of handling the really vast crowds now to be expected at St Paul's on fairly frequent occasions, and could not have viewed without apprehension the considerable loss of seating-space beneath the dome which his scheme must have involved. Right or wrong, it was inexorable: *Gregorius locutus est*. Within the next few months Church brought into Chapter a far more delicate aesthetic perception and a much deeper knowledge of Italian churches; but his own taste in architecture was by no means impeccable. In any case, Chapter was committed to its own policy before Church even received the offer of the deanery; and early in September, only a few days after his acceptance and six weeks before his installation, the choir was closed for the work of reconstruction to begin. Services were transferred, on Sundays and

[1] Street in *Cathedral Decoration*, 21.

weekdays alike, to a temporary choir on the eastern side of the dome area; a small organ was provided to accompany them.[1]

Not even yet were the minds of Chapter and the Decoration Committee wholly clear about the details of the work on which they had embarked. As late as November they were still discussing the erection of a screen across the entrance to the choir,[2] and calling for a rough model to be placed *in situ* so that Chapter might be able to judge of the effect. Decision was postponed "until additional explanations had been given by the Executive Committee as to the Chapter's intentions concerning the use of the Dome and Nave". Whether it was Chapter that was thought to need enlightenment from the Executive about its own intentions, or perhaps the public, is something of a mystery.[3] No more seems to have been heard about a new screen; probably by "screen" nothing more portentous was intended than a low partition or a brass railing. But the work was pressed on. Monuments were cleared from the western section of the choir, to make room against the piers for the bisected organ-case and the stalls of the dignitaries. (The casing of the organ on the south side of the choir is a replica of the original woodwork on the north side.) And two devices were employed in an attempt to bring the sanctuary into slightly greater prominence: the floor of the choir was raised by three steps, or fifteen inches, above the general level of the pavement, and in the far east the altar was brought a little forward from the apse. Curtains hung behind the altar made a convenient passage for vicars and choristers to pass from one choir aisle to the other without attracting notice.[4]

At this point, exactly ten years after his father had succumbed to the same disease, the Prince of Wales fell dangerously ill with typhoid fever; special prayers were said for him in Cathedral on 10 December. On his recovery, Liddon,

[1] Green, 55; Frost, 24.
[2] Cf. *supra*, p. 83.
[3] *Acta B.*, 203.
[4] Frost, 24, 26, 28; *Acta B.*, 200.

preaching in St Paul's, declared that in some previous ages, after such an event, the Queen and her nobles would have united with her loyal citizens in offering public thanksgiving in the cathedral of the metropolis; and his words were reported to Her Majesty. This was not the first invitation of the kind to reach Queen Victoria. In 1849, after the cessation of a severe epidemic of cholera, a general Day of Thanksgiving was announced, and Bishop Blomfield suggested that she should attend a public service at St Paul's. Lord John Russell, then Prime Minister, favoured the alternative of Westminster Abbey. Victoria persuaded herself that her advisers must have made some mistake; she approved of a Thanksgiving, and was prepared "to join in the public demonstration" by attending "*some* place of *public worship,* and not in her domestic chapel"; but St George's Chapel in her own castle of Windsor marked the limit of her willingness to plunge into publicity. In 1871, however, the Sovereign, melted by personal disaster and the fearful threat of its repetition, promptly acquiesced. The date was fixed for Tuesday 27 February 1872.[1]

The Cathedral was in such a mess and tumult of reconstruction already that any more made no great difference. Chapter arranged for services on a somewhat reduced scale to be held in Christ Church, Newgate Street, and refused the request of the vicars-choral for a complete holiday from vocal labour during the emigration: St Paul's itself was closed from 5 February to 23 March, except for Sunday services in March. The Office of Works took over the Cathedral and erected scaffolding to receive a congregation of 14,000 persons; the cost was borne by the Government, but Chapter was made to pay for certain galleries put up for the use of its own friends. Feverish activity must have been required on the part of the Cathedral authorities to make the choir presentable. But by Thanksgiving Day the stalls for Chapter and dignitaries were complete, with temporary benches in front

[1] Green, 59; Gregory, 183; *Letters of Queen Victoria* (1908), II, 228.

for the singers. The organ was divided indeed, but incompletely reassembled, the pedal pipes not having been connected to the console, with the astonishing consequence that while Cooper, the sub-organist, operated the manuals for the service "Father" Willis presided in person at a temporary pedal-board, and the two kept perfect time. Goss conducted; he had composed both a Te Deum and an anthem for the occasion, and received a knighthood in reward. He said he believed he was the only knight that lived in Brixton.[1]

The service began at 12.45, when the Queen, the Prince and Princess of Wales, and most of the Royal Family arrived; a pew had been created for them just to the west of the dome. Liddon had been in the church since 9.30, and had "spent about two and a half hours in making people take off their hats, and in otherwise trying to find them seats and to keep order"; the offenders were no proletarians but the invited guests of the State, since there was no admission for any of the general public. The Thanksgiving was immensely impressive both as a service and a spectacle; and the reception of Disraeli, in Opposition, by the populace, which contrasted markedly with its indifference to Gladstone, the Prime Minister, gave the first indication of his new attraction for the people in the street. For the rest of the week enormous crowds were admitted to view the fittings.[2] Then the work of clearance began.

Little damage had been done to the fabric in rearing and removing the scaffolding, but the time had come for a systematic cleaning of the church with part of the money provided by the commutation. This was a long job. Not only was there the choir to finish; work had been in progress for months beforehand on the north porch, the old "great" organ and its accessories had to be dislodged from the south transept, and the chance was seized for dealing drastically with

[1] Green, 60–4; Frost, 26–30; *Acta B.*, 228, 267 f.; Sumner, 21.

[2] Frost, 27, 29; Green, 61; Johnston, 168; Monypenny and Buckle, *Disraeli* (1929), II, 522.

the statuary; the bases of the monuments were lowered and they were deprived of the inopportune protection of iron railings, on a spike of which a man had tried to commit suicide, without success, in 1869. Operations were still proceeding at the end of 1874. Meantime Chapter had come to a resolute decision that St Paul's should not again be turned into an amphitheatre, even at the cost of abandoning the age-long annual service for the charity children:[1] temporary erections inside the Cathedral interfered with its regular and constant use for divine service, and were henceforward to be discountenanced.[2]

For weal or woe, the battle of the screens was terminated. But it was as nothing compared with the battle of chromatics which flared up with the receipt of funds from the Thanksgiving appeal. Penrose submitted a scheme of embellishment which would have concentrated most of the colour, upon which the hearts of the Decoration Committee were set, in four areas—the choir and sanctuary, the dome, the great windows which conclude the four arms of the church, and the shallow dome over the west end of the nave. This was in July 1872; and in the same month a Fine Arts Committee was appointed by the Executive, consisting of six experts under the chairmanship of the Dean. But already the fatal decision had been taken to entrust the oversight of the whole work to William Burges, an ultra-Gothic architect who entertained the strongest abhorrence for the "abominations" of Sir Christopher Wren, and had said so publicly only a year before. Expecting to be asked to furnish him with instructions, the Fine Arts Committee was pained to find itself ignored by Mr Burges. Subsequent events are summarized in *The Times* leader of 15 June 1874: "For two years the Executive Committee for the completion of St Paul's has had the rare pleasure of witnessing a continual and inevitable struggle between what may be called its two children—

[1] Cf. *supra*, p. 103.

[2] Green, 38, 55, 62, 68, 104; *Acta B.*, 239, 242, 268, 317.

almost twins in point of time—its Fine Arts Committee and its Architect." The Fine Arts Committee thereupon broke up and was discharged, and Burges reigned supreme.[1]

The essence of the Burges plan was embodied in coloured scale models and exhibited at the Royal Academy in the spring of 1874, to the consternation of nearly all beholders. The entire interior of the Cathedral was to be refaced with a veneer of polished marbles, varied with a wealth of mosaic, gilding, carving, bronzes, arabesques, friezes, and similar gauds: white was to predominate near the ground, but as the eye rose it would observe the temperature of the pigments rising with its own angle of vision, in blacks, reds, blues, greens, and gold, reaching fever-point in the saucer-domes of the roof, which were to be subdivided into panels by the addition of plaster mouldings: and as the chromatic brilliance was to increase with the height above the floor, so was its intensity to be augmented in its passage eastward through the choir to the sanctuary. A "rough estimate" set the total cost of the projected work at £400,000, of which about one tenth was actually available.[2]

The Executive Committee, including Church, Gregory, and Liddon, continued to support Burges, accepting his design as the basis for decoration of the choir and apse, though reserving for further consideration its approval of the details. The Fine Arts Committee having been disposed of in June 1874, Chapter acceded in the same month to the request of the Executive that Penrose, who had been associated with Burges in 1872 as architectural adviser for the decoration of the Cathedral, should be relieved of this responsibility from the end of the year; it also reaffirmed the policy of the Executive, Lightfoot putting on record his respectful dissent from that decision. Permission was granted for Burges to try experimental decoration of the apse "in a temporary way". But it was vain to oppose further resistance to the criticisms of

[1] Cuttings and pamphlets in *Cathedral Decoration*, 23, 42, 43, 56.

[2] *Mr Burges' Models*, in *Cathedral Decoration*, 41.

the experts and the verdict of the public, by which the whole enterprise was utterly condemned.

At the beginning of November Chapter bowed to the inevitable. It rescinded its permission to make temporary experiments, expressed its judgement that in view of the divisions of opinion all attempt to proceed with the decoration should be, for the time, suspended, and asked the Executive Committee to pay Burges for the work he had done and cancel the existing agreement with him and Penrose. Later in the month the Executive met and, though dealing tenderly with Burges' feelings, acquiesced. As with Milman, so again with Gregory, an enthusiasm for decoration, more passionate than planned, had met its end, leaving behind a legacy of confusion and waste, but little positive accomplishment except the enlargement and partition of the organ. One gain ensued. As time passed and the Cathedral recovered from the physical convulsions of the previous fifteen years, the appetite for large-scale experiment waned and there was general acceptance of the open choir.[1]

Baulked of its decorations, Chapter turned its energies towards bells, a species of which St Paul's had hitherto possessed only two to strike the quarter chimes, the large bell which rang the hours and was tolled at the death of the mighty, and a small bell in the north-west tower which was rung for service. The resolution was taken in 1873 to devote the proceeds of the sale of unwanted odds and ends to the provision of a peal of twelve bells for the north-west tower and a carillon for the south-west tower. Stainer, who had succeeded Goss as organist in 1872, was asked to visit Belgium on a tour of inspection, so that a carillon might be ordered on the best model; but nothing came of that part of the scheme. The peal materialized, through the generosity of the Corporation and various Guilds of the City. The bells were dedicated by Bishop Jackson after Evensong on All Saints' Day 1878; the ceremony was delayed by the length of the

[1] *Cathedral Decoration*, 43, 60; *Acta B.*, 388 f., 393, 405 f.

sermon customary on festivals, which was preached by an aged minor canon deputising for the absent prebendary. The first "scientific peal" was rung on them by the College Youths in 1881: it lasted for four hours and seventeen minutes, and the ringers were locked into the ringing chamber until it was finished.

In the same year a new great bell ("Great Paul") was also ordered, and arrived the following May. It had been intended to hang in the northern tower, but as it weighed nearly seventeen tons insuperable objections were discovered at the eleventh hour to the plan of hoisting it above the existing peal, and grave risks were foreseen in swinging it at such an elevation. Its destination was therefore switched to the southern tower, where it was skilfully and safely accommodated with the help of the Royal Engineers and tackle borrowed from the Ordnance. The "Dean's doorway" at the foot of the tower, and the eye-hole of the cupola over the staircase, had to be enlarged by the temporary removal of stone-work, a task accomplished without the use of obstructive scaffolding. The bell was delivered on a truck to a point some fifty feet away, and thence slid on a prepared stage into the tower. There it was grappled by powerful lifting gear and raised into position, where it hangs in a solid cage of timber resting on a ledge in the masonry. The operation of hoisting it occupied three days. It bears the inscription, suggested by Liddon, *vae mihi si non evangelizavero* (1 Cor. 9. 16); and orders were given that it should bear its witness by being chimed every weekday for five minutes from 1 o'clock. It was paid for out of accumulated profits of the crypt and cupola.[1]

[1] Gregory, 209 f.; *Acta B.*, 325, 329; *Acta C.*, 63 f., 94, 96–9, 105; Green, 145 f., 165, 167 f.; Russell *B.*, 72 f.

10

CHOIR AND MUSIC UNDER STAINER

Bells make a merry kind of music of their own, but the music which is essential to a great cathedral establishment is that which accompanies and sustains the regular offices of divine worship. In this respect Church found on his arrival at St Paul's that the tide of harmony had ebbed. The choir was small, and its numerical weakness was rendered more acute by the extreme irregularity of its attendance. The organist, John Goss, was an old man; he was born in 1800 and had held his post at St Paul's since 1838; the difficulties of his position were more than he was able to contend with.[1] After the revival of the weekly disciplinary chapter in 1870 many complaints were recorded which indicate the strains and stresses arising between him and the Succentor and the vicars; remarks of a similar kind had been entered in Gregory's private note-book during 1869.[2]

Thus, "The Succentor reported that, owing to faulty playing on the part of the organist, the service on Friday was very defective." "Succentor reported that the service on Friday evening was a failure owing to the wrong Magnificat and Nunc Dimittis being played." "The Succentor complained that there was no counter-tenor on Tuesday or Wednesday morning, and that the anthem had to be changed in the service on Thursday evening through the organist's being without a copy, while on Tuesday he played the wrong anthem." "There were only 4 adult voices and the service was a failure. The anthem had to be changed as the boys were not ready." "Mr Goss attended to explain a stoppage

[1] Cf. *supra*, pp. 21–2. [2] Cf. *supra*, p. 96.

in the service yesterday, and it was resolved that 'every deputy singing in the choir shall be requested to notify to the virger in attendance for what member of the choir he is acting as deputy' ": on the same occasion it was ruled that, if the appointed service or anthem had to be changed owing to the sudden indisposition of a singer or other urgent cause, notice must be given of the proposed change before the service began, and that "it cannot be allowed that any change should be made during the service, or during the passage from the vestries to the choir."[1]

The blame clearly could not all be laid on the unhappy Goss. The root of the trouble lay in the slackness of the administration and the traditional jealousies between different interests within the establishment. But it was also true that Goss took many outside engagements and had never been expected to give his whole time to St Paul's; his income as organist was about £250. Chapter therefore let it be known to him that for the future the large increase which was contemplated in the musical activities of the Cathedral made it desirable for its organist to render full-time service. On hearing this, in November 1871, Goss wrote a dignified and unselfish letter, not untinged with pathos, laying himself and his future at the discretion of the Dean and Chapter. It was arranged that his resignation should take effect from Lady Day 1872, that he should retain the honorary title of Organist of St Paul's, together with his office of vicar-choral (which, incidentally, being a freehold could not have been taken from him) and most of his emoluments by way of pension. The circumstances of his retirement, which he survived for another eight years, were made illustrious by the unforeseen occurrence of the Thanksgiving Service in February and his own share in its success; and he departed with his knighthood and a blaze of glory.[2] In place of Goss Chapter obtained, for a salary of £400, an undivided claim

[1] *Min.*, 15 and 29 Oct. 1870, 14 and 28 Jan. and 4 Feb. 1871.
[2] *Acta B.*, 210–14, 275 f.

upon the exertions of John Stainer. This was a gift from heaven, and Chapter clinched their bargain with him before December was out.

Stainer was an old St Paul's boy. Born in 1840, he entered the choir as probationer in 1848, and was admitted chorister in 1849, under the tuition of Coward.[1] Miss Hackett observed his talent and paid for him to have organ lessons from George Cooper, assistant organist to Goss and subsequently to Stainer himself; Coward made him organist of his own church of St Benet, Paul's Wharf, while the boy was still in the Cathedral choir. Young Stainer had a friend at the Chapel Royal, named Arthur Sullivan; the two boys spent their leisure on the penny steamers, enjoying oranges and nuts and the attractions of the Thames. By 1861 Stainer had become organist of Magdalen College, Oxford, where he made a great reputation and composed settings and anthems in tireless profusion and with a high degree of technical skill. It was due to Liddon that he was brought back from Oxford; and Chapter could not have chosen a better man for the work they wanted done. Stainer was a scholar of rare distinction, and extremely hard-working; if the kind of music required was not available he was perfectly ready to produce adaptations or original scores on demand. He was a brilliant executant and a great choir-trainer. But beyond his professional ability he was a devout Churchman, with his whole heart engaged in improving the tone of the services; he possessed the qualities so urgently needed for controlling the choir—tact, humour, modesty, and friendliness, in addition to an all-pervasive energy; and he had inside knowledge of St Paul's.[2]

Some interesting conditions were attached to Stainer's appointment. One was that he should "be authorised to provide an assistant for whom the Dean and Chapter will secure to

[1] Cf. *supra*, p. 49.

[2] *Acta B.*, 212, 215; Fellowes in *English Church Music* (R.S.C.M.), Jan. 1951; Bumpus, 174 ff., 180 (but his dates are unreliable); *Min.*, 15 July 1899; *Bundle*, 83; Frost, 68, 85; Russell *B.*, 30 f., 53–5, 85.

him a salary of £100 a year": apparently it was left to Stainer both to select and, as intermediary, to pay his assistant. Chapter went so far as to "recommend to him" George Cooper for the post, "but leave it to his option to appoint him or not as he may feel best". This showed a gratifying confidence in Stainer, but looks at first sight rather less than kind to Cooper, who had been deputy organist at the Cathedral since 1838.[1] Presumably, however, it was taken by ancient custom to be the organist's own business to provide whatever assistance he needed at the organ; it was only at the end of 1869 that mention is made of a salary being granted to Cooper from the Cathedral, and then only at the rate of £20.[2] At any rate, Cooper retained his post until he died in 1876; Stainer was then able to secure as sub-organist an Oxford pupil of his own, George Martin, who had already been serving for two years as music master in the new choir-school.[3]

A second unexpected feature of Stainer's contract was that he was promised, in part payment of his stipulated salary, the next vacancy that might occur in the post of vicar-choral. As Goss still held one of the vicariates the effective number of these freehold offices was thus reduced to four, which did not altogether please certain of the gentlemen of the choir when the reversion fell in, at the end of 1872, and they found that Stainer was appointed. It was understood that Chapter would have liked to break the association of organist and vicar, but that Stainer would not take the organ on any other terms, since he had a freehold at Oxford and wanted the same security at St Paul's. When he retired in 1888 he resigned both posts, and from that time onward the organist ceased to be technically a choirman. But it was not only with the vicars that Stainer had trouble at the start; he suffered many insults, and the Sunday evening special choir resigned in a body. He asked Chapter to spare him any criticisms for two

[1] Cf. *supra*, pp. 22–3. [2] *Cf. supra*, p. 99.
[3] *Acta B.*, 96, 225 f.; Russell *B.*, 56; Frost, 60, 64.

years, after which he guaranteed that they would be content: by the end of that period his exertions had raised the standard of the choir into universal fame. Chapter quickly showed that it was satisfied with its bargain by increasing his salary to a total of £500 from the time that he began to draw the emoluments of his vicariate.[1]

One of Stainer's first concerns was to enlarge the choir; now that it had finally emerged from its catacomb of enclosure it needed an access of vocal power in order to transmit melody throughout the vast church. He recommended an establishment of some forty boys and eighteen men (of whom twelve might suffice for any ordinary weekday). The full number of boys could not be attained until the choir school had been built; but the eight existing choristers and four probationers[2] were reinforced by the election of another dozen boys in January 1873. The problem of the men's voices was easier to solve. Stainer had at the outset five effective vicars (the sixth member of the choral foundation being the pensioned Goss) and five supernumeraries.[3] Chapter therefore decided to hold an open competition in December 1872 for the election of eight further supernumeraries, to begin work on the following Lady Day.

Several changes were introduced at the same time. Supernumeraries were in future to be called Assistant Vicars-choral. Salaries were raised, a contributory pension scheme was started, and payment was offered for deputies during the summer holidays. In return each assistant was now to give full attendance like an established freeholder of the choir; his quota of duty was fixed at two services on Sundays and great feasts, and eight out of the twelve regular weekday services; and a stiff code of rules and regulations was imposed. Some aspirants who were accustomed to more easy-going employment were frightened into withdrawing their

[1] *Acta B.*, 225, 299, 301; *Acta C.*, 187 f.; Fellowes, loc. cit.; Frost, 24 f., 39 f.; Green, 207.

[2] Cf. *supra*, p. 49.

[3] Cf. *supra*, p. 98.

applications on being shown a copy of the rules which they would have to keep. When Stainer obtained his vacancy as vicar, Chapter provided for an additional assistant vicar to remedy the consequent deficiency in the choir.[1]

The gentlemen of the choir were not accustomed to rehearsals; when faced with music they had never seen before they might cast an eye through it during one of the lessons at a previous service, but no more had been expected of them. From his first week in office Stainer started to explain to them the manner in which he wanted things done; "but then," as one of them wrote, "Stainer had such a charming way with him". The new regulations for assistant vicars included an obligation to attend one choir-practice a week: some time passed before a regular weekly practice was in fact enforced, but Stainer used to rehearse them before or after service whenever he thought a need existed. He also enormously extended the range of the Cathedral music, with the enthusiastic help of Sparrow Simpson, who was made Succentor in 1876.[2]

Stainer's own acknowledgement of Simpson's co-operation was complete and ungrudging. Simpson, he said, always consulted him in drawing up the lists of music to be sung. He had no fads, but adopted anything conducive to worship, "from the early part of the sixteenth century to the latter part of the nineteenth". He never wavered in his desire to encourage living musicians, and gave every promising composition a trial in St Paul's, even at the risk of a few failures. The only thing he could not endure was "respectable sham old music": he banned modern composers who merely imitated old masters instead of writing in an idiom of their own. As an experienced librarian he evolved an admirable method of binding and storing the contents of the rapidly expanding music library. He invariably attended the weekly

[1] Russell *B.*, 33; Frost, 36–9; *Acta B.*, 254 ff., 257, 261 ff., 301 f.

[2] Frost, 27, 31 f., 47, 63; *Acta B.*, 263; *Min.*, 11 Oct. 1873 (Succentor's Report, *ad. fin.*).

rehearsals, winning the affectionate confidence of the choir and infusing it with the freshness and vigour of his own enthusiasm. When Simpson resigned the succentorship at the end of 1885 Chapter specially recorded its sense of his "great and in some respects unprecedented services", and concurred in Stainer's judgement that without his help the vast improvement which had been effected in the worship of the Cathedral would have been impossible.[1]

Improvements made in the appearance of the choir, though they coincided with Stainer's arrival, are probably to be attributed to Liddon and Gregory. When the Cathedral reopened after the Thanksgiving Service, on 24 March 1872, it was observed that the boys were wearing cassocks under their surplices. In October it was decided to supply the choir with surplices, and to have them washed, at the expense of the Cathedral. The vicars were put into cassocks at Advent 1873. But it was on Stainer that the duty fell of reconstructing the Sunday evening voluntary choir "in such a way as he may think will best conduce to its efficiency": as already recorded,[2] he winnowed the men and swept away the women and strange children. He rehearsed the survivors every Friday evening in the Chapter House, and they were soon devoted to him, in spite of the fact that from January 1873 their duties, like the Sunday evening services, became continuous all the year round.[3]

In the same month another musical experiment inaugurated a tradition that was rapidly fixed and permanently maintained. Mention has been made on an earlier page[4] of Gregory's proposal, in which Chapter concurred, that an appropriate musical service should be arranged for Holy Week. The decision was taken in April 1871, three weeks after Westminster Abbey had observed Maundy Thursday with a performance of Bach's St Matthew Passion: but if the

[1] Simpson, 67–72; *Acta C.*, 154. [2] Cf. *supra*, p. 85.
[3] Frost, 30, 46; Green, 74, 88; Russell *B.*, 85; *Acta B.*, 242, 265.
[4] See *supra*, p. 105.

example of the Abbey possibly gave Gregory his idea, it by no means predetermined the form that it should assume, for Chapter felt great hesitation before allowing the engagement, for a performance in church, of an imported orchestra and augmented choir whose members might be of any religion or none. In 1872 Holy Week fell at the very moment of the change in organist, and perhaps for that reason, perhaps from Goss's expressed inability to undertake extra work, nothing had been set in train. However, Stainer's keenness on attempting special musical services turned the scale, and for St Paul's Day in January 1873 he obtained permission to hire orchestra and singers at his own expense for performing at evensong a selection from Mendelssohn's oratorio *St Paul*.[1]

During the rehearsal Church addressed the performers, pointing out that the proceedings were not a concert but an experiment in church services, and that it depended very much on their own behaviour whether it would ever be repeated. Capitular diffidence was overcome by the result, and Bach's Passion music duly followed in the April following. These two services continued to attract large crowds for very many years, though the special musical observance of St Paul's Day has unhappily been dropped. To them was added an Advent musical service in 1878; originally this took the form of Spohr's *Last Judgement*, later alternating with Brahms's Requiem, and subsequently changed to Handel's *Messiah*; but until Stainer's retirement this service was performed by the Cathedral choir unaided, and accompanied only by the organ. The added splendour of an orchestra was, however, given from 1873 to the annual service for the Corporation of the Sons of the Clergy, a charitable foundation dating from 1655 during the persecution of the clergy under the Commonwealth, which had agelong associations with the Cathedral. In 1888, owing to the bad state of his eyesight, Stainer retired from St Paul's. One eye had been injured in childhood; the other was struck by a tennis ball in 1875 and

[1] *Acta B.*, 171; Frost, 31, 40.

had caused him a deal of trouble since. He was succeeded as organist by Martin. In 1899 Chapter gave a dinner in Stainer's honour, to celebrate the fiftieth anniversary of his becoming a chorister of the Cathedral. A knighthood had been conferred upon him on his retirement from St Paul's in 1888, in recognition of his great services to music both in Church and State.[1]

Minor Canon Coward, who was Stainer's schoolmaster in 1849 and finally survived him by ten years, was in actual process of relinquishing his charge of the choristers' education at the very time that his former pupil returned to St Paul's as organist. The office of Almoner, to which that charge had been attached, was abolished, and its endowment was transferred to the Ecclesiastical Commissioners, as part of the commutation settlement of 1872. Chapter appointed as headmaster of the reorganized choir school the Reverend Albert Barff, a Berkshire incumbent who had previously been chaplain of the theological college at Cuddesdon while Liddon was vice-principal. Barff was a man of deep and simple piety, and considerable originality of mind, who stamped a characteristic impress on the reconstituted school, of which he was virtually the founder. He was never a minor canon, as subsequent headmasters have been, and therefore like the organist had no official status in the Cathedral hierarchy; but in 1873 Chapter assigned to the headmaster the right of occupying the Chancellor's stall in choir whenever that dignitary did not require it for his own use, since the school is included in that department of Cathedral activity which comes under the Chancellor's jurisdiction.[2]

Coward moved out of No. 1 Amen Corner at the beginning of 1873, and Barff moved in shortly after. The house had been fitted and furnished to serve not only for the tuition of all the choristers but for the lodging of the newly elected twelve,

[1] Frost, 41, 44, 62, 63 f., 68, 85; Russell *B.*, 53; Green, 81, 148; Fellowes, loc. cit.; *Min.*, 15 July 1899; *Acta C.*, 189.

[2] *Acta B.*, 234, 249, 318; Russell *B.*, 36, 43 f., 111 f.; cf. Green, 201.

The Funeral of the 1st Duke of Wellington: The Scene under the Dome, 18 November 1852

The Choir Robing at St Paul's, c. 1852

who were to receive free board and education. Existing choristers continued as before to live at their homes, for until the entire school could be permanently assembled at its new premises in Carter Lane it was impossible to do more for the remaining seniors than provide them with a daily dinner. For two years, therefore, the school was in a state of division and transition. But the new choir house was completed and occupied early in 1875, and the numbers were built up to the full complement of forty. Not the least of its amenities was a playground on the roof, where the boys enjoyed fresh air and games; members of the public in the street below were protected from voluntary or involuntary missiles by the cage of wire-netting which enclosed this elevated field of exercise. It is worth recording that, from the very first, Chapter began to show a practical concern for the future education of its choristers when their voices should break and they ceased to belong to the choir school.[1]

The new choristers who had been elected on St Paul's Day, 1873, were admitted by the Dean with a special form of service in the north chapel on 8 March. The problem of holidays immediately presented itself; it was no longer reasonable to expect the boys to sing, day in, day out, for the whole year. The fact that they were already about equally divided into boarders and non-residents may have suggested the solution; at any rate, it was decided only a week later that one half of the choristers should have leave of absence alternately on Saturday afternoons. Three months later it was agreed that they should all be excused together for one afternoon in the week, provided that Stainer could make satisfactory arrangements for singing the service with men's voices only. Accordingly Stainer and others set to work and composed responses, chants, and canticles to meet the need; for anthems they selected such passages from old cathedral anthems as happened to contain no treble part. It appears that the day

[1] *Acta B.*, 257 f., 386; Green, 74, 76; Frost, 95.

originally chosen was Wednesday, but was very shortly changed to Thursday.[1]

The larger problem of terminal holidays for the boys was solved on the same lines as that of the weekly half-holiday, though it took much longer to cut the final knot. In August and September 1873 half the choristers were granted a month's holiday in turn, leaving the other half to maintain the services in Cathedral. Presumably a similar course was followed at Christmas and Easter; later practice certainly was to send the boys away in two divisions for a week's holiday each, after the octave of the festivals. A change in the established order seems to have originated in an epidemic. In 1885 the school was visited by an outbreak of scarlet fever, and for the whole of September the choristers were absent from Cathedral. A month of men's voices, even under difficulties from the shortage of appropriate music, apparently inured the authorities to the possibility of a similar deprivation annually, for it was decided that from the summer of 1886 the whole school should be sent away on holiday together for a month. At Easter and Christmas the old arrangement was continued for several years; the first reference to a general holiday at these seasons occurs at Easter 1896, when the boys were away for a week, and thereafter an absence of ten days was granted after Epiphany and Low Sunday in each year.[2]

During the epidemic, and from the time of the decision to dispense with a full choir for a month in each year, hurried efforts were employed to procure settings of the morning canticles suited to men's voices. A shock was in store for the vicars-choral when it came to chants for the psalms. Sparrow Simpson had been followed in the office of Succentor at the close of 1885 by William Russell, one of the new minor canons, who added to his choral responsibilities by becoming

[1] *Min.*, 8 March 1873, 15 March 1873; *Acta B.*, 325; Frost, 48 f.

[2] *Min.*, 11 Oct. 1873 (Succentor's Report), Sept. 1885, 18 April 1896, 28 Nov. 1896; Bumpus, 187; Frost, 76 f.; Green, 188, 195; *Acta C.*, 162.

also headmaster of the choir school in the following October. He now persuaded Stainer, who was keenly interested in plainsong, to join him in introducing Gregorian tones for the psalms when there were only men to sing them. This was announced to the gentlemen of the choir in 1886, shortly before the boys' summer holiday was due: their dislike was unconcealed.

"If we are justified", writes one of them, "in building beautiful cathedrals for our worship, we are surely justified in singing in them the most beautiful music that can be had, instead of falling back on crude stuff composed in days when the art of music was in its infancy." The idea that Anglican chants as adapted for men's voices are beautiful may appear strange to a more susceptible delicacy than his; but there was only too much substance in the charge that the Gregorians sung in St Paul's were crude. Stainer was interested in plainsong, but did not really understand it; his errors were no great discredit to him, for at that period the tradition of plainchant was almost everywhere degenerate, and only an exceptional musician would have paid it any attention at all. But in fact he destroyed the free rhythm, as of ordinary speech, which is the essence of its proper execution, confining what ought to be a flowing melody into stiff bars, and girding it with Victorian harmonies. The product was a well-meant counterfeit of the Gregorian Muse in corsets and crinoline.[1]

The difficulty experienced in securing regularity of attendance from the gentlemen of the choir was only gradually overcome; for some time after Stainer's accession the best efforts of Chapter failed to exact punctual and reliable service. The new statute for vicars-choral enacted in 1874 [2] did not apply to existing vicars; what was more serious, from the point of view of musical efficiency, it still left future vicars with a freehold of their office, which was not abolished until the passing of the Cathedrals Measure of 1931. The state of

[1] Frost, 77 f.; Russell *B.*, 84; Green, 190; *Acta C.*, 171.

[2] Cf. *supra*, p. 99.

affairs thus produced is well illustrated by a minute entered in 1901: "News was received of the death of Mr Charles Lockey, who was admitted Vicar-Choral of the Cathedral in the year 1844; but owing to the loss of his voice he has been represented by deputy since 1859." Such a system did not conduce either to good singing or to good discipline.

The chief weapon plied by Chapter in its warfare against unpunctuality was a rigid application of the traditional, statutory system of fines, which it enforced with automatic rigour; no fine for late arrival was normally remitted unless the defaulter produced a written certificate from the railway authorities that his train had in fact been delayed. Such certificates were regularly submitted during the '70s and '80s, bearing the signature of an inspector, or the station master, or even the superintendent of the railway. In 1878, in order to prove that the late-comer had started punctually and had allowed a proper margin of time. it was resolved "that for the future no excuse from a Railway should be taken in which the exact time for the train's arrival and its actual arrival was not stated". The railway officials seem to have accepted the demands thus made upon them in good part; only in 1884 was it reported that the Metropolitan Railway Company refused to certify delays in the working of its own system.[1]

In early days the new severity provoked a measure of resistance. When Chapter decided, in June 1873, to have a formal notification posted in the vicars' vestry of those members of the choir who had lapsed in their turn of duty, the senior vicar-choral (the same Mr Francis who had rebuked Gregory's attempts to intone) [2] declared that he would pull it down, and did pull it down. Thereupon the Chapter Clerk summoned him before Chapter to explain his conduct. He admitted that he had torn down the notice, and was suspended from attendance in the choir for three months for

[1] *Suppl.*, 112 ff.; *Min.*, 4 Dec. 1901; ibid., 27 July 1878, 13 Dec. 1884, and *passim*.

[2] Cf. *supra, p.* 97.

his great insubordination and contempt of statutable authority: during the period of his suspension a deputy would be provided and the cost be deducted from his salary. Given leave to speak, he proceeded to state "that he had not been treated with proper respect, that he was not the servant of the Dean and Chapter, that at the request of Dean Mansel he prepared the new rota of services for making lapses under which he was now being called to account but did not engage to be bound by it, and he repeated his opinion that the Dean and Chapter were not justified in putting up the paper which he had torn down".[1]

This statement failed to alter Chapter's view of the incident, and his suspension was confirmed by a formal act under the Chapter seal. The delinquent then consulted a firm of solicitors, who extracted an apology from their client and themselves suggested to Chapter that it might be a good solution if he were allowed to retire from active duty upon terms. He had been admitted to office as an alto thirty years before, and was now aged 62. Chapter declined to accept the mere apology without his also paying the small sum expended on a deputy. In his turn, the defender of the independent rights of vicars declined to retire from "the performance of duties to which he has been accustomed for so many years and which he considers himself still competent to fulfil". Finally he surrendered, wrote an apology which could be shown to other members of the choir, consented to pay for the deputy, and had his sentence of suspension revoked after it had run for about a month. The entire negotiation was conducted through the respective solicitors. Two and a half years later he did indeed resign in return for a fixed pension; this was noted as a most exceptional case, since vicars normally retained their freehold until death.[2]

[1] *Acta B.*, 319 ff., 327.
[2] *Acta B.*, 328, 330–4; *Suppl.*, 162; Frost, 64.

II

PASTORAL CARE

ONE OF the spiritual attractions of St Paul's at this period was certainly its preaching; but not, for the most part, the preaching of senior members of the Cathedral staff. Liddon alone of the canons drew the crowds. A contemporary wit alleged that of the canons "there was one who could preach, but not write a sermon; another who could write but not preach; a third who could do both; and a fourth who could do neither." The interpretation is as follows. Gregory was a powerful and effective speaker in Convocation or upon a public platform, or in a village church where he spoke *ex tempore* from a stored mind and full heart; but his written sermons in Cathedral were dull. Lightfoot had plenty to say that was worth saying, but was judged to have a poor delivery; he was infinitely more effective in intimate addresses to young disciples than in the pomp and circumstance of the Cathedral pulpit. The third and ambidextrous canon was Liddon. The fourth was Claughton, the Archdeacon of London, whose talents had been exhausted by the administration of a tropical bishopric. Nor were the prebendaries, who were the most frequent recipients of the Bishop's nomination to the Sunday morning pulpit, able to afford their brethren of the Chapter much additional strength; they shared among themselves some learning and distinction, but their sermons were generally both tedious and prolonged. As the service consisted of Mattins, Litany, and Holy Communion, all sung at length and often elaborately, it was no light affliction to endure a dull sermon lasting forty minutes; and the congregation which had entered on its devotions at 10.30 was commonly detained till after 1 o'clock for their conclusion. Indeed, in 1892, after an agitation conducted by H. S. Holland, printed notice was circulated to morning preachers, inviting their attention to the fact that even with a brief discourse the service would last for two and a half hours.[1]

It was to the preachers at the special Sunday evening service (to whom a duration of thirty minutes was recommended) and on other special occasions that the Cathedral looked for a high order of eloquence and fervour, or for some compensating quality of popular attraction. Thus in 1878, when the second Lambeth Conference took place, the opportunity was seized to flood St Paul's with oversea bishops. The first Conference, held in 1867 and attended by 76 bishops, had awakened no noticeable echo on Ludgate Hill. But in the summer of 1878, with 100 apostolic orators to draw upon, Chapter manifested the increased breadth of its outlook by suspending all its normal arrangements for Sunday sermons and putting the pulpit at the disposal of American and Colonial bishops at the morning, afternoon, and evening services for the space of three entire months. The closing service of the Conference was held in the Cathedral, as happened again in 1888, when 145 bishops attended and about 500 communicants presented themselves at the concluding Eucharist. Such a concourse of visiting prelates demanded meticulous and knowledgeable organization, in which Randall Davidson, then Dean of Windsor, rendered great assistance.[2]

The season of Lent afforded regular occasion for an annual spate of preaching. The City churches had not then adopted the habit of providing midday sermons for City workers, and the field was clear for the Cathedral to put forth a great homiletic effort. Accordingly from 1882 special midday addresses were arranged for every day in Lent except Saturdays, and the most famous preachers and missioners of the

[1] Russell *B.*, 26 f., 75, 77; Gregory, 237; *Acta D.* (cover).
[2] *Acta D.* (cover); Green, 144 f., 206 f.; Russell *B.*, 94 f.

day were engaged to deliver them. Many more hearers attended than had been expected, and after the first sermon the place of delivery was changed from a movable pulpit at the west end of the church to the pulpit under the dome. The daily Lenten sermon continued far into the twentieth century. But Lenten preaching was by no means confined to the midday address. The lists of Lenten services for 1884 and 1885 have been preserved, showing that sermons accompanied Evensong on Wednesdays and Fridays, and that addresses were also given at a late evening service in crypt or north-west chapel on Tuesdays and Thursdays: for these reliance was placed largely on the new and active minor canons. In all, during each of these two years, the sermons and addresses in St Paul's on the forty weekdays between Ash Wednesday and Easter Eve amounted to sixty-one, over and above the three regular sermons on Sundays; and in addition, from 1878 the Three Hours Devotion had been conducted from noon to 3 p.m. on Good Friday. Truly may it be said that the religious public was avid of exhortation.[1]

Nevertheless, the main focus of spiritual activity in the Cathedral lay not so much in sermons as in services. In the summer of 1873 a petition was received from 58 young men, asking for a short daily evening service to be instituted in one of the chapels, "on the model of Compline, with varying hymns and lessons". A conference was held with the petitioners; Church was requested to draw up the form of service, and Barff, the headmaster, was made responsible, with some assistance and a small extra stipend, for conducting the service every weekday evening. Beginning at the following Advent, it was held in the north-west chapel (though later transferred to the crypt). A similar short service of psalms and hymns, based on Sext and compiled by Liddon, was said daily in the luncheon hour from Advent 1881. A daily Eucharist at 8 o'clock in the same chapel was started in January 1877. The devoted Virger Green, as sub-sacrist,

[1] Russell *B.*, 63 f.; *Scrap Book*, 849 ff.; Green, 140.

responsible for putting out the sacred vessels and restoring them to the safe where they were kept, thought that he would be required to make a personal attendance every morning and protested vigorously against the innovation, but was appeased on hearing that his duties might be delegated. Early Morning Prayer was then for some months said after the Eucharist, at 8.30. But by Easter the new chapel of St Faith, in the crypt, was ready for use, Morning Prayer was transferred thither, and its normal hour of 8 o'clock was restored.[1]

Services for particular uses were also devised. One for the admission of choristers after completing their probation was produced by Church in 1873. Others were drawn up by Liddon in 1881 for the solemn reception of virgers and vicars-choral on to the Cathedral foundation. These were for domestic consolation. But constant recourse was had to St Paul's for services of a diocesan character or with a wider reference to the needs of the Church at large: added to the daily choir services, which formed the first charge on the efforts of the whole body of clergy and singers, and to the numerous other regular services, they made up a most impressive total of devotional activities. Great national events received such religious recognition as was due to them. Many consecrations of bishops took place in St Paul's at this period; that of Benson to the new See of Truro, in 1877, lasted from 11 o'clock "until near 3 p.m.". There were also many confirmations: Bishop Jackson mostly employed an assistant bishop as his deputy for this purpose, but when Frederick Temple succeeded him in 1885, he confirmed in Cathedral about six times a year. A mission to London occupied a week in February 1874; it was preceded by a day of devotion in St Paul's for the clergy, several special services were held daily in Cathedral during the mission, and a service of thanksgiving followed. When the annual day of intercession for foreign missions (associated two years later with St Andrew's

[1] *Acta B.*, 326, 338; *Acta C.*, 61, 64; Green, 88, 128, 130, 165; Russell *B.*, 60, 62 f.

tide) was inaugurated in Advent 1872, St Paul's consecrated the whole day to the cause; and at different times farewell Eucharists were celebrated for Bishop West Jones of Cape Town and Bishop Steere of Zanzibar on their leaving England.[1]

The spiritual claims of individuals were not neglected. A grandchild of the Archdeacon was baptized in 1875; the last known baptism in the Cathedral had been performed in 1713, but several more followed. The Lady Mayoress was married in St Paul's in 1877, before a vast invited concourse, beside whom "the public were admitted to stand in the aisles of the nave": the citizens might well gape, for this was believed to be the first wedding in the Cathedral since about the year 1760. Deceased prebendaries received the honour of a Dead March, usually on the Sunday following their demise. But in the natural course such isolated incidents were submerged in the tide of special services undertaken on behalf of Church organizations. The Sons of the Clergy continued to celebrate their annual festival. The great missionary societies and voluntary associations of every kind were welcomed, the inter-denominational Bible Society among them. In 1873 the London Gregorian Association first held its service in St Paul's; Green notes that "the choir numbered between seven and eight hundred, besides brass instruments . . . the service began at 8 and over at 10.15". They seem to have combined in a strange fashion the arts practised by Jubal, inventor of music, and Tubal-Cain, producer of hardware.[2]

With all such open-handed encouragement of sectional interests the Cathedral made no concealment either of its own ultimate responsibility for everything that took place within the walls or of its own intrinsic character as a cathedral of the Church of England. Indeed, even outside the walls a certain stiffness was maintained: in 1888 Chapter is to be found resolving that it was inconsistent with the duties of an

[1] *Acta B.*, 309; *Acta C.*, 61; Green, 72, 91, 98, 131, 134, 180, 193.
[2] Green, 77, 105 f., 133 f. and *passim*.

assistant vicar-choral to take any part in musical services held in, or on behalf of, Roman Catholic or Protestant Dissenting chapels. Only a member of the foundation was allowed to give the blessing in Cathedral: the sole exceptions permitted were in favour of the Archbishop of the province or a diocesan bishop-suffragan when representing the Bishop of London. Once a visiting bishop who had come to preach the sermon took it upon himself, without invitation or notice, to advance and pronounce the absolution at the sung Eucharist. In the vestry afterwards he rashly remarked to Liddon that he supposed he had done right, since, as he thought, his action had added to the dignity of the service. Liddon, in his blandest tones, replied: "As a matter of fact you were not right, and we here do not feel that this service requires any such accessory to its dignity." [1]

Printed regulations were in force for choral festivals of visiting societies. Only such as were of established position, and were expressly connected with the Church of England, or at least enjoyed the patronage of the Archbishop or the Bishop, were to be accepted without special consent. The prayers at such a service were to be chanted by a minor canon; the name of the preacher had to be submitted to the Dean for approval; the proposed order of service also had to be submitted for approval at least a fortnight in advance. The society concerned had to cover all contingent expenses without any charge falling on the Cathedral; no tickets were ever to be sold; choirboys must be under the control of some responsible person.

On one occasion a well-known Church society offended against the rules, and Liddon, who was in residence, took the matter up with its director in a spirit of urbane asperity. The society had invited a preacher from Ireland, and had allowed the fact to be published before submitting the nomination to the Dean. On having his attention called to the omission the director sent a polite but brief apology, which failed entirely

[1] *Acta C.*, 195; Russell *B.*, 76.

to satisfy Liddon. "It would", he answered, "be very far from the purpose of the Dean and Chapter to wish to inflict a slight on a distinguished Irish clergyman. We shall not interfere with your proposed arrangements for the service on the 23rd. But I cannot encourage you to expect that a Society which thinks so lightly of Rules laid down after much consideration, and insisted on in all cases, will be again allowed to hold a service in S. Paul's. I have written the above after taking counsel with Canon Gregory." This elicited apologies and explanations expressive of a much more deep concern, and the offer of a personal call, at which Liddon received the director graciously. Unfortunately the service paper had not been submitted either: but this omission was also rectified, and the incident terminated peaceably.[1]

Following the commutation of the Cathedral estates, a large increase took place in the maintenance staff. Chapter was solicitous for the welfare of its employees, and in 1873 invited Sparrow Simpson, as a suitable minor canon, to give special attention to the spiritual interests of the servants of the Cathedral. It had already established a provident fund for their benefit, and shortly afterwards voted £100 towards establishing a library for their use. In 1874 the lease of a residence in Paternoster Square was purchased, and a virger and a bell-ringer were installed, so that some of the staff might be housed conveniently near the Cathedral. When the minor canons' houses were constructed a domicile for the Dean's Virger was included in the scheme. But a much wider field for social and pastoral activities existed among the young men employed in business houses in the neighbourhood, who were boarded by their firms and had perforce no roots in any parochial organization—more especially since practically none of the City incumbents resided in their parishes and very few ever held more than a Sunday service in their churches. It was for the sake of such men as these

[1] *Scrap Book*, 905 f.

that Tuesday evening lectures [1] had been given in St Paul's during the winter months since 1871, at first by members of Chapter, but later by outsiders of distinction; and it was also by them that the late evening service on weekdays, instituted in 1873, was mainly attended. One of Chapter's first considerations, therefore, when the time came to appoint new minor canons under the revised scheme of 1876,[2] was to secure priests of active habit and pastoral temper to minister to young clerks and warehousemen.[3]

The first two men selected, William Russell and H. C. Shuttleworth, abundantly proved the capacity of Chapter to exercise a fitting choice, and set the highest standard of loyalty and ability to those who came after. Russell taught in the choir school, and succeeded Barff as headmaster in 1886; he won golden opinions as a schoolmaster, but resigned on grounds of health in 1895; like Barff he was later made a prebendary. Shuttleworth (another example of Liddon's judgement) became Rector of St Nicholas, Cole Abbey, close to the Cathedral, in 1883. There he gathered a great following, especially among members of the acting profession; he subsequently combined with his parish the Professorship of Pastoral Theology at King's College. Great pains were taken by Chapter, and many inquiries were made, in order to secure the right men for the posts; and in preliminary interviews candidates had impressed on them the intense importance attached to the plans which Chapter had formed for pastoral work among men and boys in the City. Sworn in as minor canons on probation in October 1876, they were solemnly admitted to office in the Dean's vestry in December 1877, and installed in choir by the Warden of the College after the first lesson at Evensong.[4]

At once they set to work with classes and instructions and services; a good many candidates for Confirmation were

[1] Cf. *supra*, pp. 106–7. [2] Cf. *supra*, p. 127.

[3] *Acta B.*, 218, 259, 310, 326, 337, 382; Green, 93, 164; Russell *B.*, 57.

[4] *Acta C.*, 171; *Acta D.*, 84, 88; Russell *B.*, 40 f., 59; Green, 125, 136.

attracted, and Russell organized a guild of communicants. It was Shuttleworth who proposed, and was entrusted with the responsibility of conducting for the first time, the Three Hours Devotion on Good Friday in 1878. At that date the idea of spending the hours of the Passion in meditation was still thought to trail clouds, or rags, of Popery; Chapter was a little afraid of a Protestant demonstration. But Shuttleworth collected a band of his young men to sit near the pulpit and lead the unaccompanied hymns, and policemen were held in reserve in case misguided fanatics started to brawl. Nothing untoward happened; the service passed off quietly. The daily evening service was maintained for about twenty-five years and then abandoned, since fewer young warehousemen were any longer "living-in". The lunch-hour service remained the responsibility of the minor canons until commuted, after the second world war, for a choral service twice a week. But the bulk of the new work was pivoted not on the material edifice of the Cathedral, but on meetings held in business and private houses, and in the Chapter House.[1]

Since much of Russell's time was occupied with his duties as second master in the choir school, most of the outside evangelism fell to Shuttleworth. His report on his activities for the preceding twelvemonth, made to the Dean at the end of 1880, illustrates the kind of work in which he was engaged. He delivered many lectures—two or three times a week during the winter months—in the large warehouses of the Churchyard, Holborn, and the neighbourhood, but occasionally also as far afield as Camberwell or Hackney. The subjects were mostly secular, such as "Heroism", "The Age of Elizabeth", "Charles Kingsley", or "Books to Read, and Others". But as the audience got to know him he did his best to introduce some religious or moral issue, and sometimes he was expressly invited to speak about religion. He also conducted classes in his own house, and on Saturday afternoons,

[1] Russell *B.*, 58 f., 60, 64 f.; Green, 140.

except in the dark and dreary season, took parties round the Cathedral. In such ways he made many friends and interested many young men in St Paul's. Whether his lectures accomplished any greater good than the acknowledged benefit of bringing a number of young people into personal relations with a clergyman, he rather seems to have doubted: "I do not think that St Paul's attracts the great body of young City men." He had noticed, however, that whenever he took duty in one of the City churches his acquaintance from the warehouses used to follow and sit at his feet, for what that might be worth. It seems clear that though a few young men were drawn by his efforts into the orbit of the Cathedral services, he found them as a rule somewhat overwhelmed by the enormity and solemnity of St Paul's; he wanted to secure a vantage-ground with an atmosphere at once more definitely religious than that of the warehouses and more snug and seductive than that afforded by the illimitable spaces, retarding echoes, and spiritual restraints of the great church.

He had attempted, as desired by the Dean, to do something for the men employed in the Cathedral. "It is quite the most difficult task I have yet tried to carry out." He had established friendly intercourse, and induced a few to attend his Bible class, but that marked the limit of his success. A broader and apparently a faintly alarming prospect had, however, opened in quite another direction. Nurses from St Bartholomew's Hospital had attended his course of Lent lectures at the late evening service in the crypt chapel, and the Matron had written to ask that the instructions might be continued. Accordingly he had given a course of addresses on the deepening of the spiritual life. A large number of young women had also been present at one of his warehouse lectures. Some had even come to him to be prepared for Confirmation. Perhaps this indicated an opening for a ministry to young women living and working around the Cathedral. But he thought they possibly had less need of help than the young men; he knew very little about them or of the conditions of their lives; and it was plain that any effort in this direction would require very careful management.

On one subject Shuttleworth was lamentably clear, that the musical soirées held at the Chapter House had been voted by the young men to be "so awfully slow". The Dean and Chapter had, of their goodness, invited any of the warehousemen who cared to inscribe their names in a book at the Chapter House to music, conversation, and light refreshments. Their guests fully recognized the honour of thus meeting the Dean and the Chapter; but most of them were too shy to take part in conversation which had obviously been over their heads, and many neither appreciated music nor the kind of social intercourse which delighted the highbrows. In an attempt to remedy this defect a course of scientific lectures had been introduced in the preceding year, without effecting any improvement on the usual plan, for the lectures had been difficult to follow, and much too long, altogether apart from the fact that they destroyed the social character of the entertainment. Accordingly Shuttleworth recommended the adoption of a scheme proposed by Mr Kelly, another minor canon recently appointed. This was that the music at the soirées should be interspersed with readings, "not always of a grave character". If this suggestion was ever carried out the parties must have been considerably brightened. Shuttleworth himself is described as "rather full of fun". Kelly wrote comedies for the Cathedral choristers to act, and the new-style minor canons collaborated in words and music of the songs and parodies with which the plays were enriched.[1]

In concluding his report, Shuttleworth broached the notion of founding a club and reading-room for his young men, if premises could be secured. In 1883, the year in which Shuttleworth left St Paul's, this project actually came to fruition, Chapter making an initial grant of £200 towards expenses, with hope of more to follow. Rules were framed, and a committee was formed under the presidency of a minor canon.

[1] Gregory, 198; Russell *B.*, 58; *Scrap Book*, 894 ff.

But the club did not flourish quite in accordance with the expectations of its promoters, and in 1892 it was closed: the members were asked to transfer themselves either to a similar institution conducted by the Church of England Young Men's Society or to a club of Shuttleworth's connected with St Nicholas, Cole Abbey, to both of which Chapter voted a small annual grant. It may be that the atmosphere of the club was found excessively improving. But in any case young men were ceasing to be resident in such numbers on the ground, and the day of usefulness for clubs within the City had passed its meridian.

Nevertheless, while the conditions remained favourable, the Cathedral had made great and successful efforts to provide pastoral benefits for those who spent their lives under its shadow. The credit for inaugurating them goes to Chapter, but the honour of their performance is rightly due to the indefatigable members of the reformed College. That the minor canons still had plenty of business to occupy them is perhaps to be inferred from a decision also taken in 1892. The Sub-dean of the Chapels Royal had written to inquire about the possible appointment of some one of the minor canons of St Paul's to his staff as priest-in-ordinary to the Queen. Chapter discussed the matter, and resolved that the offer must be declined.[1]

[1] Russell *B.*, 59; *Acta C.*, 101; *Acta D.*, 47 f., 52, 60; *Report* in *Scrap Book*, 907 f.

12

VIRGERS AND MISCREANTS

WORK is seldom accomplished without encountering some friction, and St Paul's continued to meet its share of difficulties. During the long course of reorganization and reform the prebendaries had been confronted with a show of resolution; the minor canons were at last being reduced to a natural but possibly undue degree of subjection; and the obstructive impulses of the vicars-choral were in process of being quelled. It was also necessary to deal with the disorderly affections of lesser mortals, particularly of the virgers. A number of inefficient employees were now being dismissed or pensioned off, and in May 1872 the turn came of a virger named Leef; he had been admitted to office in 1843, was aged between 70 and 80, and was almost totally deaf and unfit for further duty. Chapter therefore proposed to him that he should execute a formal resignation of his office, embodying an equally formal undertaking on the part of Chapter that he should receive a pension for life of £230 a year.

These terms would seem to have been easy enough. Leef's tenure dated back to the old days when virgers were not stipendiaries, but drew their emoluments almost wholly from the fees charged to tourists for visiting various parts of the Cathedral; and from such dues or their commuted values he was receiving on the average an annual income of £290, whereas the new-style virgers were paid a direct salary of only £110. And at first he agreed to accept the offer made him. But with the litigiousness that seems at one time or another to have permeated most ranks in the Cathedral hierarchy, he consulted a solicitor and was advised to withdraw his acceptance. He now claimed to be irremovable, on the ground that his appointment conferred on him a freehold; he went further and alleged that he was under no obligation, in the event of incapacity, even to provide a deputy to do his work; in brief, he refused to resign. Thereupon Chapter stated a case to Counsel for a legal opinion on the matter; and from the documents submitted an extremely interesting light is thrown on certain historical aspects of a virger's standing in St Paul's Cathedral.[1]

The express wording of the ancient statutes leaves no doubt about the conditional character of a virger's appointment. It was ordained in 1282 that the virgers should hand back their wands to the Dean every year on Michaelmas Day; he should then inquire into their past conduct and either dismiss them or, if they were found trustworthy, restore their wands; in no circumstances were they permitted to claim an unrestricted tenure of their office. The same rules are repeated in the Epitome of the statutes, drawn up by Dean Colet at the beginning of the sixteenth century, from which Chapter quoted the relevant passage to the learned Counsel; it contained the added direction that virgers were to carry out their duties in their own proper persons, not by deputies, which Counsel regarded as a further pointer contrary to the thesis that they held a freehold ministerial office. As late as 1724, when Bishop Gibson conducted a visitation of the Cathedral, two of the questions included in his articles were whether the virgers were "chosen every year", and whether each of them did "execute the office in his own person". But vested interests tend to take root: even in 1282 certain persons had been claiming freeholds to protect themselves from the consequences of their misdeeds: and even in the face of positive statutes there was just a chance that contrary custom might be held to have modified the force of ecclesiastical law.[2]

In addition, somebody had remembered or discovered a

[1] *Acta B.*, 246, 265, 281 f.; Green, 72.

[2] *Statt.*, 91, 224 f., 303.

very awkward precedent. In 1778 a virger was dismissed for gross misconduct. He then submitted the following apology:

> Whereas I Henry Argent late Virger of Saint Paul's Cathedral have given great offense to the Dean and Chapter by my drunkenness and repeated misbehaviour and by personal rudeness and insolence to them for which I have justly and statutably been removed from my place and all the benefits and advantages thereunto belonging I the said Henry Argent do here on my bended knees in the presence of the Dean and Chapter and the other Virgers of the said Cathedral Church acknowledge my faults, most humbly beg pardon of the Dean and Chapter and beseech them to have compassion upon me, and to restore me to my place And I do hereby promise and engage never more to be guilty of the like offenses but to be sober and regular in the discharge of my Office and to pay all due submission and obedience to the injunctions of the Dean and Chapter.

In view of so unqualified an expression of repentance (though presumably dictated by Chapter and phrased by its Clerk) the errant virger was forgiven. He was obliged actually to read his confession publicly on his bended knees and to subscribe it in writing; after which Chapter reinstated him in solemn form. It must have been a deeply affecting scene. Unhappily his flesh proved as weak as his spirit, for three years later in 1781, he was once more removed from his office "for a long series of irregular, disorderly, disobedient behaviour", and it was ordered that he never be restored again. Still more unhappily for Chapter, he took his case to the Court of King's Bench, which granted a *mandamus* in 1783 to reinstate him in his virgership and compel his successor not merely to retire from a post to which he had been duly appointed, but to hand over to Argent all the profits which he had received while holding it. In the event, Argent continued in his virgership till his death in 1794.[1] It is interesting to note, as further evidence of the prevailing contempt for statutes, that the successor thus rudely displaced had

[1] *Muniments, V*, 199.

been officiating for some time before 1781 as Argent's deputy.

The story now reverts to 1872. What Chapter would have liked to know was the grounds on which the King's Bench had caused Argent to be restored to office ninety years before. But although the case had been briefly reported, the report failed to state the reasons for the Court's decision, and so left a pretty field for legal argument. In the end, Counsel's opinion on this point proved to be reassuring, though not at all conclusive. It looked, he confessed, as if the Court had treated Argent as enjoying a higher status than that of mere servant to whom notice might be given at the will of his employers. On the other hand, since no mention was made of any opportunity being given him, when dismissed for the second time, of testifying in his own defence, it was possible that his dismissal had been quashed on the merely technical ground of non-observance of the proper forms of procedure: there was certainly no direct proof of lifelong tenure. The undoubted facts that Chapter had tamely submitted to the *mandamus* and that Argent's unfortunate successor had therefore had to wait till 1791 before admission to the next vacancy,[1] seem not to have impressed the expert legal mind; they were passed over in a silence which was, perhaps, in the circumstances discreet.

But Chapter's main attention was concentrated on the capitular Muniment Books (one of which was missing) and their record of the exact manner and conditions of Leef's own appointment as virger in 1843. The evidence disclosed therein showed that Leef had appeared in the Chapter House, before Sydney Smith, canon residentiary, in the presence of the deputy registrar of the Cathedral, and there exhibited a duly executed presentation of himself to the office of virger, issued to him by the Treasurer (within whose province it lay to present virgers after they had been nominated to him by Chapter), and humbly prayed "to be admitted to the said

[1] *Muniments*, V, 156.

Office of Virger and right and justice to be administered to him in the premises". Whereupon he was required to take "the Oaths of Allegiance and Supremacy and Canonical Obedience and duly to execute the Office of one of the Virgers of the said Cathedral Church". He also had to subscribe a paper pledging him to appear at the Chapter House annually on Audit Day and resign his virger's rod "according to the Antient Rites and Statutes of the said Cathedral Church"; and likewise acknowledging that he held his post subject to the will and pleasure of the Dean and Chapter; and further agreeing to submit to any modification in the accustomed profits of his office which Chapter might be pleased to ordain. On his completion of these, by no means insignificant, undertakings the canon-in-residence "graciously admitted the said David Leef to and in the said Office".

Some additional facts also came to light in the examination of the Muniment Books. The subscription of the engagement which (*prima facie* at least) debarred Leef from raising any future claim to a freehold was an innovation started in the early part of the nineteenth century; the exact date of its introduction was unknown in 1872, owing to the disappearance of the missing Muniment Book. It had not been customary before the period in question, but certainly had been imposed on the two virgers immediately preceding and on the one immediately following Leef. It looked uncommonly like a device to circumvent any untoward consequences of the case of Henry Argent. By a most unusual disposition of historical circumstances more is known about the matter now, for the Muniment Book that was missing in 1872 is unaccountably extant in the Library to-day. From this it may be seen that virgers were admitted in the old form twice in 1781 (the second occasion being that on which Argent was replaced after his dismissal) and once in each of the years 1791, 1794, 1797, 1798, 1817, and 1820. It was not until the next vacancy, which occurred in 1833, that conditions were imposed which expressly limited the tenure of the office. As has been stated in an earlier chapter, that was part of the attempt to tighten the screw of Cathedral discipline, initiated soon after Sydney Smith's admission to Chapter.[1]

Virgers admitted in 1833 and again in 1839 subscribed a paper in which they merely promised to resign if called upon to do so by the Dean and Chapter.[2] It was only in July 1843, when the next virger fell to be admitted, who happened to be Leef, that the full pressure was exerted and a financial condition was imposed: he was to be entitled to all and singular the fees and profits to the said office of old time belonging "or to such portion of them as the said Dean and Chapter may now or hereafter think fit and right". This was a beautifully indefinite and entirely different proposition, reflecting the attempt made under the management of Hale between 1843 and 1845 to introduce a new principle and system of employment for subordinate members of the Cathedral foundation—an attempt which broke down under the legal resistance offered by the vicars-choral and the refusal of the Ecclesiastical Commissioners to advance the necessary finance.[3] Chapter was quickly compelled to confer the same status on new vicars as on their seniors. But the position of the virgers was nothing like so strong, and two further admissions of virgers were made in March and April 1845, in similar form to Leef's. Nevertheless, after Chapter's final defeat by the vicars in 1847 no further inroad was made on the traditional status or profits of the virgers, and the manner of their admission quietly reverted to the ancient form as it had stood before 1833.[4]

So much for the manner of Leef's appointment and for the motives underlying its novelty. Chapter in 1872 seems to have been imperfectly aware of the full extent of the novelty,

[1] *Muniments*, V, 40 f., 47 f., 156, 199; VI, 12, 36, 140, 181; VII, 77 f.; cf. *supra*, p. 44.

[2] *Muniments*, VII, 77 f., 129.

[3] Cf. *supra*, pp. 45 ff., 53 ff.

[4] Cf. *supra*, pp. 46 f.; *Muniments*, VII, 199 f., 201, 255 *et post.*

and still less well-informed about the reasons for it. But it had itself quite recently taken precautions similar to those attempted by Hale, when a new virger was appointed in July 1871, just before the death of Mansel. It does not appear that the new virger signed any compromising document on that occasion. But he was graciously admitted as before to the office of virger "together with all the rights and privileges other than such as are of a pecuniary nature belonging to the said Office", to hold the said office during the goodwill and pleasure of Chapter but no longer, at the yearly stipend of £110 "in lieu of all fees payments and perquisites to the said Office heretofore belonging or accustomably received by the holder thereof". If Leef were now able to sustain the claims which he had put forward, Chapter might bid farewell to all its carefully devised arrangements for a reformed system of virgers.

What Chapter had had principally in mind in framing its new regulations was not so much the expectation that virgers might lay claim to actual freehold tenure, as the desire to bring them under reasonable control and above all to substitute for the accustomable perquisites of crypt and cupola a fixed and regular stipend. Whether fees or freehold were in question, claimants could base their pretensions only on the force of custom. But the dreadful precedent of Argent showed how great the danger was that custom might prove strong enough to override all regulations, ancient or modern. And when Chapter found that the requirement of a written engagement, such as had been exacted for a period from Leef and other virgers, had been quietly abandoned in subsequent appointments, it began to feel the ground rock under its feet. Did the abandonment imply that Chapter had then come to entertain doubts about its legal competence to impose conditions? Could it be the case that, notwithstanding statutes and regulations and forms of appointment, established customs had bound so tough a growth around the capitular oak as to preclude Chapter from all right either to vary the form of admission to a virgership or to change the accustomed terms of a virger's employment? Had the reformed Cathedral lost all power of controlling a body of unreformed virgers, short, at any rate, of procuring a special Act of Parliament?

This was the real question upon which, together with the general problem of the wisest practical course to pursue, Chapter requested Counsel to advise it. Little, it may be imagined, did Leef comprehend how grave a shock he had administered to his employers. The situation was, however, restored by the combined wisdom of Counsel and resolution of his clients. Counsel advised that Leef was in a cleft stick. Either the virgers had a freehold, and in that case he had never been properly appointed to the office: or else, if his appointment as actually made was good in law, then he merely held his post at the will of the Dean and Chapter. Since the precedent of Argent was by no means legally conclusive, he thought on the whole that Chapter would be safe if it proceeded to remove Leef from office on the ground of physical incapacity for his duties: but great care should be taken first of all to summon him to appear and show cause why he should not be removed on the specific ground alleged. If, after this, Leef were to obtain a *mandamus* for his restoration, Chapter would probably be able to make a good return.

Counsel's opinion was dated 30 October 1872. Three days later Chapter decided to act on it, and so informed Leef, on whose solicitor a formal notice was served to the same effect. The solicitor replied that on reconsideration Leef was now prepared to accept Chapter's original offer of a pension. But Chapter meant to make no mistake and refused to accept anything short of absolute and unconditional resignation. Leef submitted, and his deed of resignation (opening with the invocation "In the name of God, Amen") was drawn and executed with all the terrors and complications of the law, sustained by proctors and notary public, witnesses and seals and signatures. Having thus asserted and vindicated its right to dismiss a virger for sufficient cause, Chapter brought the business to a satisfactory conclusion by securing to him the proffered pension during his natural life.[1]

The great practical importance of establishing the right of dismissal was shown by a case of misconduct which had occurred earlier in the year. Another of the virgers had celebrated the Day of Thanksgiving for the recovery of the Prince of Wales, in the previous February, with a bout of loyal intoxication. In such circumstances his fault was reckoned comparatively venial; he was brought before Chapter, admonished, and made to suffer no harsher penalty. But two years later he created further scandal. A passer-by, who seems to have recognized him, saw him one Sunday evening drunk in the street in the company of some unsuitable character, and asked the police to take charge of him; he was therefore brought into the police station in Fleet Street at 10 p.m. by a sergeant and a constable, "not searched, property 1/8 and an umbrella, detained till sober, discharged at 6 a.m.". The facts were reported to the Dean's Virger. Chapter informed the culprit that they intended to get rid of him and that he would shortly hear from the Chapter Clerk.[2]

Everybody now knew precisely the procedure to be followed. The virger was summoned to appear and show cause in his defence. He attended and admitted his guilt. The constable and sergeant of police, accompanied by their inspector and the passer-by, came and deposed, in his presence, to his state of helpless intoxication on the night in question: the Chapter House was virtually converted into a police court. At the end of it all he was dismissed from the service of the Cathedral. Thereupon Chapter intimated its unwillingness to throw him and his family on the world without resource; and with a leniency which seems amazing, since the man is said to have been only 36, suggested that if he gave them the safeguard of an unconditional resignation they would secure

[1] *Acta B.*, 270, 281–99. [2] *Acta B.*, 229, 393 f.

to him and his family a pension for his life of £150. In answer to such an offer it was hardly surprising that "he expressed his perfect readiness to resign". So the same formalities as had embellished the departure of Leef were re-enacted in all their dreadful solemnity, and the peccant pensioner went off with £150 per annum, of which £20 was to be paid to himself directly and £130 (by equal weekly instalments) to his wife, "for her separate use independent of you and your debts control or interference". He had been a virger for less than seven years. The way of the sinner may be hard, but nobody can accuse Chapter of being unmerciful to his dependants. His successor merely got the bake-meats of the funeral—£120 a year and a tenure at the pleasure of the Chapter.[1]

But the whole of Chapter's troubles did not arise from within the establishment. There were also some that came upon them from without. Thus complaint was made in the autumn of 1876 of the theft of umbrellas during service-time, continuing over a period of several months. A man was charged and sentenced at Guildhall to fourteen days hard labour for one such offence. Some years later a man and a boy successively taken into custody for stealing a pigeon from the garden had a better run of luck, being both dismissed with a caution; the action of the court must be considered merciful, since it is understood that wild pigeons within the City, though of less value than umbrellas, are the property of the Lord Mayor. A man threw ink about the floor of the Cathedral on two or three occasions in 1886; he was fined forty shillings or fourteen days imprisonment. In 1878 a discharged lunatic threw himself down from the Whispering Gallery; he was taken to hospital in a cab but died on the way, and in consequence of the incident an extra guard-rail was fixed in the gallery. In 1890, on a Sunday morning, while a prebendary was preaching a sermon, a man shot himself in the Cathedral with a revolver; and a few

[1] *Acta B.*, 395–8, 400–5; *Muniments*, VIII, 151 f.

months afterwards another shot himself at midnight outside the church, under the west portico. About the same period the western steps were chosen for a less gruesome misdemeanour; a man was arrested for attempting to hold a meeting there without permission, and was bound over to keep the peace for six months.[1]

One most persistent nuisance was an unfortunate person named Freund. Between 1882 and 1889 he was convicted in the Lord Mayor's court no fewer than six times, once for preaching outside the Cathedral and five times for creating a disturbance during services. On the first occasion he was sent to a lunatic asylum; on the next (when he had been preaching) he was thought sane enough to be awarded seven days imprisonment; but for interrupting another preacher's sermon, on the third occasion, he was once more committed to the asylum. After that, it was a month or months in prison for him every time, twice in 1885 and finally, after he had aggravated his disturbance with an assault, in 1889.[2]

Protestant objectors seem to have confined their attentions to the paschal season. In 1878 their threatened demonstration against the Three Hours service had failed to materialize. In the following year Chapter was once more on its guard, and policemen were concealed in the crypt, after a convenient custom regularly honoured when fear of disturbances were entertained. Nothing more alarming occurred than the distribution of tracts in the street. But serious and exciting brawls took place during service-time in 1883 and 1885. The first happened at Evensong on Easter Eve, when a man ran up the choir, sprang on the altar and proceeded to hurl cross and candlesticks and flowers to the floor. He was pursued by Gregory and some of the gentlemen of the choir, and conducted to the crypt to await the arrival of the police, shouting as he went, "Protestants to the rescue". H. S. Holland records the tradition that Gregory crammed his

[1] Green, 126, 137, 195, 215, 216, 218, 219.
[2] Green, 166, 169, 174, 181, 189, 209.

handkerchief down the culprit's throat, and "the pace", he writes, "at which Gregory [then aged 64] got off his surplice while running to catch the man was what especially struck awe in the beholders". The protester was fined £5, which was promptly paid by his Protestant supporters.

The second incident occurred in the north-west chapel on Good Friday, when the Dean had completed the offertory and was reading the prayer for the Church at the Eucharist then customary in St Paul's on that day. A demonstrator rushed to the credence and smashed the wine cruet with his umbrella; he then flew to the altar and knocked over the sacred vessels. Holland was himself present at this scene, and thus describes the consequence. "By the time I reached the man, there was no portion of his person which was not already occupied by somebody; and Gregory was seated firmly about his head, holding his face against the floor, and tightening his clutch whenever the poor man found space enough to get his mouth clear and to whisper 'Bless you, my brothers'." After an inquiry into the state of his mind, this offender went to prison for a month.[1] For the next three years, by an arrangement with the Commissioner of City Police, plain-clothes constables were regularly stationed in the Cathedral to guard against disorders.

A different kind of demonstration was staged in St Paul's on a Sunday in February 1887 by an army of political Socialists who in Trafalgar Square and elsewhere had been holding protest meetings against the Government, under the leadership of John Burns. On the preceding Sunday they had attended Westminster Abbey. They now wrote to the canon-in-residence to announce their intention of visiting St Paul's, and to request that either the Archbishop of Canterbury or the Bishop of London should be put up to preach to them. The canon was Dr Gifford, who had stepped into the archidiaconal shoes in 1884. He answered that the normal arrangement, by which he was due to preach himself, could not be

[1] Green, 140, 151, 170 f., 185; Gregory, 212 f., 259 f.; *Acta C.*, 201.

altered. However, the Socialists arrived on the Sunday afternoon and filled not only every part of the Cathedral but, with the accompanying crowd, a considerable stretch of Ludgate Hill. One of their leaders came to the vestry and asked that a service might be provided for those unable to gain admittance; whereupon Gregory, never at a loss when action was demanded, took a prebendary, a minor canon, and four choristers to the west portico and there conducted a short service. The crowd then dispersed, and Gregory's band of stalwarts returned to their seats in choir.

Meantime, inside the Cathedral, Evensong was being sung amid some noise and disorder. When preaching time was reached Gifford delivered what Gregory described as an admirable sermon; it was on the text, "The rich and poor meet together: the Lord is the maker of them all" (Prov. 22. 2), and was accompanied by occasional hissing, hooting, and cheering from the congregation. The Lord Mayor was present in his stall, and the City constabulary once more occupied the crypt in force, without, however, being called upon to make arrests. After this display of firmness on the part of St Paul's the demonstrators desisted from any further prosecution of their threatened campaign of social-democratic church-attendance. But had it only happened that Holland had been in residence a different sermon might have been delivered: Holland's sympathies were passionately engaged in support of the protesters, whom he thought to be labouring under genuine grievances, and against the policy of repression favoured by the Government. Certainly he would have bid them demonstrate in the street, if they wished, but in the church he would have drawn them to lay politics aside and submit their very pressing troubles to the righteous judgement of God.[1]

[1] Gregory, 214 f.; Green, 198; Frost, 91; Russell *B.*, 81; Prestige, 79.

13

THE CHAPTER IN THE '80s

THE PRODIGIOUS work of reforming and modernizing St Paul's, and re-establishing it both as a self-contained and self-governing institution and as a great public witness and religious force, had been the work of a team. Its members had differed widely in gifts and temperament, and to a certain extent in theological complexion, but not at all about the objects and methods of their reform. In particular, Gregory was the financier and administrator, who had plotted the direction and governed the development of a great movement which, though it started under the inspiration of Milman, had in his hands produced only a wayward surge of experiments. Liddon served as spiritual and liturgical expert who set the tone of the unceasing round of services; in Holland's words, "he brought to the Cathedral the sense of beauty, passion and romance . . . and gave it a spiritual ideal". He also brought to it Stainer, Barff, and Shuttleworth. But lest anybody should imagine that the tone he set was "Ritualistic", it is worth remarking that not till January 1898, more than seven years after his death, were copes ordered to be worn (and then only at morning service on five great feasts in the year), or coloured stoles enjoined at early celebrations of Holy Communion. Behind these two loomed the shy presence of the Dean, clothed with authority and awe, displaying in his drawn features "the unearthly refinement of a scholar-saint" (the words are Hensley Henson's), and armed with literary distinction, intellectual judgement, and moral grandeur. Before three such incomparable lights the European reputation of international scholars, such as were Lightfoot and Stubbs, might seem to contribute little further brightness to the Cathedral, and the pleasant nonentity of an archdeacon in episcopal orders melted into the shadows.[1]

The lure of the episcopate was in fact dangled before them all. Church, but for his frail health and resolute negation, might have been Archbishop of Canterbury instead of Benson on Tait's death in 1882. Gregory, it was understood, could have gone to Cape Town instead of his friend West Jones in 1874, or to Brechin in 1876. Liddon refused Brechin, Edinburgh, and St Albans, and fought strenuously in 1885 to avoid an imminent danger of being nominated for Lincoln or Salisbury. Only Lightfoot and Stubbs succumbed, the first in 1879, the second in 1884. But their defection made room for one whose fertility of ideas and enormous influence, direct and indirect, upon his generation far outweighed the value to the Cathedral of their massive but more sedentary scholarship; and in Henry Scott Holland St Paul's received one of the most brilliant, as also one of the most devoted, of its distinguished personalities.[2]

Holland's appointment to the canonry was again the work of Gladstone; and though the Cathedral has material reason to be thankful to Disraeli for picking Gregory and Stubbs and to Salisbury for selecting, in 1890, the then unknown Newbolt in the place of Liddon, there would almost seem to have been a special providence in operation linking the fortunes of St Paul's at the critical moments of its regeneration with the agency of Gladstone's pontifical statesmanship. By 1884 neither Church nor Liddon could count on much reserve of physical strength: one or both might drop off before very long. The archdeacons of the period, appointed by the Bishop, were of no great service: Gifford was a scholar and was well-liked, but was not in full sympathy with the rest of Chapter, being a decided Evangelical, and like his predecessor he found the work too much for him; he retired in 1889. There

[1] *Bundle*, 83; *Acta D.*, 126; *More Letters of H. H. Henson*, No. 94.

[2] Church, 307; Gregory, 239; Johnston, 243, 310–18, 327 f., 376.

remained only Gregory. He was indeed the rock on whom the whole foundation rested. But the Cathedral needed something more than a foundation. It required imagination, and a high degree of directive intelligence, and a power of theological teaching, and a gift for attracting and sustaining the religious interest of a wide public, and also, if the great revival were not to run the risk of collapse, a force of continuity to carry forward the work so well begun. All this was secured when Gladstone sent Holland to Amen Court.[1]

Holland was 37 when he received the canonry. He had run a dazzling course from boyhood, without himself being dazzled or spoilt. He loved equally music and poetry and athletics, took a brilliant degree in 1870, and at the end of the year was elected to a Studentship at Christ Church, where his task was to teach philosophy. Religious philosophy was the inspiration and passion of his intellectual life: "We all wanted", writes Stephen Paget his biographer, "to get to Plato and St John; and here was a man, not much older than ourselves, who had got to them—pushing his way, with a laugh and a shove of the shoulders, through all our difficulties." What Holland wrote of Justin Martyr might have been said of himself: he had always pursued philosophy with the strictly religious aim of attaining thereby the highest spiritual happiness in communing with God; the certified knowledge of God, therefore, professed by the prophets and made manifest in Christ, came to him as the crown of his existing aspiration. Holland's infectious hilarity fascinated the rising generation, and his torrential oratory, vivid with imagery and sparkling with epigrams, carried his younger hearers away. But his very brilliance roused the dark suspicions of professional intellectuals. To the end of his career his "fireworks" detracted from his reputation with those who wanted academic subjects treated in an academic way; they refused to take him seriously because of what they called his rhetoric and his journalism; and his life was far too fully

[1] *Russell B.*, 80 f.

occupied with a press of immediate practical concerns to leave him any chance of writing the great leisured and systematic books of which he was capable. His dealings with theology oddly recall his attitude to marriage: he took "intense enjoyment of all the multitude of little loves which are given me", but shrank from undertaking the high and noble, all-embracing honour and obligation of wedlock, profoundly though he admired its effect on other people: he could not bring himself to concentrate his affections on any one earthly object. So he was content to ignite intellectual tinder and to detonate ideas, to illuminate the earthly pilgrimage of the oppressed and the bewildered with the light of true religion, and to cut blazing trails for other men to follow.[1]

He was a devout friend and personal disciple of the Oxford philosopher T. H. Green. Holland's mind was ever open to receive new aspects of truth and fact, truly liberal and forward-looking not only in the way in which he entertained fresh knowledge but in the insight with which he appreciated its values and strove to assimilate it into his system of reality. How forward-looking was his mind, and how practical were his judgements, when he was in his prime, cannot be better illustrated than by the verdict which he passed on political Liberalism in 1897. A generation before its ultimate decline into impotence, he put his finger on its weakness: the party was too closely tied to "the Nonconformist capitalist". The evidence lay in its readiness to acquiesce in attacks made on the Church of England, which by that time contained an aggressive Liberal or Radical wing, and in its fatal loss of touch with Labour.

Together with some friends he forwarded a protest to Liberal headquarters. The Liberals, it said, were failing to relieve "the social pressure" on the working classes: "We are convinced that without a definite policy to relieve this pressure the Liberal party will die. . . . Mere skill in Parliamentary tactics cannot replace the moral force and religious spirit that

[1] Paget, 83, 97, 248 f.; cf. 167, *Bundle*, 66 f.

have, before now, given life to the Liberal creed." Yet, as the writers saw events, official Liberalism seemed to be out of touch with Labour. "The rich Liberal capitalist is not necessarily more in sympathy with the workers than the rich Tory capitalist. Parliament is still made up for the most part of wealthy men; nor does official Liberalism show much readiness to concede a fair share of representation to Labour men. This is suicidal and unjust." It was in fact the obstinate claim of Liberals to be the exclusive spokesmen of reform, and their disinclination to let Labour speak for itself, that brought about their political downfall a quarter of a century later. This was an astonishing piece of prescience, and the more significant because the judgement it expressed was essentially social rather than political in character.[1]

Holland himself was both a Liberal in politics and a Liberal Catholic in religion. He clung to the Gospel, and derived from it a social gospel which was a genuine gospel and not merely an economic programme; he had an absorbing interest in people. "Imagine", he exclaimed at a dinner party, "putting up a stained glass window to Faith, Hope, and Political Economy." The qualities which he demanded of others, and exhibited in himself, were personal qualities and thus at bottom religious. His intimates at Oxford had been the members of the group led by Talbot and Illingworth and Francis Paget (who had married Church's daughter in 1883) and Gore. It was Holland who devised their annual meeting, started in 1875, to which he gave the title of "the holy party". To the end of his life his swift transitions from gay to grave and his intermingling of humour and religion were apt to be startling: he habitually referred to virgers' wands as "holy pokers", and to cress-sandwiches as "Nebuchadnezzars", after the king in the Book of Daniel who was "made to eat grass as oxen". The reason simply was that for him no part of life was untouched by spirituality; things great and small alike were penetrated by personal religion.[2]

[1] Paget, 211 f.; cf. *Bundle*, 193. [2] Paget, 73, 81; *Bundle*, 64 f.

So on the one hand he distributed his germinative ideas with the prodigality of a primitive sower, scattering the seed broadcast; he launched them with an exuberant joy in words, and clothed them with a flamboyant and irrepressible humour. He bubbled with an intellectual vitality deep and extensive as the light; thoughts gushed from his mind for Gore and others to work up into disquisitions and treatises.[1] On the other hand, he insisted on these thoughts being given a practical application and testing. He had a horror of becoming merely academic. Of his dear friend Paget he could write that in one phase of his life he "was stiffening up a little: the academic crust was creeping over him: Oxford was playing its evil part". It can easily be imagined therefore how deep a joy it was to Holland himself to be called away from Oxford to dabble in the seething cauldron of London. But London was no novelty to him. Just before his ordination, in September 1872, he had contrasted academic apologetics with the realities of a London slum—instead of trying to grapple with "subtle indistinct viciousness of tendency", a priest in the East End would be seeing "actual living, actual dying, actual sinning, real good hearty vice, naked sin: drunkenness, murder, revelling, and such like".[2]

Another letter written at the same time expressed the wish that resident tutors at Oxford could "get woke up to a sense of life and death". A new democracy was rising into power over which no religion had any hold: Christian intellectuals "ought *above all* to have touched the new spirit of irregulated democracy and to know what it wants, what it feels the need of but is angry at finding no satisfaction for: this is quite as important as the more intellectual infidelity". So after ordination Holland spent the next Holy Week at Hoxton, preaching in church and, with more response, round the streets. "It was intensely exciting, and, we were inclined to say, very successful. The crowd gathered in a moment, a real live dirty crowd of roughs and streety women; they followed

[1] Cf. Gore in Prestige, 99, 157. [2] Paget, 61, 167; *Bundle*, 66.

us—they sang a bit; they listened with extraordinary intentness and solemnity." He was quite as much at home in Hoxton as he was in Christ Church. In the following December, 1873, still a deacon, he preached for the first time in St Paul's at the special evening service, and seems to have felt pretty well at home there too. "I enjoyed it very much myself—and managed to be heard: and the place looks so splendid with that mass of people." The invitation had come from Liddon who, unfortunately, was not altogether pleased: Holland had allowed himself to utter paradoxes about the nature of God which Liddon found (as he found so many things) rather disquieting. Holland himself described his sermon ruefully as "pantheistic".[1]

There was much more reason for Liddon's disquiet than the immaturity of a young man's attempts to philosophize, although Liddon habitually kept himself so close within his own shell that neither he nor the young men of the holy party realized the full depth of their division until the publication of *Lux Mundi* in 1889.[2] For two High Churchmen whose views about practical religion were so closely allied, and who were now to be colleagues in promoting religion in the heart of London, Holland and Liddon present a profound contrast both in temperament and in theological outlook. Liddon was a pessimist, for ever looking backward and striving to defend the past; Holland was an optimist, whose eyes were set upon the future, for ever trying to snatch the initiative and take the offensive.

It was providential that the new canon of 1884, who for the next quarter of a century was to assume the principal share in partnering Gregory and building on the spiritual foundations which Liddon had helped so greatly to lay, possessed both the will and the ability to advance with the changing years: for the impulse which had been so powerfully begun would never have been kept in motion by a directorate which was purely conservative and static in its

[1] Paget, 61, 68 f., 74. [2] Johnston, 364, 368.

principles: the religious life and influence of the Cathedral had to develop if they were to satisfy the needs of the times and of the people. Liddon was incapable of development. He had great gifts. But in a rapidly changing world it was somewhat idle to protest against all change; and if the world, as he believed, was going to the dogs, little was to be gained by offering it religion only with the associations and under the restrictions that it had already determined to discard. The old tune of Catholic Christianity needed to be transposed once more into a different key.

The broad ground of Liddon's belief might be said, without excessive exaggeration, to be the Bible as interpreted by Dr Pusey. Pusey had dallied once, in his youth, with German literary and historical criticism of Holy Scripture, and shrunk back appalled at the gulf which it seemed to open before his feet. Both he and Liddon had come to adopt an intensely literalistic view of Biblical revelation and a rigidly authoritarian conception of the wisdom with which it has pleased God to endow the Church in forming theological judgements. For them the sacred text was in every part and in every sense infallible, and the interpretations put upon its teaching by the Church were equally final and sacrosanct, not relatively but absolutely, beyond any restatement or discussion.[1] Their whole bent was to put on the same uniform level of directly revealed truth not only the great Christian doctrines about God and man but also the inferences which can properly be drawn from them; together with the very words and phrases in which such truths have been conveyed, through man, to man's intelligence. Liddon's public function had therefore come to be, in large measure, the defence of formulas: he was convinced that any deviation, even in the use made of a formula, involved a fatal disparagement of the Church's right to teach.

Lightfoot used to protest against Liddon's "Oxford logic". When faced with opposition Liddon, with relentless concen-

[1] Cf. Johnston, 364 f.

tration on a narrow line of deductive inference, used to prophesy the dreadful consequences which would follow if his adversaries did not desist: "If you begin to slide down an inclined plane, you cannot stop in the middle merely by wishing earnestly to do so." Having thus foreseen the worst, he threw himself into despondency and isolation without waiting to see whether his prophecies of gloom came true. His friend Francis Paget accounted for this habit by calling attention to the complete absence from Liddon's life of any burden of administration or government either in parish or university; it had never been his duty to exercise responsibility or make important decisions on his own authority, and so he had missed the practical discipline of mind which comes from having to adjust oneself to stubborn wills and circumstantial hindrances. He was what Holland trembled at the thought of becoming, a super-conscientious theoretician. So he continued sacrificially to entrench the outposts of religion against frontal assault while the enemy adopted new lines of philosophical approach, outflanking his traditional defences, and threatened the very citadel of faith.[1]

Holland brought reinforcements of a very different temper to St Paul's and, from the position which he established there, to the Church at large. If the general tendency of thought was drifting from a transcendental towards an immanentist emphasis, he preferred to search the current mood to see what points of contact and support it might present for Christianity. Accordingly, without disparaging the living authority genuinely resident in the Church, he laid stress on the value of intuitive insight and on the undoubted development which takes place in the rational appreciation of revealed truth.[2] If again the interest of the enfranchised masses was shifting from politics (so far as the masses had ever cared for politics) to industrial and economic problems, it seemed to him and to his friends essential to give the greatest possible

[1] F. Paget in Johnston, 394–8; cf. Liddon in Paget, 112.
[2] Cf. section III of his essay in *Lux Mundi*.

prominence to the Christian doctrine of man no less than to the Christian doctrine of God. If Christianity was right in claiming that God had become Man, there must be something in mankind intrinsically capable of responding to revelation, and "the Man" Christ Jesus must contain "the solution of all human problems".[1]

Holland firmly believed in conducting a war of spiritual manoeuvre. Instead of wasting his strength in the defence of outposts he would carry the war into the enemy's country, march round his rear, and take him in reverse. It was an incalculable blessing to St Paul's that in place of two great scholars in succession, who were largely absentees, it secured in Holland a great resident theologian who was both sympathetically abreast (if not in advance) of the thought of his day, and also capable of preaching to the people who were swayed by it a fully Christian interpretation of its values. His own feeling about his canonry was expressed in characteristic style in a letter to Gore shortly after his nomination had been published: "It is so noble to look up at the great Dome—and know that it beats, now, like a great Heart—in London—a home for all who watch after God. To help to make it as a *heart*, a Christian *heart*, to great London—this is one's prayer." [2]

Holland did not preach ecclesiastical controversy and party-politics, still less mere topical sensations, in church; he kept the pulpit for the fundamental truths and principles of Christianity. But he made the fullest use of press and platform to point the applications which he drew from basic Christianity, and his house in Amen Court was a centre of literary and social propaganda. It was there that the contributors to *Lux Mundi* met in 1888 in order to read, discuss, and criticize the first drafts of the essays which were to raise such a storm at the end of the following year, when Liberal Catholicism in the Church of England was revealed to the world as embodying not merely High Church doctrine but

[1] Paget, 171.
[2] Prestige, 59; cf. 30 f., 46.

still Higher Criticism of Biblical documents. It was also in Holland's house that the meetings were held, in 1889, which led to the foundation of the Christian Social Union, of which he was made Chairman of committee, with Westcott as the first President; its three objects were to claim for the Christian law the ultimate authority to rule social practice, to encourage common study of the way to apply Christian moral truths to the social and economic problems of the day, and to present Christ as the enemy of wrong and selfishness and as the power of righteousness and love. The Union proceeded to investigate with critical care and to denounce with vigour a number of social and industrial abuses. And in 1896 appeared the first number of *The Commonwealth*, a Christian social magazine into which Holland threw all his exuberance and in the pages of which he was free to say exactly what he liked on any or every topic of current interest.[1] All this could not take place without bearing somewhat markedly on the part played by the Cathedral in the religious life of London.

London was Holland's life, and St Paul's its heart. The See of Glasgow, for which he was asked in 1888 to let himself be nominated, could never be in serious question. His clear vocation was to arouse enthusiasm for Christian causes and to guide it into wise channels by appropriate organization. On the platform he was magnificent. He used to say himself that he had a "funny face"; his school-friends had called him "Monkey". But his face was funny in another sense too, for it crinkled and sparkled with fun. Unlike some modern professors and evangelists he was incapable of making religion appear dull; he could not but be light-hearted and merry about all the things for which he cared most deeply; and on the platform he felt no restraint in indulging his preference for religious gaiety. His audiences found him infectious. Not only on behalf of the more mundane enterprises of the Christian Social Union did he burgeon into a riot of quip and

[1] Prestige, 91, 98; Paget, 169 f., 173, 206.

epigram; for years he took the chair at great annual evening meetings of the Junior Clergy Missionary Association (which he was chiefly responsible for founding) and of the Universities' Mission to Central Africa, and entranced vast audiences who were attracted in large part by his magnetism. For foreign missions, as for social reform, he must appeal to the people, for, as he said, "it is the home people who decide what the impress of England shall be on the story of the world".[1]

But the roots of his joy and inspiration drew abiding sustenance from the Cathedral and its services. He has sketched, as few others could, the ideals for St Paul's which he shared with Chapter as a whole. "It was essential that the worship carried on in the central church of London should be continuous as the life which it was needed to sanctify . . . felt as an incessant pressure throughout the thronging occupation of the week: men, when they turned in at the doors, must find it continually happening." That worship "must uplift something of an ideal; it must be honourable, seemly, reverent; it must show that . . . men are putting their very best into the acts by which they hold communion with their God and Saviour". Above all, the "central Eucharistic Act of the Church's Communion with God must occupy the house which was built to enshrine it . . . must be always at hand . . . must be brought out of the corner in which it has hitherto lurked—the privilege of a secluded knot . . . must show itself as the culminating moment of public worship". Again, at St Paul's "with its Palladian spaciousness", "set upon the central platform in the midst of enormous populations . . . the appeal should be wide-winged": not only capable of "drawing multitudes under its spell", but also "given freely . . . no limitation of the use of the cathedral by the suggestion of payment, or of reserved or appropriated seats . . . no challenging virgers, no obstruction to free movement . . . no shaking of the money-bag". And lastly, the Cathedral "must

[1] Paget, 10, 167, 196 f.; Russell *B.*, 90.

be brought into sensitive touch with the multitudinous forms of diocesan life", become a central hearth at which Churchmen from the parishes might warm their hearts "by the glow of a felt fellowship; missions, committees, guilds, leagues, societies, associations . . . in corporate acts of worship, before the one altar, under the mothering dome".[1]

The choirboys adored him, and he wrote them, in 1892, an intensely Chestertonian poem about the dome, long before Chesterton had published a line:

> That is the egg that hatched us,
> Hung up there in the sky;
> We were the happy White-birds
> Baked in the big blue Pie. . . .

It doubtless expresses his own feelings far more accurately than it does the extraverted yearnings of cold-blooded choristers:

> Home again! Home again!
> Beneath the big blue Dome again!
> Ah, would we ne'er might roam again,
> But sing the songs of home again,
> Under the blessed Dome.

St Paul's was at least the author's "very very own" spiritual home:

> . . . Domum, Dulce Domum,
> And Dome and Home in one.

The dome fascinated him: "his love of St Paul's resolves itself, again and again, into his love of the dome". The reason suggested by his biographer presents an obvious truth, that ranks and troops of spires can only point the way to heaven so long as the beholder stays outside the edifice to which his spire is attached, but the dome of St Paul's is equally delightful outside and inside. Yet Holland's passion for the dome was surely far more than aesthetic or even than symbolic; he

[1] Holland in Church, 211–13.

loved it, craved for it, returned to it, and brooded over it because of all the acts and processes, heavenly and earthly, which the lovely dome covered, sheltered, and unified.[1]

He attended the daily services with regularity, though, being but human, the interminable length of some of them occasionally exhausted him: after one such event he came home, dropped on the sofa, and exclaimed, with a deep sigh, "I've been in church ever since I can remember." His sermons in Cathedral were extremely well attended, especially in his later years, when he had acquired a wide following of his own. Yet for multitude of hearers, it is recorded by a contemporary, there can be no comparison between Liddon and Holland: never has St Paul's presented such a spectacle of regular and eager listeners since Liddon's voice was silent. Liddon had a voice of silvery tone peculiarly adapted to the acoustic eccentricities of St Paul's, together with exceptional gifts for expounding Scripture so as to make it live in the minds of his audience and illustrate their own spiritual life. Holland was a more philosophical preacher, with deeper subtlety of thought and argument; his utterance was rapid, his language exuberant, he piled up epithets as though to overwhelm dispute by a culminating weight of missile fancies; his message opened unfamiliar applications to practical life—on every ground his sermons required a much closer attention in the hearer than might ordinarily be expected for a more conventional style of discourse. But his originality deserved attention and his thought challenged thought.[2]

The person in Chapter who was most nearly akin to Holland intellectually was the Dean. Both possessed a keen interest in all knowledge and rejoiced in those discoveries of the mind in which their age took pride—not only in knowledge for its own sake, but in knowledge as framed in the general scheme of God's universe and pointing to the ways of God. Neither was theologically afraid of intellectual novelty,

[1] Paget, 151 f.   [2] Paget, 153, 155–8; Russell *B.*, 92.

as Liddon was. But Church lived in almost impenetrable self-effacement, expressing himself in print, not on the platform; never could he be conceived as reaching out to the public with Holland's joyous abandonment, challenging and heckled and enjoying every moment of the scrap. Church was too balanced a critic, too scrupulously anxious to inspect the back and sides of every problem, too nicely apprehensive to be fair to all parties, for such work as that: a man must needs have in him some elements, at least, of the partisan in order to make a bonny fighter. So far from being a partisan, Church was a personified Conscience, and sometimes paid the penalty of his greatness of soul, like Hamlet, when facing a practical dilemma. He could not habitually command the intuitive immediacy of resolution which qualified Holland's delicacy and sensitiveness: "I am sufficiently prone to scepticism", wrote Church in 1877 with reference to the burning problem of State interference in ecclesiastical affairs, "to doubt all absolute theories as to right on either side." [1]

Thus though in general sympathy with the new school of theological artillery which exploded on the world in *Lux Mundi*, Church was critical of what he thought the violent overstatement of its case. Not that he was incapable of taking sides, especially when he seemed to detect injustice or presumption. He had been indignant at the tyranny proposed on Newman in 1845. His anger was aroused by the unfair judicial condemnation of a Ritualist in 1856, though personally he was quite uninterested in ritualism: "It is this determination, in courts of justice, to find a meaning and a direction where there is none, and to close questions which at the least are open ones, which is enough to drive fair and quiet men into savage thoughts and feelings." He came out openly in opposition to the Public Worship Regulation Act in 1874, and in a private letter denounced "the ignorance of some, the pride of others, the suspicious injustice of even wise and good men" (such as, no doubt, Archbishop Tait),

[1] Church, 253.

which within six months had threatened with disruption the Church which "at the beginning of the year stood for the strongest and most hopeful Church in Christendom". It was a strange reversal that ranged him, almost in despair, alongside Liddon, who was preaching a divine confidence and prophesying that "we shall live to see the drowned Egyptians on the sea-shore even yet". *The Guardian* took the other side in the controversy, and the Dean ceased to write for the paper; from 1874 to 1883 his pen, which had done so much to shape and support it, was withdrawn from its service.[1]

For eight years Church continued to protest against the "unjust, unconstitutional and oppressive" persecution of the Ritualists under the Act, while labouring behind the scenes for peace, until Tait on his deathbed arranged at long last a truce. But Church was shaken in conscience because he could only protest verbally; no part of the oppression fell upon his own back. Ought not a man in high office like himself to prove the reality of his abhorrence of the "grotesquely one-sided" way in which the Church of England was being misgoverned by resigning the deanery, abandoning comfort and security, and finding another job? This scrupulous desire to clear his own soul of complicity was thoroughly Tractarian. It had bulked large in the mind of Newman in 1845, driving him towards secession. Liddon and Pusey again, during 1871 and 1872, had proclaimed to the bishops that they would leave the Church of England if impious hands were laid on the Athanasian Creed. Everybody knew they meant what they said, and that other secessions would follow; only the Ritualists would "take their own line of caring for nothing", stay in till they were thrown out, and be a thorn of disaffection in the apostolic flesh.[2] But that occasion had passed safely off. Dean Church was now faced not with a clear-cut issue which would be decided, one way or the other, at a definite moment,

[1] Prestige, 104 f.; F. Paget in Church, Preface, xxi f.; Church, 57, 147 f., 244; Lathbury, *Dean Church* (1905), 112 f., 134.

[2] *Life of Pusey*, IV, 233, 235, 240, 246.

but with a continuing episcopal policy of unjust coercion; and he began to think that the only remedy might be a sacrifice comparable to the purge of 1845. In 1877 he was seriously considering resignation. Happily for St Paul's and all concerned he was persuaded that this course would tend to shatter confidence in the Church of England to so great a degree as to cause worse evils than it could mend; and he remained at his post.[1]

Some other capitular consciences were less delicate than the Dean's. In 1881 the then bishop-archdeacon nominated his nephew for a Chapter living, as established custom gave him a perfect right to do. Gregory and Stubbs, who were both present, seem to have raised no objection. The Dean, however, though he declined, in the absence of any prohibiting regulation, to vote against the proposal, entered a solemn record of his disapproval, and Liddon joined him; it was "highly inexpedient" in the general interests of the Church that Chapter patronage should be bestowed on relatives of the patrons. Worse happened in 1882, when in similar circumstances Gregory nominated his own son: Stubbs was present, but not the Archdeacon. Again the Dean and Liddon recorded their disapprobation in the most formal manner, and "with the deepest regret". Since on both occasions Liddon made a separate protest, in which he used the word "dissent" instead of "disapproval", it would appear that, unlike the Dean, he actually voted against acceptance of the nominations.[2]

There certainly was a stratum of insensitivity in Gregory's composition. Once in Church's absence he presided at the tea-party given annually to members of the works staff, and obviously hurt the feelings of the guests by delivering a lecture on punctilious discharge of Cathedral duties. It was left to Holland to restore good humour by a racy speech, in which he chaffed canons, choristers, virgers, and workmen in turn for thinking that their own part in maintaining the

[1] Church, 259 f. [2] *Acta C.*, 65 f., 82 f.

Cathedral was the only one that really mattered. What Gregory thought of Holland's political enterprises can scarcely be imagined. Gregory "never ceased", says Holland, "to look upon himself as Tom Keble's man", and Tom Keble's men belonged to a strict and rigid school: "they were tough Tories". Gregory readily adopted any improvement in the mechanical devices which make for practical efficiency in daily life, but resisted intransigently certain of the big changes that were coming over organized society, especially in the field of education and local government. Holland's policy was for Churchmen to accept inevitable changes and try to infiltrate into the new order, since Christians also are citizens and have the right to use what influence they can command: but Gregory could not be brought to compromise himself by acquiescence in events of which he deeply disapproved: he too was a Tractarian.[1]

Naturally, as the Dean's health began to give way, it was upon this tough, rugged, constant, honest, practical man of business (and the term includes Christian business) that he came to rely in ever greater measure. Church's constitution was unequal to the sulphurous fogs of a London winter. From 1886 onward his medical advisers sent him away at the end of each year until spring had returned, either to the south of France or, more accessibly, to Dover. On these occasions he handed over his responsibilities to Gregory as senior canon, with a generous confidence that perhaps he could not have felt in any other member of Chapter. In the Proxy which he executed he named Gregory as his "Proctor or substitute" for all Cathedral business: "and do hereby give and grant to him a general power for me and in my name place and stead to call meetings of the Chapter for the transaction of general business connected with the said Cathedral and to appear thereat and preside in my name and to do all and singular matters and things which in and about the premises shall be necessary or in anywise convenient in my name in the same

[1] Russell *B.*, 89 f.; Holland in Gregory, 258, 261 f.

St Paul's Cathedral: In the Nave Looking towards the Organ, c. 1852

Richard William Church, Dean 1871–90

Robert Gregory, Dean 1891–1911

manner as I myself could do was I personally present. And I promise to ratify and confirm all and whatsoever my said Proctor shall do." Trust could hardly have been carried to extremer lengths.[1]

Church was greatly stricken by the death of his only son in January 1888. The loss of several old and close friends followed on this bereavement, and in August 1890 Newman died. The intimacy between Church and Newman, suspended but not broken in 1846, had been renewed in 1864, when Newman asked him to read the proof-sheets of his *Apologia*. They had met again for the first time in 1865, and in 1872 Liddon had made his first acquaintance with Newman at a dinner-party in the deanery; "his manner", noted Liddon, "was quite that of Mr Keble in its simplicity and intensity." Church was now engaged in revising the proofs of his own *Oxford Movement*, and the Cardinal's death brought a special sorrow. Liddon also was seriously ill, though apparently recovering; but in the next month came news of his unexpectedly sudden death. Church was very feeble, but insisted on taking part in the funeral: it was the last time that he officiated in St Paul's, and he had to have a deputy in reserve in case his strength should fail. After that he went downhill rapidly. His last few weeks were spent at Dover, where he died on 9 December. He was buried at Whatley, by his own request; and left strict charge that no memorial should be raised to him except a stone inscribed with two verses of the *Dies Irae*.[2]

[1] *Acta C.*, 176 f.; cf. Gregory, 217.

[2] Church, 167, 169, 328–31, 338 f., 344–50; Johnston, 170; Russell *B.*, 96 f.

14

BYZANTINE SPLENDOURS

On Church's death all London, and interested persons in regions far beyond, felt that there could be only one fit successor to the deanery. That one was Gregory. For twenty-two years he had been a dominating force in St Paul's and a tower of strength for all its enterprises. In age he was nearly 72; but years counted for little in a man so tough, so vigorous, and so experienced. His natural powers were not abated. He still had in him, as events were to prove, another twenty years of service, which remained, until near the end, as strenuous and unceasing as it had ever been. Lord Salisbury, then Prime Minister, could hardly have looked elsewhere in nominating a new Dean; as Stubbs, by this time Bishop of Oxford, observed, Lord Salisbury "has had no choice". Gregory received the offer on Christmas Eve, and accepted it so promptly that the appointment was announced next day. The chorus of approval was led by the Archbishop of Canterbury (Benson), who voiced the sentiments of all in writing "to express deep satisfaction that the devoted lover and servant of St Paul's should succeed to the Deanery". Canterbury Convocation was in session in the following February, when Gregory was installed; and the Lower House, of which he had for many years been an active and effective member, adjourned in order to be present in Cathedral at the installation.[1]

In view of Gregory's long-standing and aggressive desire to carry out the programme of "embellishment" projected for the Cathedral since the days of Milman, it is not surprising that his first thoughts as Dean were bent towards that

[1] Gregory, 216, 232 f.; Green, 218.

quarter. The Decoration Committee had been in abeyance since the end of 1874;[1] Burges, its High Priest, had died in 1881. But the money which had been collected still continued in existence, and Gregory was now determined to spend it. His feelings were already known. During the last few years of Church's life the matter had been under discussion, and more than once he had generously pressed Gregory to go ahead. But Gregory, quite rightly, had declined to saddle Church with the responsibility for possibly controversial measures in which the poor state of Church's health disabled him from taking any really active part. Nevertheless, a large sum had already been expended on capitular initiative and partly from capitular resources, both on improvements and repairs to the Cathedral and its property and on the erection of a magnificent reredos at the east end of the choir.[2]

First of all, a new chapel was fitted up in the eastern part of the crypt, with altar, marble steps, and mosaic pavement, and came into use in 1877. It is known as St Faith's, after a medieval parish church demolished in 1256 to make room for an extension of the old Cathedral, when the parishioners were granted parochial rights in the crypt of St Paul's by way of compensation. This chapel, which can accommodate several hundred people while retaining an atmosphere of homely intimacy, has proved extremely useful for services and lectures for which the western chapels were too small or the dome too grandiose.[3]

Between 1879 and 1883 the fabric of the church was receiving attentions of a thoroughness exceeding the normal routine. Extensive replacements were made of marble pavement, and the choir, which had subsisted with a temporary floor since 1859,[4] was paved again with marble. A new system for blowing the organ, invented by Willis, was installed, and the new great bell was hung. Walls and ceilings were cleaned down. The mosaic floor of the Wellington

[1] Cf. *supra*, p. 146.
[2] Gregory, 217.
[3] Green, 130; Sinclair, 55, 475.
[4] Cf. *supra*, p. 83.

chamber in the crypt was completed; its manufacture had occupied the enforced leisure of inmates of the female convict prison at Woking. The granite pavement outside the entrance to the north transept was renewed. Joints in the external masonry were stopped with a new oil cement. A vertical fissure, half an inch wide, in one of the columns of the west front demanded peculiar care and contrivance, but was successfully repaired. A big job was entailed in recasting and relaying some 24,000 square feet of lead on various sections of the roof, and renewing 4000 feet of flashings. In connection with this work a casting chamber was established in the crypt, since cast lead was difficult to obtain, the trade preferring milled lead, which was thought less suitable for the task. Among other repairs to the masonry, inside and out, must be mentioned that of cramping and securing fractured steps of the beautiful Geometrical Staircase in the south-west tower; twenty-one steps had parted company with the wall and were found to be supported by little more than abstract contiguity with their neighbours. Finally, wire guards were fixed to exclude pigeons from frequenting the porticoes; the nuisance they caused had been increasing year by year. The guards, unhappily, proved only partially successful in their object.[1]

Meantime, additional protection had to be given to the estate at Tillingham. Many centuries earlier the Cathedral had suffered the total loss of one of its prebendal estates, situated at Walton-on-the-Naze in Essex, which was inundated by the sea about the time of the Norman Conquest; the stall in question still bears the title of *Consumpta per Mare*. The estate at Tillingham, on the nearer side of the Blackwater, is guarded from similar encroachment by a sea-wall; it received extensive damage in recent times from the disastrous flood that ravaged the coast of East Anglia in 1953, when the wall was breached. Considerable sums were spent on strengthening the wall in 1882, and again, after dangerous

[1] *Acta C.*, 17 ff., 30 ff., 52–6, 69 ff., 95 f.

storms, in 1887; it was breached in 1898 and serious loss ensued. But repairs were effected, and this historic property of St Paul's yet remains, after thirteen and a half centuries, on the landward side of the beleaguering waves.[1]

Another set of problems was presented in connection with the Chapter House, built by Wren in the Churchyard to the north of the Cathedral. When Thomas Hall succeeded Sellon as Receiver in 1869 he was allowed, in accordance with long custom, to take up quarters in the Chapter House for his personal accommodation, with the reservation that Chapter might resume the rooms for its own purposes at some future date. On Lightfoot's appointment to a canonry in 1871 notice was given to the Receiver that the rooms would be required: the canonical house at No. 1 Amen Corner was in the occupation of the choir school, and as Lightfoot was a bachelor, and resident for most of his time at Cambridge, the Chapter House sufficiently provided for his needs. The Receiver was informed, in answer to his protest, that the volume of his work would be diminished by the forthcoming commutation of the estates, and that he would have to find a domicile at his own charges after the summer of 1872; and Lightfoot took possession. Stubbs, who succeeded Lightfoot, occupied No. 1 Amen Court, but early in his tenancy made an important discovery in the roof of the Chapter House. He was searching for some missing registers, and on climbing through a trap-door into the garret he found a mass of ancient charters, leases, wills, letters, and miscellaneous papers which had apparently last been seen by mortal eye two centuries before. So easy is it for a corporate body to lose its own muniments on its own premises.[2]

The three Wren houses in Amen Court being now assigned to the holders of the three ancient stalls, no capitular house was available for the Archdeacon of London. No inconvenience was caused by this deficiency till 1884, as the

[1] Sinclair, 110; *Acta C.*, 80 f., 181; *Acta D.*, 134.

[2] *Acta B.*, 236 ff.; Hutton, 197.

Archdeacon preferred to live outside the City. But at the end of 1884, when Gifford succeeded to the office, some fresh arrangement had to be devised. The rooms in the Chapter House previously occupied by Lightfoot and then by Dr Martin, the sub-organist,[1] which constituted the only living-space that Chapter had to spare, were inadequate to Gifford's requirements. The first plan was to exchange the Chapter House for some more commodious premises. The Mercers' Company had at its disposal the buildings of St Paul's School, at the east of the Churchyard, which were being vacated on the removal of the school to Hammersmith; so negotiations were opened for acquiring part of them in return for the Chapter House. But this scheme proved impracticable. In the following July Frederick Temple, newly translated to the bishopric of London, asked if he might purchase the Chapter House: he wanted to live in the City in order to be near the Cathedral. Gregory was strongly sympathetic towards the idea, but the request had to be declined, because Chapter could not afford to buy an alternative site for a new Chapter House at the enormous prices ruling for land in the neighbourhood of St Paul's.[2]

It was therefore determined to enlarge the existing Chapter House by adding a new top story, and to assign canonical lodging therein to the Archdeacon. Accordingly Gifford took up his abode there, and was followed by Sinclair, his successor. In 1912, when funds were short and there had been a recent change of Archdeacon, a project was discussed of selling the Chapter House to the Ecclesiastical Commissioners; correspondence was exchanged, but the matter came to nothing. By 1920 the first world war had greatly reduced the value of money and consequently also the purchasing power of endowments. At the same time St Paul's was faced with an immense outlay for preserving the fabric. So most of the

[1] Cf. *supra*, p. 151.

[2] Gregory, 214, 245; *Acta C.*, 125, 139 f.; Frost, 73 f.

Chapter House was leased at a large rental to a bank, which remained in occupation till the House was burned out in the second world war. The Archdeacon was provided with a home in the best of the minor canons' houses in Amen Court.[1]

During the '80s, amid so many preoccupations, and with the dust of controversy which had been raised by the designs of Burges only gradually settling, Chapter was content to let the Decoration Committee and its plans for embellishing the Cathedral languish. The Committee's one independent project was to substitute for Thornhill's paintings of incidents in the life of St Paul, on the inner dome, a series of designs to illustrate the Book of Revelation. Eminent artists prepared trial cartoons, which were actually suspended over Thornhill's pictures in 1883. But they failed to give satisfaction, either on the score of fitness or on that of expense; and the idea was dropped. However, while the Committee was dallying with the dome, Chapter itself, in April 1883, invited the gifted G. F. Bodley, R.A., to submit designs for a new high altar and appropriate surroundings.

Bodley promptly produced suggestions for a splendid and elaborate reredos in marbles of many colours. The central feature was to be a sculptured group of figures representing the crucifixion of the Saviour, set in a frame of wreathed and twisted columns, with pediment over and crowned with statuary. This towering erection, reaching to the clerestory, was truly calculated to provide an impressive termination to the choir, and one, moreover, which should strike an unmistakably religious note; the fact that it would gravely obscure the apse with which Wren had designed to close his vista, does not seem to have occasioned remark. A still more serious foreclosure upon Wren's architectural design was proposed, though only as a dispensable garnish, in the addition of solid

[1] Green, 188, 210; *Acta C.*, 140, 173; *Min.*, 3 Feb. 1912, 16 March 1912; *Acta D.*, 254.

marble screens joining the reredos to the piers of the sanctuary on either side.[1]

The novelty of Bodley's ideas demanded some degree of acclimatization. Liddon's first inclination was for a simpler design. But the more he studied Bodley's proposals the more he liked them; the central Calvary put out an exquisite attraction to his sense of religious fitness, and he convinced himself without undue reluctance that Bodley's instinct for the scale and details of the whole composition was to be trusted. In November authority was given for Bodley to prepare a model of his reredos; in the following January his design was accepted by Chapter. Not until November 1884, however, did Gregory, at Chapter's request, produce a statement of the cash available to pay for its execution, from which it appeared that the main project could be financed in roughly equal parts from gifts earmarked for this particular branch of the embellishment, and from capitular profits and floating balance. In the following July it was resolved, in accordance with the wishes of Bodley and his partner, Garner, to make an opportunity for judging the effect of the reredos by putting up a "cartoon" of it in the Cathedral. Chapter clearly did not possess means to pay for more than the central portion of the full design; accordingly the help of the Decoration Committee was enlisted, with happy consequences. Not only was that riven body almost unanimously reunited in approval of the plans, but it consented to bear the whole cost of the quadrant wings on either side, and of the marble floor and steps of the sanctuary, amounting in all to more than the expenditure estimated for the central section of the reredos.[2]

The work of erection began in August 1886. For a short period the entire choir was closed and the altar temporarily placed outside the entrance; later a wooden screen was fixed between the stalls, and the western part of the choir was

[1] Sinclair, 475; *Acta C.*, 71, 103; Gregory, 206 f.

[2] Johnston, 329; Gregory, 207 ff.; *Acta C.*, 106 f., 125 f., 138, 150.

brought into use. The usual Advent oratorio was omitted, and the Bishop transferred his ordination to St James's, Piccadilly. The reredos was completed in time to be dedicated on St Paul's Day, 25 January 1888. Later in the same year a large additional sum was expended on refacing with marble the stone flutings of the pilasters in the sanctuary; and the original altar rails, a beautifully executed piece of iron-work by Wren's craftsman Tijou, were moved westwards to form a low screen across the entrance to the choir. All in all, the reredos and its accompaniments cost nearly £40,000. Finally a new high altar was given in 1891 by Liddon's sister, and the Jesus chapel, formed in the apse behind the reredos and ultimately containing Liddon's monument, was dedicated at the end of the year.[1]

No sooner had the reredos been placed in position than it became the target for attack. The intolerant and litigious Puritanism of a section of Protestant Churchmen, which had already distressed Church and aroused the antagonism of Gregory and Liddon, objected to the representation of the Redeemer on the cross as being an object of superstitious regard. Proceedings were therefore instituted to have it removed, under the provisions of the Public Worship Regulation Act, the charter of secular dictatorship. Temple, having as Bishop of London a right under the Act to veto the prosecution, exercised it. Thereupon the promoters applied to the ordinary secular courts for a *mandamus* to override his veto. The case was heard in November 1888; a reserved judgement was delivered in June 1889 against the Bishop and the Dean and Chapter, who appealed to the House of Lords. The appeal was heard in December, when judgement was again reserved. In the following Holy Week Temple displayed his solidarity with his Cathedral by himself conducting the Three Hours devotion in St Paul's. It was not until July 1891 that the House of Lords made known its decision, but when

[1] Frost, 80 f.; Green, 195 ff., 202; Gregory, 218, 220; *Acta C.*, 200; *Acta D.* (inset), 81.

it came it was satisfactory. The Calvary was determined to be not a crucifix and superstitious but a historical representation of a group of figures: the Gospel triumphed over secular legalism by a legal technicality.[1] Half a century later the reredos was so badly shaken by a bomb, which exploded in the roof above it during the second world war, that Chapter decided to remove it and substitute a baldachino; a few of the statues that had not been damaged are preserved in the crypt chapels.

Much had therefore been accomplished, largely under Gregory's inspiration, before he became Dean; "the decoration of the Cathedral", as he wrote in his autobiography, "was thus fairly commenced." Within a few days of his appointment the suggestion was made to him that Sir William Richmond (as he afterwards became) should be asked to design a scheme of decoration for the choir. Gregory, feeling that his hands were now free, took up the proposal with characteristic alacrity. The Decoration Committee was summoned to concur; as early as March 1891 preparatory work was started and scaffolding began to go up in the Cathedral, though not until June did the Decoration Committee approve, and Chapter endorse, the terms of a contract with Richmond to cover his activities for the next three years. It was decided to fill arches, clerestory, and ceilings with gilding and colour and to panel the area with brilliant glass mosaics. By November 1892 the easternmost saucer dome of the choir was finished and inspected. By March 1894 work was sufficiently advanced for numerous parties of royal and civic visitors to be conducted up the scaffolds by the Dean and the canons to get a close view of the results. During Easter week thousands were admitted daily to the choir in order to behold and marvel, and the sun shone brightly on the mosaics for the public delectation. The roof was finished by March 1896, and the last craftsman left the choir, now

[1] *Acta C.*, 198; Russell *B.*, 70; Green, 208 f., 211, 213, 222; Sinclair, 349.

glowing in accomplished splendour, one year later. The great work was done at last.[1]

More, however, than the decoration of the choir alone had already accompanied that achievement, and more still was to follow after. The series of mosaics representing prophets and evangelists in the spandrels of the dome, which had been begun by Milman,[2] was now completed; and the niches in the drum were filled, between 1892 and 1894, with statues of the eight principal doctors of the Church. In 1893 a new reredos, and Liddon's monument, were placed in the Jesus chapel. Mosaics were inserted in the quarter-domes under the Whispering Gallery between 1898 and 1901, through the generosity of City companies. Not till August 1907 was all the work of decoration finished in the aisles of the choir and the last of the scaffolding finally removed. Most of the stained glass with which, during this period, the choir had been enriched and darkened, was blown out of the windows by the bombardments of the second world war. With this exception and improvement, the great object conceived by Milman and accomplished by Gregory remains intact, a vision of Byzantine splendour covering the entire eastern section of the church with a mantle of coloured magnificence. Even Burges may be held to have his memorial in the finished product, for, as he designed, the half-dome of the apse is filled with a gigantic figure, in mosaic, of Christ imparting his benediction on the scene.[3]

Forrest Browne, who took a personal and practical interest in the mosaics and watched with delight the whole process of ornamentation taking shape before his eyes, left a careful account of the technique employed. Mosaics are of two kinds.

[1] Gregory, 209, 217 f.; Green, 219; *Acta D.*, 35 f.; *Min.*, 19 Nov. 1892, March 1894, 28 March 1896, 11 April 1896, 6 March 1897.

[2] Cf. *supra*, p. 82.

[3] *Acta C.*, 200; *Min.*, 6 Aug. 1892, 28 Oct. 1893, 5 Nov. 1898, 3 Aug. 1907; Gregory, 219; *Mr Burges' Models* in *Cathedral Decoration*, 41 (p. 15); Green, 258.

In the one, the small coloured blocks or tesserae with which the pattern or picture is built up are laid flat, and produce a smooth surface not immediately distinguishable from a fresco painted on the wall. This is the modern Italian style, and had been followed by the foreign craftsmen who worked on the spandrels between the arches of the dome. But Richmond, who had made a long study of Byzantine mosaics, determined to adopt the more ancient style, in which the tesserae are set at different angles so as to catch and reflect the light; the resultant surface is rough and the effect is much more brilliantly decorative. His method of working was marked by extreme care. He first of all submitted small coloured designs, which were subsequently enlarged to full scale; the full-sized cartoons were then, for the most part, actually hung in their projected place in the Cathedral, in order to judge the effect. The various parts of the design were next transferred to tracing paper from which the craftsmen worked. A portion of the surface to be decorated was coated with cement, but no more than could be covered with tesserae in a single day while the cement remained soft and pliable. The craftsman pierced the tracing with a bradawl to mark the lines of the pattern on the prepared surface, and pressed the tesserae into position one by one. It was a long and calculated operation.

The tesserae themselves were made of thick glass in a variety of tints. It came in flat cakes; these were cut up into blocks about half an inch in breadth in a workshop which had been established, together with drawing-offices and store-rooms, in the galleries over the aisles of the choir. In the early stages a great number of different colours were in use; by 1894 this had been reduced to a hundred and fifty, as it was found that in the frequently murky atmosphere of London extreme delicacy of treatment was wasted, and tones and outlines needed to be more strongly marked. By 1896 the number of stock tints was reduced to fifty. The workmen were all British. More than a score of craftsmen were engaged in fixing the tesserae, mostly trained in Richmond's own studio. It was a ticklish business to design and erect the scaffolding necessary to reach the less accessible parts of the building; but Penrose and the able Clerk of the Works had had considerable experience in such "contrivance", and the regular works staff managed the whole affair without a single accident. So saints and angels, birds and beasts, fish and flowers sprang into glowing life, and the Cathedral was glorified.[1]

Apart from pure embellishment two other undertakings of importance had been carried out. The clock in the south-west tower showed signs of wear, and in 1893 a new clock was installed under the superintendence of Lord Grimthorpe. Grimthorpe was a man of varied parts—Protestant partisan, restorer of St Albans Abbey, and notable expert on clock-making. Gregory, whose heart was set on procuring a new and better clock for St Paul's, enlisted Grimthorpe's enthusiastic aid; schemes for illuminated dials and for more elaborately tuneful chimes fell through on the score of expense. Between 1897 and 1900, however, the organ was once more enlarged and partially rebuilt, at a cost of £3000, temporarily borrowed from the Decoration Fund. That Fund itself had recently needed to be replenished: embellishment of the order then in execution costs an immense amount of money. By 1894 the balance accrued from the old appeal had been exhausted and a new appeal was launched. But with the exhilarating evidence before its eyes of progress actually in the making, the public responded generously; at the service held on 2 December 1897 to commemorate the opening of the choir of new St Paul's for public worship exactly two centuries before, the collection was given to the Decoration Fund and amounted to £1000. Finance was not as yet a crippling embarrassment.[2]

Throughout the long course of restoring and decorating St

[1] Browne, 318; cf. Sinclair, 378–82, and Newbolt, 216 ff.

[2] Sinclair, 430 f.; Russell *B.*, 105 f.; Sumner, 22 f.; *Acta D.*, 81, 105, 124; *Min.*, 2 Dec. 1897.

Paul's the same Surveyor had held office, from the early days of Milman until the completion of the mosaics in the choir. Then in 1897, after forty-five years of long-suffering and devotion, Penrose resigned.[1] He had been appointed by the Trustees in 1852, at a salary of £75, increased to £150 in 1860 when the first (or Milman's) spate of reconstruction was in full flow and the Trustees were still in possession of considerable sums. But after the second reconstructive burst had been initiated under Mansel, the funds of the Trustees were virtually exhausted,[2] and full control of the revenue, whether derived from endowments or from public generosity, had fallen into the hands of Chapter. A fresh arrangement was therefore made with Penrose in 1880, by which Chapter became his paymaster: in return for his salary of £150 he agreed to oversee all regular maintenance work on the Cathedral, but he was promised a commission on all new works for which he might be asked to prepare plans, Chapter making it quite plain that other architects might be employed for special undertakings if it should so desire—as indeed it did employ Bodley for the reredos and Richmond for the last and purely Gregorian torrent of decorative action.[3]

Penrose, though a man of brilliant attainments and unquestionable loyalty, had not altogether succeeded in winning Gregory's confidence. He had, so Holland records, "a wavering manner and a tendency to indecision"; on such proclivities Gregory's weight fell somewhat heavily. Gregory hated having to deal with anybody who did not know his own mind or allowed his judgement to be swayed by the arguments of the last speaker: "I would prefer to be contradicted ten times over, and reasons given for it, rather than have to do with a man of that type." But when Penrose retired Chapter was generous in its appreciation not only of his unflagging activity, but of his initiative, professional skill, and "unfailing good temper". There must have been times

[1] Cf. *supra*, pp. 62, 82. [2] Cf. *supra*, pp. 125–6.
[3] *Acta C.*, 59 f.; *Acta D.*, 105.

when he needed all he had of the last and not least precious commodity.

He was succeeded by Somers Clarke, not as "a resident Surveyor such as has been hitherto employed", but as "consulting architect", with a small retaining fee in return for making two reports on the fabric in each year, and the usual professional remuneration for such advice and plans as he might be called on to supply. In 1906, when Somers Clarke retired, Chapter appointed in his place Mervyn Macartney, on similar terms, but setting out with greater particularity both his duties, rights, and fees, and also his relations with the Clerk of the Works.[1] Another victory, though on a minor scale and in a comparatively unimportant field, had been secured for centralized administration. More and more the efficient working of the Cathedral had come to depend on the existence of able and strong and active men in Chapter—working unitedly in harmonious co-operation with one another and with their subordinate officers, and devoting their primary energies to the service of St Paul's—and, as a corollary, on the presence among them of a Dean capable of business and qualified to make his influence felt.

[1] *Acta D.*, 112 f., 117 f., 213; Gregory, 229, 259.

15

RELIGION AND THE PUBLIC

As CANON, Gregory had been instrumental, in Holland's words, "in providing the opportunities which others could use and in securing the resources which were available for others to apply". When he became Dean, nothing essential was changed, but the scope of his activities was enlarged. He continued till extreme old age to manage the business and finances of the Cathedral in the office of Chapter Treasurer, and was constant in attendance at its services. He took an unconcealed delight in the decorations which he was then able to put in hand. "There was a pleasant irony, which he himself enjoyed, in the fact that he should have been called to supervise a matter so entirely outside his natural bent and skill." While his colleagues wavered on the edge of an aesthetic decision, Gregory called upon them, to their horror, for an instantaneous vote. He selected his artist, trusted the judgement of his chosen expert and, with his long experience of the frustrations of divided counsel, plunged ahead.

In every practical question he demanded instant attention to detail. When asked to give his sentence he would invariably make a personal inspection: "Let's go and see it." He pursued the same course on his visits to the farms and buildings on the Tillingham estate as in his oversight of the Cathedral fabric. His theory was that though he might know nothing of the immediate problem, yet if he probed into the situation with awkward questions he would certainly be furnished, sooner or later, with unnecessarily full and apologetic explanations which would infallibly point him towards the weak spot; and thus the shrewd old man would know exactly where he ought to direct investigations.[1]

Church's disposition had been too retiring, and his health in his later years too feeble, to admit of his entering greatly into the life of the City. Here Gregory presented a marked contrast. He made many friends among the leading men and threw himself with hearty enjoyment and good will into the social delights that accompany metropolitan commerce, dining frequently with City companies and bringing St Paul's into a fruitful association with their members. He interested them in his plans for the Cathedral, and it was largely through the generosity of some of them that he was able to found scholarships for choristers, on leaving the choir school, to pursue their further education; the welfare of the boys lay very close to his heart. But indeed his influence in the City, and the uncommon respect which he enjoyed in that quarter, were of long standing. Once, while he was still a canon, a merchant came to ask him for advice. The unfortunate man had been left a fortune of some £70,000, which he did not want to keep and scarcely knew how to dispose of to the best advantage. But he and Gregory between them arranged to give the lot away.[2]

The Dean was also on the best of terms with successive Bishops of London. Jackson, with whom in early days he had had what Sydney Smith used to call a "collision",[3] came to know and understand his quality. Temple (1885–96) held him in high regard; their rough and gruff goodness was a common bond. On one occasion, when Temple was expected to attend a service in Cathedral, he arrived two minutes late, only to find proceedings in full swing. On their return to the vestry he protested; but the only reply he got from Gregory was: "When the clock strikes we begin." It was the kind of answer that he could appreciate, and he never came late again. On Temple's translation to Canterbury the See of

[1] Gregory, 241 f., 244, 253 f.; Russell *B.*, 103 f.
[2] Gregory, 242 f., 248; Russell *B.*, 104 f. [3] Cf. *supra*, pp. 107 f.

London was filled for four all too short years (1897–1901) by Mandell Creighton, an inspiring historian and teacher, whose strong convictions were matched with an understanding tolerance and enlivened by an equally unusual sense of humour and epigrammatic sparkle. For him Gregory entertained a cordial admiration which drew forth a corresponding affection from the Bishop, and they worked together in the deepest possible accord. If Gregory sometimes displayed something of the character of an irresistible force, he knew both how to avoid unnecessary conflict with other forces of a similar potency, and how to unite his own powers with those of others in a common effort. He was too wise not to recognize wisdom in others, and strong enough to value strength.[1]

His Chapter included three new members. Sinclair had received the archdeaconry in 1889; he took a real interest in the Cathedral. Newbolt, in mind very much a parochial version of the Liddon archetype, of whom more falls to be said later, was appointed in place of Liddon in the autumn of 1890, though he was not fully resident until the following summer. Gregory's own canonry was filled by the keen and active Browne from Cambridge, in whom the professorial tradition was renewed in a manner that secured to St Paul's a first charge on the work and affections of its holder. Thus though the men changed, outlook and policy and tradition were maintained. And for another twenty years the vivid and generous spirit of Holland was found at Gregory's right hand, always his loyal supporter and towards the end his principal prop and stay. The sun which Gladstone had hung in the Cathedral firmament suffered no eclipse.

Holland was now cutting a great figure both in London and in the Church beyond. His overflowing energy seemed almost boundless. The hub of his life was the Cathedral, but his radial activities stretched in every direction. An impenitent Liberal whose faith in the existing Liberal Party was

[1] Gregory, 241, 245.

thickly clouded with a doubt, he flung himself into social and political adventures. He preached social righteousness from the platforms of the Christian Social Union and proclaimed political judgements, some of them extremely unpopular, in the columns of *The Commonwealth*. He founded the Maurice Hostel as a "C.S.U. settlement" in Hoxton in 1898, and poured his soul into the support of its innumerable activities and the provision of its illimitable needs: the inaugural meeting was held in St Paul's Chapter House. He loathed the national self-idolatry of the baser Imperialism and denounced the "savage swagger" and "vile passion" which attended the outbreak of the South African War. When the Liberals came into power he fiercely criticized the uncomprehending bias against the Church of England which was manifested in their Education Bill, but his heart and purse were opened in sympathy with the unemployed who marched to London through the rain, five hundred strong, from Leicester in 1905. He made mistakes and was sometimes deceived and disappointed. But his passionate enthusiasm for justice, championship of the oppressed, and fervour in the spread of Christianity, sprung as they were from a dogmatic spiritual faith in God, drew a great following from the public to St Paul's and attracted more select groups of men with influence to Amen Court.[1]

Among the new members of Chapter the outstanding figure was that of W. C. E. Newbolt, both on account of his successful experiments in pastoral work and because he long outstayed his colleagues, retaining his canonry till 1930. He had been trained in a curacy under the great Butler, at Wantage, that model of parochial system where Liddon had earlier spent a brief apprenticeship. He then served a village church in Gloucestershire and a working-class parish at Malvern Link. After twenty years in parochial work he was given charge, in 1888, of the Theological College at Ely, to train future parish priests. When, less than two years later, he was

[1] Paget, 214 f., 226 ff.; cf. 207.

called to St Paul's some surprise was felt at his proposed departure. Since Church was at Dover and nearing his end, Newbolt came to Town and had an interview with Gregory, to ask whether there was any chance of his combining St Paul's with an extended tenure of the Principalship of Ely. Gregory "snubbed" that idea firmly and at once. So Newbolt took a partial residence in December, thereby earning the right to say that he had served for ten days under Dean Church, and promised to stay no longer at Ely than was necessary for a successor to be found to take over the College.[1]

Newbolt's most distinctive contribution to the life of the Cathedral was in his development of the pastoral work hitherto conducted mainly by the minor canons. As finally reorganized by him it took two forms, the Lecture Society and the Amen Court Guild. The former took its origin from a private class which met in the Chapter House. In 1893 it was decided to expand the class into a society, and with Gregory's approval its meetings were transferred in 1894 to the crypt of the Cathedral, where through the winter months courses of lectures were delivered to any men who cared to join, on the general subject of "Catholic faith and practice". Holland, Browne, and other canons lent their aid, and as time passed many well-known teachers from London and the universities were invited to take part. After ten years, with a membership of more than a hundred, the society won consent for renaming itself the St Paul's Lecture Society. By 1914 it had over four hundred members, with an average weekly attendance exceeding two hundred; and it has survived the shock of two world wars. Its first secretary, Edgar Hodgkinson, served continuously till 1949.

But Newbolt was not the man to be content with purely educational work. When the time came for creating a constitution for the Society, it embodied a second object besides lecturing, to which the founder himself was inclined to

[1] Newbolt *passim,* esp. 173 f., 178; Green, 216; Russell *B.,* 101 f.

ascribe an even greater importance: this was the organization of retreats for laymen. Since Sunday was the one day in the week when men in business could be free, he arranged week-end retreats in the Cathedral. He justly observed that worshippers attending the ordinary Sunday services under the dome might be surprised to know that from time to time other services were being conducted simultaneously in the upper regions of the church. He had the Trophy Room, over St Dunstan's chapel, fitted up for the purpose, and there, immune from all but the most penetrating notes of the Cathedral organ, offices were sung and addresses delivered to the retreatants. The Library served for the use of the conductor of the retreat: those who so desired might, in the intervals of their own services, share in the worship of the general congregation from the western gallery, which commands a distant but impressive view of the choir. Meals for the retreatants were provided in the convenient and hospitable apartments of the Chapter House.[1]

Newbolt's second enterprise, the Amen Court Guild, also originated in a private assembly, of a less formal kind and of more restricted scope, since its object was devotion rather than instruction. It catered more strictly for young men working, and for the most part living, in the City. Early in 1898 a small body of young warehousemen began to gather once a week in Newbolt's study at No. 3 Amen Court. He offered them spiritual teaching and elucidation of the Bible, and prepared some of them for Confirmation. They numbered about nine or ten, but devised neither organization nor social pursuits. This class continued for some years, until in May 1901 its adherents were slightly startled by his proposal that they should form themselves into a guild with definite membership and simple rules. They enrolled themselves, however, and the Bible class became the Amen Court Guild. The first rule is extremely interesting. It provided that membership should be limited to ten persons, though any member

[1] Newbolt, 206 f.; *St Paul's Lecture Society* leaflet.

might bring a friend by permission of the President, who of course was Newbolt. With admirable foresight he determined that the Guild should never lose its homely and informal character.[1]

Its members were imbued with an active and missionary spirit: they duly brought their friends. A nice problem then arose, as between the principle of restrictive homeliness and the claims of expanding aspiration. Before the end of the year an "associate" was admitted, supernumerary to the sacred ten, and a solution of the constitutional difficulty had been found: the decision was taken to form a second Branch at No. 9 Amen Court, under the direction of one of the minor canons. Thus was the method established of creating what would later have been called "cells"—a practice which in substance must be as old as any form of human society, but had all the interest of novelty as a piece of self-conscious organization at the opening of the twentieth century.

By the end of 1902 three Branches were in existence, with seventy-two names on the roll, and the rule had been altered to admit of "groups of ten members, and others who are called Associates". New members were taken from the waiting list of associates as vacancies occurred. When a member left London, as many did, to take up a business post in the provinces or to try his fortunes in the Colonies or, as happened to several, to train for the priesthood, his name was transferred to a roll of honorary membership; touch was not lost, and his friends in the Guild continued to follow his career with lively interest. So the Guild grew, till it numbered half a dozen branches and four hundred members and associates. But always it remained an association of domestic cells. Each Branch met weekly in the private house of one of the Cathedral staff or of a neighbouring City priest (most of those concerned had previously been minor canons of St Paul's) and took its title from the house in which it assembled. The one exception to the rule of domesticity was the Chapter House

[1] *A.C.G. Occasional Papers* (1909), 5 f.

Branch, consisting of honorary members from the suburbs, which met only once a month.[1]

The devotional character of the Guild was well maintained. Newbolt took six years to expound St Luke's Gospel to No. 3 and, having finished that, began upon St Matthew. An annual corporate Communion for all members was arranged in St Paul's, and an annual Quiet Day was held in the Trophy Room. The young men discussed among themselves such subjects as "Our Responsibilities as Churchmen", and outsiders addressed them on edifying and instructive topics. But social amenities were also quickly introduced. Debates and country rambles were organized, and a quarterly social gathering in the Chapter House. The club room belonging to Chapter [2] in Carter Lane was put at the disposal of the Guild and furnished with books and magazines. In 1908 publication started of the *Occasional Papers,* after great hesitation and not without some financial stress, to keep scattered members informed of Guild events. As early as 1903 members united to exhibit their talents in a concert, which was so successful that it came to be repeated annually and proved the mainstay of the Guild finances. The men themselves were keen to bear a part in managing their own affairs. The cellular system was well adjusted to combine the advantages of intimacy and of corporate action.[3]

But perhaps the most remarkable of all the Guild's undertakings was the Mission of 1908. The idea was first projected at the Annual General Meeting of the Guild in November 1906. A Mission Committee was next formed of members from each Branch, together with a representative of the Bishop's Evangelistic Council and another from the City branch of the Church of England Men's Society. The Bishop himself, the missionary-hearted Winnington-Ingram, who

[1] *Occasional Papers* (1909), 6, 23 f., cf. 1908, p. 11; Newbolt, 207 f.

[2] Cf. *supra*, p. 172.

[3] *Occasional Papers* (1908), 32, 59, (1909) 6, 23 f., (1910) 5 f.; Newbolt, 208.

from being Bishop of Stepney and junior canon of St Paul's had been promoted Bishop of London in 1901, promised to be present and to speak at the opening meeting. The use of the City of London School was secured for a week in the latter part of January 1908. As missioner the committee enlisted Fr Paul Bull, of the Community of the Resurrection at Mirfield, who had made a great name as an Army chaplain during the South African War and had on various occasions ridden into action alongside his men.[1] After a year of preparation and prayer the great day came. Twelve hundred men attended the opening; a large and increasing weekday audience was attracted; and many fresh recruits were added to the Guild. The anniversary of the Mission was celebrated with a Quiet Day, to which the Bishop came and gave the addresses. In January 1910 another Mission was conducted for ten days in Christ Church, Newgate Street; the Bishop again opened the proceedings, and Paul Bull preached nightly to an average of two hundred men, standing on a table at the chancel steps. The Guild showed plenty of initiative, and its light shone before men.[2]

Newbolt's pastoral work was unofficial and, in a sense, independent of the Cathedral, though strongly encouraged and supported by the authorities. Meantime, the Cathedral itself was bearing, in its own more spectacular fashion, witness to the claims of religion on the national life. The service to celebrate Queen Victoria's Jubilee, on 21 June 1887, had been held in Westminster Abbey, St Paul's merely lending its choir and providing a special service for the City two days later. (To commemorate the latter event the Lord Mayor presented a handsome new set of prayer books for use in the choir, which were still doing duty after nearly seventy years of wear.) But ten years later St Paul's came into its own, when the Diamond Jubilee was observed with great solemnities, in the arrangement of which Holland, acting on behalf of

[1] Paul Bull, *God and our Soldiers*, 149 f.

[2] *Occasional Papers* (1908), 3, 16, (1909) 3, 67, (1910) 2 ff.

Chapter, had displayed unsuspected powers of organization and business. The anniversary of the Accession fell on a Sunday. On that day St Paul's was filled with a glittering assemblage, headed by the Prince and Princess of Wales and including most of the uncrowned royalty of England and half that of Europe, together with the Russian Orthodox Archbishop of Finland, the diplomatic corps and a portentous array of gowns and wigs. Two hundred barristers alone walked in procession to the dome.[1]

All this magnificence, however, was thrown into eclipse by the great ceremony at noon on the following Tuesday, when the aged Queen drove in person to the Cathedral to give thanks to God for the sixty years of her reign. She was too infirm to make the steep ascent of the western approach, so the service was held on the steps outside the Cathedral. The top of Ludgate Hill was turned into a vast arena, banked with stands for the spectators. One enterprising firm of contractors temporarily demolished a shop in the Churchyard to erect seating, under agreement to rebuild it afterwards, and *Punch* inquired whether the scaffolds round St Paul's were in preparation for pulling down the church in order to accommodate more sight-seers.

It was arranged that the Queen should sit in her carriage at ground level between the Cathedral and the statue of Queen Anne. The greatest prelates joined the Dean and Chapter on a platform to receive her. The steps and portico were crammed with choristers and honoured guests, and bright with Beefeaters and Gentlemen-at-Arms. The imperial majesty of England was supported by the pomp and panoply of foreign royalty and the military lustre of the British and Indian Armies. The Dean and Chapter wore splendid copes (for the first time), with skull-caps of Cardinal-red velvet. The Lambeth Conference had brought bishops to London from every quarter of the globe, and more than a hundred of them

[1] Frost, 79; Green, 200; Newbolt, 182, 266; *Min.* following 19 June 1897.

were present to adorn the gorgeous scene. The concourse on the steps was so compressed that places for the Cathedral clergy to stand were marked out with chalk. Most of the ticket-holders had been in position before 10 o'clock. But the sun shone out, the decorations shimmered, the stands towered luminously with gaily coloured frocks, bands played, and processions marched. And when the Queen arrived the choirs sang a hearty Te Deum, a few prayers were said, the Archbishop of Canterbury gave the blessing, the Old Hundredth (abbreviated) was taken up with fervour by the vast crowd. The entire service lasted only twenty minutes.[1]

An immense amount of work had gone into the preparation for a ceremony so novel of its kind and so unprecedented in the place in which it was held. Fresh complications cropped up at the eleventh hour, owing to the failure of the Lord Chamberlain's Office to consult the Cathedral in advance. Browne was in residence, and had obtained the sanction of Chapter for the Dean and himself to deal with any such emergency, so everything was settled peacefully except the question whether there was room on the steps to spare for Beefeaters. On this matter the emergency committee enjoyed the luxury of a violent conflict of opinion, and contrary orders were issued by the two parties; but Browne got his way. Gregory, so far from bearing malice, persuaded himself that the arrangement was of his own making. Few men in Gregory's day could boast that they had succeeded in overruling the Dean of St Paul's. The preliminaries concluded with a full rehearsal of the service on the site, on the previous evening. The Churchyard and the galleries were packed with people, as if for the actual thanksgiving; they listened with close attention, though "sometimes with applause", and joined in the hymn. Eyewitnesses from the Cathedral were profoundly impressed. Two curious facts emerged about the training of the horses in the State carriage. One of the noble

[1] *Min.* following 19 June 1897; Newbolt, 264 ff.; *The Guardian*, 24 June 1897, p. 1007; Green, 290.

beasts was habitually bored by long halts, and always lay down on such occasions unless constantly reminded of its dignity and duty; its groom therefore stood by to stimulate its attention with a pin. Another suffered from the opposite defect, and would only stand still if fed by its groom from a surreptitious bag of sugar.[1]

The Chapter copes, to which allusion has been made, were offered as a gift for use at the Jubilee and on such other occasions as Chapter might appoint: the only cope worn in Cathedral hitherto had been the Bishop's at his ordinations. At the same time a processional cross was also offered, to add distinction to St Paul's day and other feasts. They had not been accepted without opposition on the part of the Archdeacon; both cross and copes were very heavy and magnificent, but his objection was presumably doctrinal. About the same time a costly set of altar-plate—four chalices and patens and two flagons, all in gold—was offered anonymously and accepted. The donor's name was subsequently disclosed, and horror overtook the Chapter when the fact came out that he was in serious trouble with the law and possessed considerably more creditors than cash. It was felt to be morally incumbent that the chalices, or their value, should be returned for the benefit of defrauded creditors. So Holland gave or raised the sum, it was said, of £1500 which the plate had cost, and redeemed the tainted offering by a voluntary sacrifice.[2] The plate was melted down and refashioned to the architectonic designs of Sir Edward Lutyens in 1934.

Time speeds by. The second centenary of the foundation of the Society for Promoting Christian Knowledge was celebrated in St Paul's in 1898; that of the kindred Society for the Propagation of the Gospel was kept in 1900. In the same year at the Welsh festival service "twelve harps were used". The Church Congress, an annual voluntary platform for

[1] Browne, 354–8; Newbolt, 265 f.

[2] *Acta D.*, 111; Paget, 148 f.; Newbolt, 226.

ecclesiastical discussion, which had been founded in 1861, first held its sessions in London during 1899, attracting a membership of 8000; the opening and closing services took place in St Paul's. Next month Robert Green, virger and diarist, retired after forty-seven years of faithful service and was appointed honorary virger. Meantime Church and nation had been confronted with yet graver issues by the outbreak of the South African War. The City raised a force of City Imperial Volunteers; during January 1900 two farewell services were held for contingents of them leaving for the front, and the Lord Mayor attended both. Thanksgivings were offered in due course for the relief of Ladysmith and Mafeking; at the end of October the C.I.V. were back at home and 1500 of the regiment came to an impressive thanksgiving service. Cathedral and City prayed and rejoiced in concert.[1]

Queen Victoria died early in 1901, three days before St Paul's day. The whole nation was plunged into mourning, black clothes replacing colours on the streets of London suburbs. The patronal festival of the Cathedral was transferred to 8 February. Special supplications were offered daily after Evensong, until the funeral on 2 February; the church was crowded every day. A solemn Requiem was sung for the dead Queen on 1 February, and on the following afternoon a memorial service was held at the same hour as her burial was taking place at Windsor. Nine years later a similar procedure marked the obsequies of Edward VII, but Whit-Sunday, which fell within the period of mourning, was observed with the usual solemnities. At the time fixed for his Coronation, in 1902, all preparations were in train for special celebrations, including a service to be attended by the King and Queen after their crowning. But the King fell sick with appendicitis, the Coronation had to be postponed, and the proposed rejoicings were once more turned to supplications.

[1] Green, 298, 323, 327; *Min.*, 13 and 20 Jan. 1900, 3 and 10 March 1900, 19 May 1900, 16 June 1900, 4 Nov. 1900; *D.E.C.H.* (1st ed., 1912), 153; *Acta D.*, 139 f.

Their Majesties came to St Paul's, however, in the following October to give public thanks for the King's recovery.[1]

Another royal occasion arose through the initiative of Archdeacon Sinclair, who conceived the notion of giving to the Order of St Michael and St George a spiritual home in the Cathedral, in the same sort of way as the Order of the Bath is domesticated in Westminster Abbey. The plan was greeted with a certain amount of capitular scepticism. It was by no means easy to hit on a location at once suitable to the Order and convenient to St Paul's. But all difficulties were overcome, and in 1901 Chapter offered the Order the use of the south-west chapel, formerly the consistory court, then the matrix of the Wellington monument, and only recently converted to a baptistery. The font was moved to the south transept, and a scheme of decoration, rather over-elaborate for the confined space in which it is displayed, was carried out under the supervision of the Cathedral Surveyor. The King came in state to the opening of the chapel in 1906, accompanied by knights arrayed in Solomonian glory; and the chapel, hung with banners of chivalry, provides a focus both for the annual service of the Order and for other more intimate festivities.[2]

But the Cathedral does not exist solely to ornament the State connection. Its other activities continued unabated. The daily round of worship was sustained with all the dignity of which its resources permitted. Special services were celebrated of great variety and in incredible profusion. It has been recorded that in the twelve months from October 1906 to September 1907 the Cathedral was thrown open on behalf of something like ninety different causes or societies, some of which returned on several distinct occasions in the course of the year. Great congregations came throughout Holy Week in 1902 to the addresses delivered by the Bishop;

[1] *Min.*, 26 Jan. 1901, 2 and 9 Feb. 1901, 5 July 1902, 1 Nov. 1902, 7, 14, 22 May 1910; *Acta D.*, 165 f.; Newbolt, 267–71.

[2] Sinclair, 391 ff.; Newbolt, 230, 271.

incidentally on Easter Eve the choir was lighted for the first time by electricity. The Archbishop preached in the following month at a farewell service for the scholars of Christ's Hospital, on their leaving London for Horsham. In 1904 the thirteenth centenary was observed of the consecration of St Mellitus, the first Bishop of London. At the two hundred and fiftieth festival of the Sons of the Clergy in the same year the collection for the charity amounted to no less than £10,700.

In 1908 the Lambeth Conference of 242 bishops was preceded by a Pan-Anglican Congress of 7000 delegates, lay and clerical, from all parts of the world: thanksgiving services were held in St Paul's both for the bishops and for the Congress, and the former were granted the freedom of the Cathedral pulpit on Sunday mornings and evenings throughout June, July, and August. Finally, in 1910, through the munificence of a parliamentary benefactor, a memorial of the medieval Paul's Cross, from which so many provocative sermons had been launched, was erected in the Churchyard near its ancient site. At the opening, some of the bystanders mistook the platform which surrounds the monument for the basin of a fountain, to the disappointment of those who may have hoped to see it, when vacated by the Bishop and the canons, replenished with decorative jets. It bears its witness to historical memories, but without liquid supplement.[1]

A few select minutes of the Chapter present so exquisite a flavour that they should be extricated from the storage of the files. In the spring of 1895 influenza was "very prevalent". As a remedy against infection "eucalyptus oil was placed on the stoves to fumigate the Cathedral". Luckily the Archdeacon does not seem to have confused the scent with that of frankincense. The singing of the services by men only, in the absence of the boys, gave fresh cause for complaint in 1906. "The men's services have been most unsatisfactory all

[1] Sinclair, 483 ff.; *Min.*, 29 March 1902, 19 April 1902, 23 April 1904, 7 May 1904, 27 Jan. 1908, 11 April 1908, 6 Aug. 1908; Newbolt, 232 f.

the week—sung with no heart, and most untuneful." Accordingly "the Chapter requests the Precentor to confer with the organist and succentor with a view to the better rendering of the services in the absence of the boys, which in their opinion requires a radical reform".

Ritualism in a Chapter living created deep concern to Bishop-Canon Lang: "The Bishop of Stepney brought up the lamentable condition of St Clement's, City Road, where the Latin Mass was constantly said by wilful curates in its entirety, besides other purely Roman devotions." In 1908 "it was finally agreed that the Horse on the D. of W.'s monument should look East." A story lies behind this entry. Long-drawn efforts were being made to complete Stevens's memorial to the Duke of Wellington by putting up the equestrian statue which he had designed for its summit.[1] For some inexplicable reason controversy raged between those who favoured an eastward position for the quadruped and those who wanted it to face towards the western doors. It is alleged in Cathedral tradition that Newbolt supported the latter proposal on the purely symbolic ground that the Duke might then properly be taken as beating a retreat from the prebendaries' sermons. Certain it is that a decree was passed in the next year that "the Master of the Charterhouse should not be asked to preach again, as he is absolutely inaudible".[2]

[1] Cf. *supra*, p. 79.

[2] *Min.*, 2 and 9 March 1895, 21 and 28 April 1906, 10 Nov. 1906, 27 Jan. 1908, 26 June 1909.

16

THE END OF AN ERA

THE REIGN of Edward VII marked the meridian development of Victorian civilization: Edwardians were merely Victorians written in coarser, grosser script. The recurrent but typically Victorian fallacy that human society had at last achieved a stable constitution was firmly established in Edwardian minds. Internal stresses certainly were manifested; but confidence was felt that every difficulty could be overcome by much the same devices as had succeeded heretofore. Little did politicians imagine that within a very few years such misplaced confidence would reduce the powerful and dominant Liberal Party to a heap of political rubble. A cloud, as yet no larger (but no smaller) than a man's mailed fist, did indeed hang over the foreign horizon, if a prophet looked from the Carmel of Liberal victory across the North Sea. But a Liberal once so prescient as Holland now refused contemptuously to recognize the danger of German Imperialism. His articles in *The Commonwealth,* down to the very outbreak of war, raged against "bloated armaments" and mocked at "the German scare", but had not one word of comment on the Sarajevo murders or the crisis of August 1914: the issue of that month announced a congress to be held at Basle with papers to be read on "Christianity and Universal Peace".[1] The mass of Englishmen continued to indulge its assurance of security, or if not that, at least its confidence in the outcome. Nobody imagined the shattering effect of the prolonged struggle on Western European society, still less the frightful consequences on the Asiatic border of the example,

[1] Paget, 207.

so nearly triumphant, set by imperial ruthlessness in central Europe.

The situation inside St Paul's resembled that in the nation at large. The Cathedral represented fully and accurately the opulent piety of the Victorian middle classes in their most truly religious vein, and, with limitations, in their most intelligent apprehension of Christianity. Its services exerted a wide and in some respects disastrous influence on the worship of parish churches which were in no sort of condition, materially or otherwise, to carry out successfully the imitation of cathedral solemnity which they too often attempted. But the achievements of 1911 amounted to no more than realization of the ideals of 1871. Victorianism had flowered in St Paul's for forty years and continued to put forth glorious bloom, but nothing had been introduced which might justly be described as embodying a new strain either in thought or in devotion.

Yet new ideas had been disseminated and were taking root within the Church of England; their shoots lay only just below the surface of the soil. The "Modernism" falsely so called which Harnack taught in Protestant Germany, and the Modernism properly so named which Loisy proclaimed in Roman Catholic France, filled no small place in the minds of certain of the rising theological generation in England and were destined to create no small stir. The school of *Lux Mundi*, which was represented in St Paul's by Holland and to some extent by the younger bishop-canons, was implacably opposed to both Modernisms, especially the former, which emerged earlier and more shockingly into the open. The time was fully ripe for the appointment to Chapter of a younger intellectual capable of renewing the work which Holland had performed a quarter of a century before, appraising in a constructive way the crudities of the new theological movements and garnering whatever sweetness lay in the cover of their ostentatious petals and innutritious foliage.

But no such character of combined insight, grasp, and sympathy emerged.

Again, a deliberate revolution in accepted ideals of public worship was already present to the minds of Anglo-Catholic enthusiasts, who hoped both to civilize and enrich Anglican tradition under Latin inspiration and in the same act to Anglicize certain of the Latinisms of their Ritualist forerunners. The heralds of their revolt were busy; their banners would shortly be unfurled. It would not have been easy to discover anywhere, in the last decade of Victorianism before the first world war, a leader of sufficient commanding talents and position to mediate between the new movement and official Churchmanship; but certainly none such was to be found at St Paul's. During the '70s the old Chapter under Church, though it contained no Ritualist, had shown sufficient insight to defend Ritualists against misrepresentation and injustice. But now young iconoclasts were active who knew not Stainer and cared nothing for the devotionally featureless musicianship and Brahmsical ecclesiastical sentiment that marked the current convention of worship.[1] Such men thought the Cathedral services too long and slow, too pompous and provincial. Their contempt was not altogether without reason. Alexander recalled in his old age that when he joined the Chapter, in 1909, the canons' sermons on Sunday afternoons still customarily lasted for forty minutes, though he promptly cut his own discourses to a mere twenty-five. Even in religion, Victorianism was not enough: some of its finest fruits were overgrown a lot too much.

Material problems also stood by the threshold of St Paul's and were beginning to knock at the great doors. As yet there was no serious lack of funds for regular uses. While a stream of gifts poured into Chapter's hands to complete the great

[1] This sweeping observation must not be taken as directed against Brahms personally, but against the sloppy pietism of very much lesser men who floundered in the track of German master-musicians.

decorative schemes of the '90s, an outward flow had been maintained of benefactions from the Cathedral for repairs and improvements to churches, parsonages, and schools which had a claim on capitular generosity. Alms were collected as a matter of course at Holy Communion, the proceeds being devoted to charity at the discretion of the several members of Chapter. But at other services the public was at liberty to worship in St Paul's without being pressed for contributions towards its upkeep; there was, in Holland's phrase, "no shaking of the money-bag". When a collection was taken it was not to benefit the Cathedral but in support of some extraneous cause; such levies were exceptional, though in 1903 some increase was permitted in their frequency. Regular collections were established only in 1918, to meet the rising cost of wages and materials.[1] For all the normal purposes of Cathedral expenditure the proceeds of the commutation still sufficed. But anxiety for the stability of the fabric had begun to be felt, and in the 1900s, when the long and costly process of decoration was drawing to an end, instead of closing its appeal accounts with a sense of relief from financial pressure, Chapter had to raise large sums for major repairs of an extraordinary kind. The state of the fabric resembled that of social institutions; neither was by any means so secure as had been thought.

The threat of constructional instability arose partly from outside causes, and partly from weaknesses that had developed in the actual fabric of the church. The first danger declared itself earlier; but injurious consequences were in fact averted owing to the vigilance with which it was watched by successive Surveyors. Before Wren built the Cathedral, he took careful soundings of the subsoil. He saw that the foundations of the old cathedral had been laid on a layer of firm pot-earth, but the layer had a thickness of only four to six feet; below it were various strata of sand and

[1] *Acta D.*, 25 f., 175 f.; *Min.*, 12 Jan. 1918; cf. *supra*, p. 198 *ad fin.*

gravel, not sufficiently stable to support the immense weight of a great church, and in order to reach a reliable basis underneath in the natural hard London clay he would have had to sink his foundations forty feet or more. Accordingly he decided to build on the pot-earth, which gave him all the support that he required so long as nothing occurred to interfere with the subsoil. But under conditions which have developed since Wren's day the subsoil is peculiarly liable to disturbance, not directly, but through interference with the water which permeates its fine sands. Should the subterranean flow be obstructed or diverted, scouring may ensue and the layers of quick sands be washed away; if deep excavations are made near the Cathedral and pumps are used to dispose of the water in the subsoil, the fine sands will probably be drawn out with the water. In either case the foundations of the Cathedral would be endangered.

This danger had long been realized. Great alarm had been caused in 1831, when Copleston was Dean and Cockerell was Surveyor, by an attempt to construct a deep sewer to the south of St Paul's. With the aid of representations from the foremost engineers of the day the City authorities were persuaded to stop the work, though not before a great deal of water had been pumped away. Half a century later public works presented a recurrent threat to the Cathedral. Opposition had to be organized in 1890 and 1891 to the Bill then before Parliament authorizing a Central London Railway under Newgate Street; in consequence the original scheme was modified. In 1901 a close watch was being kept on proposals for a Piccadilly and City Tube to run under Carter Lane; this project was eventually abandoned. Six years later the London County Council planned to lay a new sewer passing within forty feet of the south-west corner of St Paul's; after much anxiety had been expressed the Council diverted the course of the sewer to a safer distance. A still more serious danger was threatened by the scheme, initiated in 1910, to excavate a subway less than twenty-five yards from the east end of the church, for a service of tramcars linking Cheapside with a proposed new bridge over the Thames.[1]

Violent public controversy broke out at the end of 1912 when the details of the plan were revealed, and bitter attacks were levelled against anyone who might dare to interpose false alarms for the safety of the Cathedral between the people and their trams. The opposition to the subway was directed by Alexander, who had been elected Chapter Treasurer in February 1911, and Mervyn Macartney, Surveyor since 1906. This scheme also was abandoned. But two good things came out of it. Macartney's apprehensions for the safety of the fabric led him to make the most careful surveys, which revealed for the first time the true state of the dome and its supports. And the idea was suggested of safeguarding the Cathedral for the future by declaring a "sacred area" round it within which no deep construction should be permitted. This plan required legislation, and was not carried out till after the complete restoration of the Cathedral, finished in 1930. At that date, however, the suggestion was renewed. The City Corporation promoted a Bill in Parliament to give it effect, and the Bill passed both Houses of the legislature in the course of 1935. The Cathedral subsoil therefore now enjoys the protection of the law.[2]

The second danger, which arose from internal pressures and deterioration of material, was active and urgent. Somers Clarke, Surveyor from 1897 to 1906, reported in 1902 that movement had been observed in the western portico. The arch under the pediment was opening out laterally, and the entire west front showed some tendency to break away from the nave and incline in the direction of Ludgate Hill. It was found necessary to rebuild the arch and to tie the west front securely to the main building with metal rods. It was also

[1] *Journal of R.I.B.A.*, 9 Aug. 1930, p. 663; *Acta D.*, 17, 28 f., 148 f.; *Min.*, 19 Nov. 1910.

[2] *Press cuttings* (Alexander's collection), Dec. 1912–Feb. 1913; *The Times* (leader), 29 Nov. 1930.

discovered that, owing to settlement in the dome structure, masonry had been dislocated and fractured in the region of the drum and colonnade immediately below the dome, and water had percolated through the pavement of the Stone Gallery, causing corrosion of Wren's iron ties and cramps and further damage to the stonework. Some settlement was known to have taken place in Wren's own time, and no great concern was occasioned by the existence of cracks in walls and piers and buttresses, so long as they showed no sign of enlargement.[1] A commission of experts in 1907 took a hopeful view of the situation. A sum of £30,000 was provided, half by Chapter and half by gift from the Ecclesiastical Commissioners, to carry out such restoration as was thought necessary; and confidence was restored.[2]

But Macartney was not satisfied. He read the cracks as tangible writing on the wall, and called in Sir Francis Fox, an eminent engineer. His report, published in *The Times* of 1 January 1913, disclosed that the entire dome was on the move; superstructure and foundations alike needed strengthening. All idea of proceeding with the subway for the trams was hurriedly cast aside. An appeal was issued early in 1914, followed by other appeals in 1922 and 1925, as the full gravity of the danger was more accurately measured by the extremely delicate instruments installed in the Cathedral.[3] Work proceeded continuously for sixteen years, at an ultimate cost of some £450,000, raised under the pertinacious leadership of Alexander, with valuable assistance from *The Times*. The buttresses of the dome were repaired. The interior of the eight supporting piers, crushed by the weight of the

[1] Cf. *supra*, p. 63.

[2] *Journal of R.I.B.A.*, 661 f.; *Acta D.*, 170, 176, 222, 225; cf. Sinclair, 478.

[3] These instruments remain in permanent operation in and around St Paul's, and are maintained at very considerable cost to the Cathedral funds. The entire fabric is thus under continuous observation, and measurements as fine as a thousandth part of a foot have actually been recorded.

dome and cupola, was grouted with cement under high pressure, which rendered them virtually monolithic. New chains of stainless steel were wrapped round the dome to prevent it spreading, and ties were inserted in the structure to bind all firmly together. Everywhere damaged stone was renewed and rusted cramps were replaced. The decay of more than two centuries was overtaken at last, and the Cathedral was pronounced safe—always provided that no further subsidence was caused by drainage from the subsoil. The anxieties and efforts of these long years of restoration were borne in a far less care-free temper than the almost casual optimism of the great Victorian decorators. Here was no confident cry for embellishment, but a more sober sense of stark need to preserve from ruin the inherited glories of antiquity.[1]

But of all these developments Gregory and his Chapter were unaware. Their minds still moved within the orbit traced in the early phases of the great revival. The work then accomplished had abiding values and continued to flourish, with prolific exuberance, but without the power of readjustment for which the dawning of a new age really called. The substitution of Alexander for the series of bishop-canons in 1909 was indeed a providential mercy; he organized the salvation of the fabric. But not even he could overcome the financial stringency caused by the fall in the purchasing power of money; cash payments which provided ample margin for Cathedral needs in 1872 could no longer be stretched to cover necessities in a post-war economy. This problem, however, still lay below the lip of the horizon. It was in ideas rather than endowments that the Cathedral was as yet impoverished.

Newbolt, so energetic on the pastoral side both before and after the first world war, was less a man of thought than of action, and drew his inspiration from the past rather than the future. Holland was losing his flair; his heart was growing

[1] *Journal of R.I.B.A.*, 656, 665–75; *Press cuttings* (Alexander's collection).

bigger than his head. The entire Cathedral was still dominated by the figure of Gregory. Gregory had become a living legend, loyally fostered and diffused by Holland, who had now been thrust into the same position of prop and stay to the aged Dean as Gregory himself had once occupied in relation to the ailing Richard Church. The "dear old man" was the embodiment of the Cathedral tradition. "The venerable figure, bowed under the white hair, moving with helping hands to and fro through the Cathedral to which he had given his life and love, had won for Robert Gregory a romantic interest in these later years. All London watched him pass in and out; and he laid hold of the public imagination." He certainly laid hold of Holland's.[1]

But Gregory was no mere figure-head. The whole Cathedral revolved round him in obedience to the system which he had done so much to forge. His natural force was abated but by no means extinguished: the old volcano could still erupt. It became a recognized duty that two of his colleagues should support him down the steps of the Cathedral and across the traffic-swept Churchyard to the deanery. They observed that Gregory used to show great impatience if their progress was at all impeded at the doors: he wondered why it was that at whatever hour he might be trying to get out of the church there must always be somebody else trying to get in. Alexander, only partially acclimatized to the atmosphere of hero-worship, could comment on his outspokenness ("not always that of a diplomatist") and his obstinacy: "If there were those (as there were) who questioned his wisdom in lingering at his post so long, they must at least recognise the intensity of a devotion which made him reluctant to break a tie of more than forty years." It was quite in character that during an illness, when the doctors told him to lie on his right side, he persisted in lying on his left—"in order that he might the better hear the bells of St Paul's". The minute book alludes to one startling instance of his

[1] Holland in Gregory, 250, 253.

gruffness in extreme old age: "the resignation of the Succentor was before the Chapter on account of the Dean having spoken abruptly to him at Evensong yesterday; they agreed not to accept it, to explain, and express regret." One may suspect that the Succentor was behaving unreasonably in wishing to resign; but Gregory's colleagues loyally shielded their Dean from the consequences of his own impulsiveness. At the date of this incident the old warrior was four days short of 90, and on his birthday the bells of the Cathedral were rung in his honour.[1]

Nevertheless these later exhibitions of the old vehemence were rare: out of the strong, as Alexander states, had come forth sweetness (though this lion was not yet dead!) and the gnarled limbs of the old forest oak had been softened by the touch of lichen and moss. The latter simile was far from inappropriate. The broad face with its rugged features and grim mouth wore an expression of kindliness; the long white hair, combed out on either side and falling nearly to his shoulders, framed it in a quietude of peaceful expectancy. He was emphatic in his thanks for any small attention. He took the greatest pleasure in visits from Bishop Winnington-Ingram, towards whom he always showed a respect which was the more touching in that it was rendered by the aged to the young. Till 1906 he was exemplary in his attendance at Cathedral. In 1907 he had a severe illness, after which he seldom appeared at Chapter meetings; but he still frequented the daily services as regularly as his health permitted. At the end of 1904 he had resigned the Chapter Treasurership to Holland, who confesses that he never expected the Dean, even in retirement, to keep his hands off the well-loved job. He was greatly mistaken. Gregory was content with everything since everything was going right, and never once attempted to interfere with his successor's administration.[2]

[1] Newbolt, 173; Alexander in *Amen Ct. Occas. Papers,* Dec. 1911, p. 40; cf. Holland in Gregory, 251; *Min.,* 6 and 13 Feb. 1909.

[2] Alexander, loc. cit.; Gregory, 240, 246, 255; Sinclair, 375 f.

Holland's description of his tranquil age and joyful acquiescence is no doubt idealized, but speaks volumes in a few sentences. "It was an immense surprise to us—this power of total surrender in one who could not, in younger days, set limits to his urgent activities. So old age brought to him new gifts. He was changed and mellowed. Peace and tenderness and resignation did their quiet and beautiful work upon him, until the long day ended. He had done: he could go home. The discipline of life had been attained. After that he was absorbed in the interest of the unseen world." The Cathedral was in Holland's hands and Gregory was perfectly satisfied: there was no need for him to exert himself while he yet lived, and Holland would naturally be appointed his successor when he died, as he himself had succeeded to Church. Holland definitely states that Gregory had all this in mind and had discussed the matter with him, not once nor twice. "The dear old man hung on so long out of affection for me. It seemed to him all right, as long as I was there to whom he was used. He has always wished me to succeed him. He has said so over and over again." Holland in turn had never thought of leaving St Paul's. He had been feeling " 'nervy' of late, under strain", but not from any difficulties connected with his position at the Cathedral. His flutters rather acted as an additional inducement to remain where he was.[1]

Then, out of the blue, the bolt fell. Towards the end of 1910 Asquith, the Prime Minister, offered Holland the Regius Professorship of Divinity at Oxford. Holland's published letters on the subject show two odd features: an unexpected readiness to consider a move, once the idea had been presented in a concrete form, and an unexplained silence on the possible effects of his acceptance on the situation at St Paul's. Presumably he talked to Gregory about it; but if so, there is only the vaguest hint that the old man's wish for him to step into the deanery had "got blurred through illness". His position was difficult: he carried all the responsibilities of a dean

[1] Gregory, 255 f.; Paget, 236 f., 238.

with none of the authority, and so long as he remained Gregory showed no sign of retiring. Holland's own reaction to the professorship was strongly negative: it seemed to him "too absurd and incredible" that he could assume the leadership of the theological faculty, badly as in fact fresh leadership was needed at the time. He was almost 64. "For thirty years I have ceased to have the power to read or study . . . I could not do it. I should feel myself a scandal." He had no material in stock to form into a course of lectures; he had never had time to pursue any special line of theological research of which the products might screen the "whole realms of theology of which I am blankly ignorant". But his old Oxford friends, Talbot and Gore and T. B. Strong, the Dean of Christ Church, pressed him hard, and he allowed himself to be persuaded, diffidently, wonderingly. His strength for the new enterprise lay, as they and Asquith doubtless judged, not in any store of theological learning but in his flaming intellectual vitality, his gift for teaching doctrine on convincing philosophic postulates, and his prophetic passion for applying religious convictions to the actual problems of contemporary life.[1]

He accepted the professorship in December, wound up his affairs at the Cathedral in the course of the next three months, and by April 1911 was established at Christ Church. It cost him dear to abandon London and St Paul's and the immense affection poured upon him there. He disguised his sorrow with a characteristic display of hilarity: when the moment came to leave Amen Court he smote on the knocker, said "Goodbye, old door", and went. But his departure was too much for Gregory to face. Without Holland's companionship and support he felt that the hour had struck for himself also. He sent in his resignation of the deanery during February, to take effect on 1 May. He asked that he might be allowed to end his days after retirement in his old home in Dean's Court, and this request was readily granted as

[1] Paget, 236 ff.

part of the pension he had so truly earned. He continued to attend service in the choir. But in July he began visibly to fail, and on 2 August 1911 he passed to his rest.[1] Before he died St Paul's had received another dean, another canon in the place of Holland, and another archdeacon. The old order, with its singular unanimity of purpose and spirit, had been broken up. An assemblage of largely untried individuals had the responsibility of grappling with problems hitherto unforeseen, as wild skies lit the opening of a new and troubled era of national and ecclesiastical time.

[1] Paget, loc. cit.; Gregory, 247, 264 ff.

APPENDIX

Unpublished Letters of Sydney Smith

SINCE the publication, in 1953, of Mr Nowell C. Smith's comprehensive *Letters of Sydney Smith*, several further letters of the witty canon have come to light in the Cathedral. The first and longest was written in reply to one from Blomfield in which the Bishop commented with some indignation on Sydney's first *Letter to Archdeacon Singleton*. It well illustrates its author's independence of judgement and freedom of expression towards men in power. There is no date on the manuscript except that endorsed (presumably on its receipt by Blomfield) "Rev. S. Smith A. 10 Feb.". The year was 1837 and the address 33 Charles St, Berkeley Square. The text is as follows:

My dear Lord

I hope there was no incivility in my last letter. I certainly did not mean that there should be any; your situation in life perhaps, accustoms you to a tone of submission & inferiority from your Correspondents, which neither you, nor any man living shall ever experience from me.

You knew perfectly well what Ld. J. Russell meant by attention to my own interests,—you ought not in your letter to me to have used any ambiguous terms, which might convey another meaning,—or having done so, & being call'd upon for an explanation, it should have been given frankly & immediately.

When I ask you about facts, you deviate into intentions;—I have never said a syllable to you about my concern for the vested rights & patronage of Chapters in general, but whether I had asked anything from Lord John for myself & my own Cathedral which was not extended to all other Prebendaries

& Cathedrals. You know very well I did not, & so you ought immediately to have said.

For the history of what past at the Commission, Lord John Russell & yourself are in complete opposition to each other.

Lord John Russell can have no interest to misrepresent, he was commission'd to negociate with me & did negociate immediately upon the breaking up of the meeting.

As to what you say respecting what you individually proposed at the meetings, it really amounts to nothing at all; a Person of your influence & authority can easily cause motions affecting your own interest to be proposed by others.

In speaking of the Bills as they came from the Commission I speak of the first unamended bills that were laid before the House; *they* only can shew the animus of the Commission. I will look over them diligently & see whether I have committed the mistakes you impute to me.

By your own shewing it appears that where the Population is 2000, & and the Income 400, you can without the least complaint of the Parish, & on the contrary, with every certificate of their perfect satisfaction, thrust in a Curate upon the Incumbent, & compel him to pay £80 a year to this Curate; & would not this ruin many a country clergyman? I may be wrong in the sum, but I am right in the consequence.

It seems then, that the imaginary foundation as you call it, has some substance, that you did attempt to thrust in a Curate, & were defeated in an action at law; I will read over the trial, & see if I agree in the causes of your defeat; my recollection of it is totally different.—The story I introduced which I solemnly assure you is not my own, was not intended to illustrate this foundation, but to connect the rebuff you met with, with the provisions of the present bill, a connexion which you will excuse me for saying I firmly believe in.—You deny having made use of the expression that it should be law &c &c [1]; I will take care to record your denial in my next edition; but pray excuse me if I ask you whether this is not a little hazardous. You & I, are in the habit of saying short, sharp things, which other people remember, but we forget;—Perhaps you forget that you

[1] "The Bishop of London is said to have declared, after his trial, that *if it was not Law, it should soon be Law*"—Singleton, I, 198.

said at your own table (not before me) "that the only use of Deans was to ask the Canons to dinner, & the only use of the Canons was to accept the invitation."—Now don't imagine I am about to allude publickly to this expression of yours, *I have not the most remote intention of so doing*, I consider the communication as *strictly private*, & I only mention it to shew you, that many such sallies fall from a quick & concentrated mind like yours, which produce every impression upon the Hearer, & are totally forgotten by the Speaker.

It seems I had a lucky escape in not mentioning the livings which you were to give up to the Bishop of Rochester, but that you only intended to get four of our best livings amounting to 4000 a year, without making for them any compensation whatever. You put yourself in a much worse predicament than that in which Lord John Russell has placed you, but the real fact is, I treated the whole thing as the rumour of an idle project which had occupied the Commission for a moment, but which had past by. If I had been in possession of your own statement of facts, & with your permission to use it, it certainly would not have lessened the severity of my animadversions.

What consideration your Bills have had generally by the Bishops, I can know nothing of, nor is it to the purpose; They emanate from the Commission, were laid before Parliament as their Bills, & the Commission must enjoy the good or bear the evil report which they occasion.

I remain my dear Lord with respect, your obedt. Servt.,

Sydney Smith

The other seven letters hitherto unpublished relate to the dinner provided on Sundays by the canon in residence and Sydney Smith's proposal, made in 1839, that it should be discontinued: the matter is mentioned above on page 12. These letters are addressed to the Warden of the College of Minor Canons. The first runs thus:

Dear Sr,

The hour of dining is so inconvenient and so little accommodated to the State of the Times that it would be better perhaps for all parties that a money payment should be substituted. Will it be agreeable to the Minor Canons to receive 10L each and to abolish the Dinners—If they agree to this the same proposition will be made to the Vicars Choral—pray be so good at the first Meeting of the M. Canons to lay this proposal before them & to return me their answer. The 120L may be at their pleasure divided pr Head or according to their attendances on Sunday. I think the latter would be the fairer plan—but this as they please. I am impowrd by the Chapter to make this Communication.

Yours truely
Sydney Smith

33 Charles St
Berkley Square

April 10
1839

The agreement cannot take place of course without the Consent of the Vicars Choral—between the Chapter and their Guests—would it not be better to have one meeting for both bodies—the offer would then be 180L—

After nearly a fortnight had elapsed without an answer, Sydney wrote again:

Dear Sr,

pray tell me if you will be so good as to bring the Subject of the dinners before the Mr Canons and to let me know when I am likely to have an answer.

Yrs very truely
Sydney Smith

33 Charles St Berkley Square
April 22, 1839

The Warden replied the same day, stating that a meeting would be held shortly, and that in the time of Dean Van Mildert (1820–6) the hour of the dinner had been postponed, to suit everybody's convenience, until after Evensong. Sydney wrote back immediately:

Dear Sr,

I think you are mistaken as to the alteration of hours in V Milderts time it was proposed by the Dean V.M. but not acceded to by others.

Yours truely
Sydney Smith

April 23, 1839

On 26 April the Warden communicated the decision of the College. He said politely but firmly that the minor canons did not feel themselves warranted in giving up "a custom and a privilege which have been long established, and which the Members of our Body have always highly esteemed". Two months then passed. When Sydney came into residence for July he had a new suggestion to offer, and took the opportunity to explain his position at some length:

July 2d 1839. 33 Charles St Berkley Square

My dear Sr,

The Sunday dinners between the Services are extremely inconvenient. My Eyes are failing very fast as is my general health. I find great difficulty in reading my Sermon in the bad light of St Pauls and I want the time immediately before the Service to impress my Sermon on my memory. I am (as you all know) a very temperate man but it is almost impossible as Master of the House to sit down among my Guests without eating & drinking to a certain extent and to do so at the very unusual hour of half past one and to preach after it invariably gives me a bad head ache.

The same dinner it may be urged might take place after the Services—but then all plea for a Sunday dinner is over—and if the manners of the age are not favorable to parties on a Sunday it would be unwise in a body of Clergymen not to respect public opinion on such subjects.

If I continued my dinners I should be under the necessity of absenting myself from them an incivility and want of respect to my reverend Brethren of which I could not consent to be guilty, and I should feel also that dinners carried on without my presence degraded my house to the level of a Tavern—

I hope therefore it will not be disagreeable to the Minor Canons and Vicars Choral If I convert these dinners into a Money payment.

I have accurate Books of the Expences of dinners since I have been Canon of St Pauls (books open to the inspection of any gentleman who has a Wish to see them) I find from these accounts that the Average Expence of each dinner has been including Wine 3L–3S and the Average Number of Guests (excluding those not belonging to the Cathedral) has been seven.

I shall place in the hands of Mr Sellon at the beginning of each Residence four pounds for each Sunday the month Contains & have already placed 16L for the present Month payable to the joint order of the Warden and any one of the Vicars Choral.

It has been a great pleasure to me to have seen at my table so many gentlemanlike & agreeable men I have really been honord & pleasd by their Company and I sincerely hope I shall retain their friendship and good will.

I beg you to make this Communication to the Minor Canons and Vicars Choral & remain my dr Sr Yours truely.

Sydney Smith

Members of the College seem to have received the communication with expressions of disfavour, for only four days later the Warden got two more letters from Sydney, and yet another on the day after. It is interesting to observe how absolutely Sydney accepted the validity of an obligation which rested solely upon custom: in St Paul's, and doubtless elsewhere, custom had a way of overriding even plain statute, as reforming Chapters sometimes found to their cost.

Dear Sr,

I am afraid the Mr Canons have mistaken Courteous language for hesitation as to my own rights.

I shall be heartily sorry to have any difference of opinion with Gentlemen I so much respect & regard but I really think I am not arrogant in saying that every man is the Master of his own house, & the judge of whom he will or will not receive— I have no right to save money by abolishing an old

Custom but where the question is who shall be my guests and who shall not I have a perfect right to chuse between the Custom & the pecuniary Value of the Custom—

I am Sr Yrs truely

Sydney Smith

July 6, 1839.

33 Charles St

The next letter is undated but was received by the Warden on the same day as the foregoing:

Dear Sr,

Why could not some Mr Canon farm these dinners as Mr Hall does for Dr Blomberg— he receives 3L for each dinner I pay 4L.

The more I reflect upon it the more I am struck with the Singularity of compelling a man to give you a dinner who says it is unpleasant & inconvenient to him to do so, and who moreover offers a fair equivalent. I am surprised that you are not struck by the unusual Style of this proceeding.

Yours truely

Sydney Smith

The last letter followed next day, and illustrates the generosity and kindness that accompanied Sydney's insistence on providing the wherewithal for Sunday dinners to be held anywhere but in his own house, even though the College remained obdurate in its rejection of all compromise:

Dear Sr,

One point I missed in my Letters to you, and rectified this omission by a message through my friend Mr Bennet. & which for the purpose of greater accuracy I put upon paper—

I consider the *Paulini prandentes* to dislike the idea of a Money payment. it is my intention therefore to invite them four times to my own house to dinner between this & the end of July 1840— & to continue my invitation to every Member of the Paul Pran— always— once for every Residence. & I hope these dinners will be in *all respects* preferable to our hasty dinners on Sunday— at any future time if the Paul Pran (a term I use to avoid circumlocution) prefer a commutation for Money either with the whole Chapter or with me individually it can easily be done—

I remain dear Sr
Very truely Yrs—
Sydney Smith

July 7, 1839.
33 Charles St Berkley Square.

I am forced to postpone my invitation till my return to Town in February 1840, because I am changing Houses & both are dismantled but this will not occur again.

Two more letters may conveniently be included here. Though not "hitherto unpublished", they are charming notes which bear upon social relations at St Paul's, and somehow escaped the vigilance of Mr Nowell Smith. Both were addressed to Richard Barham, and are reproduced here as printed in his *Life* (Vol. II, pp. 134 and 171). The first was sent in acknowledgement of a friendly gift of pheasants:

39 Green Street, November 15, 1841

Many thanks, my dear Sir, for your kind present of game. If there is a pure and elevated pleasure in this world, it is the roast pheasant and bread sauce—barn door fowls for dissenters, but for the real churchman, the thirty-nine times articled clerk—the pheasant, the pheasant!

Ever yours,
Sydney Smith

The second accompanied the annual grant of £20 for the Cathedral library:

April 6, 1844

Dear Barham,—

I send this order for 20*l*., a sum which, with your care and discretion, will soon raise the library at St Paul's to a level with that of Alexandria in ancient times; I don't mean its level after combustion, but before.

Yours truly,
Sydney Smith

INDEX

ACCOMMODATION, 2–3, increased, 83 ff.
Administration, 26 ff., 58–72
Admission fee, 29–31, 67
Alexander, Canon S. A., Chapter Treasurer, 123; 238, 241, 242, salvation of the fabric, 243
Almoner, 4, 156
Alms, alms-boxes, 81, 239
Amen Corner, 8–9, 40, 49, 51, 89, 90, 92, becomes Amen Court, 127, documents discovered, 209
Amen Court Guild, 225 ff.
Anne, Queen, 102, 110, 229
Architect, *see* Surveyor
Architecture, classical and Gothic, 134 ff.
Argent, H., virger, litigation, 176 ff.
Attwood, T., organist, 4, 6

BARFF, A., 156, 164
Barham, R. H., 6–8, friendship with S. Smith, 8–9, Senior Cardinal, 23; 42, 87
Barnes Common, 89
Barry, Sir C., architect, 84
Beckwith, E. G. A., Succentor, 21
Belli, C. A., Precentor, 9–10, 128
Bells, 25, 146–7, 207, 244
Benson, Archbishop, 188, 206
Bishop, J. C., organ-builder, 83
Blomberg, Dr, 14, 57
Blomfield, Bishop, 2, on ecclesiastical reform, 32 ff.; and St Ambrose, 36; 37, 51, 62, 63, 74–5, 90
Bodley, G. F., R.A., 84, 211–13
Brahms, J., 238
British and Foreign Bible Society, 100
Browne, Canon G. F., 122, 215, 222, 224, 230.
Bull, Fr Paul, 228
Burges, W., architect, plans for embellishment, 144–6; 207, 211, 215
Burials, 78

CALVARY, 211–12, controversy, 213–14
Canon-in-residence, duties, 10–13, 122
Canons, minor, or petty (*see also* Cupola money), 6, feud with S. Smith, 8, 10–12; 21, 53 ff., conducting visitors and reform of emoluments, 56, 64–6, 67 ff., 76; 97–8, 115, 126 ff., 174
Canons, residentiary, 6, 9, 10 ff., 25, 32, 35, 50, 51, 52, 53, reform of emoluments, 56, 64, 65, 109, 174
Cantlers, 128–9
Cardinals, 6, 22, 23
Cathedrals Act, 1840, 10, 36, 53, 64, 65
Cathedrals Measure, 1931, 159
Champneys, Canon W. W., 61, 90
Chancellor, 9
Chapter, the *passim, see esp.* 187–205
Chapter Fund, 24, 40
Chapter House, *passim, see esp.* 209–11
Charity Schools' Service, 102–4, 143
Charles I, King, and Restoration, 130
Choir, *see under* Music
Christ's Hospital, moved to Horsham, 234
Christian Social Union, 197
Church, R. W., Dean (*see esp.* 200–5), early career, 117–18; 119, 140, 155, 187, 188, 202, 204–5
Church Congress, 231
Churchyard, alterations to, 110–11
City Companies, 23, 82, 210, 221
City of London School, 228
Clarke, Somers, Surveyor, 138, 219, 233, 241
Claughton, Archdeacon, 162
Cleaning of Cathedral, 42–3, 99
"Clergyman, A", 134 ff.
Clock, 25, 26, 217

Clubs, lectures, etc., 171–3, 224 ff.
Cockerell, Mr, Surveyor (1819–52), 26, 62
Colet, J., Dean, 175
Commonwealth, The, 197, 223, 236
Condition of Cathedral in 1831, "a marble waste", cold, dirt, etc., 2–3
Cooper, G., assistant organist, 22–3, 99, 151
Copleston, E., Dean, 5, his distinction, 13–14; 51, 57, 95
Coward, J. H., minor canon, succeeds Hale as Almoner, 49; 127–8, 156
Creighton, Mandell, Bishop, 222
Crypt, 11, 42, 55, 63, 70, 71, 77, 78–9, 147, 180, 207
Cupola, money and Fund, fees for showing, 54–5, 56, 63, 67 ff., 70, 76, 88, 115, 147

DALE, Canon T., 62, 90, 114
Davidson, Randall, 163
Dean, election of, 10, reform of emoluments, 56
Decoration Committee and Fund, 112, 132 ff., 141, 144, 207, 211, 212, 214, 217
Demonstrations, hostile, 184–6
Dickens, C., 7, 73
Documents discovered, 209
Dome, the, 41, 63, embellishment, 82, 132–47 *passim*, 199–200, 215, "on the move", 242, repairs to, 242–3
Donations by St Paul's, 87, 238
Donations to St Paul's, 78, 82, 100, 106, 132, 231, 234, 238
Dress, clerical and choristers', 95, 108, 154, 187, 229, 231

EALDLAND, 128
East London Church Fund, 91
Ecclesiastical Commission Act, 1868, 72
Ecclesiastical Commission, 28, establishment and reports, 31 ff.; 52–7, 63, 67 ff., 109, 110, 113 ff., 121, 123 ff., 179, 210, 242
Ecclesiastical Revenues Commission, 31
Edinburgh Review, The, 1, 18
Educational work and teaching (*see also* Lectures), 109, 129, 137, 224
Education Bill, Liddon critical, 223
Edward VII, King, 232, 236
Embellishment and repairs, 42–3, 82, 100, 109, 111–13, 124, rival plans, 132–47, "confusion and waste", 146, 206–19
Environment, *see under* Property
Estates and endowments, commutation of, 110, 113–14, 115, 123 ff., 143, 168
Evangelism, 147, 170
Executions at Newgate, public, 9, the last in 1868, 90

FABRIC, Fund, and its Trustees, 24 ff., Surveyor of the F., 25, separated from Chapter Fund, 40; 50–1, 52, 62, cracks in, 63; 69, 83, 86, 95, 116, 124, expenditure of Fund, 125–6, 207 ff.; 218, anxiety over and repairs to, 239–43
Fenians, explosion caused by, and measures taken, 63, 90
Finance, 24 ff., "preternaturally complex", 50 ff.; 67–72, commutation (*see also* Estates), 117–31, "not yet crippling", 217; 238–9, stringency, 243
Fine Arts Committee, 144–5
Fire, the Great, 24, 130
Fire, precautions against, 27, 63, 89
Foundations and subsoil, anxiety over, 239–41
Fox, Sir F., engineer, report on deterioration of fabric, 242
Freund, convictions, etc., 184

GAISFORD, T., holds sinecure prebend, 9
Geometrical Staircase, 56, 208
George I, King, 103
George III, King, 14

George IV, King, 14, 126
Gladstone, S., 112
Gladstone, W. E., 112, 120, 123, 188, 222
Goss, J., organist, 1838–72, 6, 21 ff., 85, 99, 143, 148–9, 151, 152
Green, R. R., virger, 1852–99, and sub-sacrist, xii, 3, and *passim*, retires, 232
Gregorian chants, 159
Gregory, R. (*see esp.* 92–106), "a momentous figure", 90, canon, 92, early career, and character, 92–3, his mean installation, 93–4, begins as he means to go on, 94 ff., improvement of services, 95 ff., "no Ritualist", 107–8, Treasurer, 109, embellishment and improvement of Cathedral and environment, 110–13, 140, Chapter Treasurer, 116; 119, 162, 184–6, 187, 189, 203–5, Dean, 206, 206–19, practical and punctual, 220–2, his aides, 222, 243, a living legend but no figurehead, 244–5, tranquil age, 246, death, 248
Grimthorpe, Lord, 217

HACKETT, Maria, and choir-school, 5, 23, 150
Hale, Archdeacon (*see esp.* 39–57), Master of the Charterhouse, 21, 51, correspondence with S. Smith on remuneration, 51–2, struggle with Eccl. Commission, 53–5, 60, his many dignities, 61; 72, 84, 93, 94, 95, death, 105; 114, 179
Hall, T., Receiver, 91, 209
Hawes, W., Almoner and vicar-choral, 4–5, 21, 23, 47, 48
Heating of Cathedral, 27, 42, 125
Henry VIII, King, 65
Higher Criticism, 197
Hodgkinson, E., 224
Hodgson, Canon C., 91
Holland, Canon H. S., quoted *passim* (*see esp.* 189–93, 195–200), xii, 109, 121, 163, his liberalism, 190–1, 222–3; 204, 224, 228, 236, 237, succeeds Gregory as Chapter Treasurer, 245, Regius Professorship of Divinity at Oxford, reasons for accepting, 246–7
Howley, Archbishop, 10, 34, 37
Hughes, Canon T., 14
Hymns Ancient and Modern, introduced, 106

Ingoldsby Legends, 6–8

JACKSON, Bishop, 91, 107, 221
James II, King, 130
Jesus Chapel, 213, 215

KEBLE, J., 13, 31, 58, 59, 92
Keble, T., 92, 93, 204
Kelly, minor canon, 172
Kitchener, Lord, 95

LANG, C., bishop-canon, 123, 235
Lectures and Lecture Society, 106, 170, 172, 224
Lee, J. B., Steward, 91
Leef, D., virger, litigation, 174–82
Leighton, Lord, P.R.A., 79
Liberal Catholicism, 191, 196
Library, 6, 7, 27, 55, 56, 87–8, 225
Liddon, Canon H. P. (*see esp.* 100–2, 193–5), 15, 62, 105, 106, 107, 108, 119, 132, 162, 167–8, 187, 200, 202, 203, 205, 212, 213, 223
Lightfoot, Canon J. B. (*see esp.* 119), 90, 106, 162, 187, 188
Lighting of Cathedral, 2, gas-, 41, 75–8, electric, 78, 234
Lutyens, Sir E., 231
Lux Mundi, 193, 196, 201, 237

MACARTNEY, M., Surveyor, 219, 241, 242
Mansel, Dean, 90, 108, 113, 114, 117, 133
Martin, G., organist, 151, 156, 210
Maurice, F., 117, 223

Melvill, Canon H., a master of rhetoric, 62; 90, reported death and death, 105
Mendelssohn, F., 4, 22
Mercers' Company, 210
Milman, H. H., Dean (*see esp.* 58–69 *passim*, 73–91), 19–20, on admission fee, 31, distinguished earlier career and friends, 58–9, reasons for selection, 60; 66, 67, 69, retirement and death, 90; 92, 93, 109, 111, 133, 134, 187
Minor Canonries Act, 1875, 66, 126
Missions, 198, 227–8
Model, the, Wren's favourite design for the Cathedral, 88, another model, 88–9
Modernism, 237
Morgan, J. P., 78
Morning Chapel, the, 42, redecorated, and services in, 105–6
Mosaics, 82, 215–16
Music and choir (*see also* Vicars-choral), 4–6, 20–4, régime of choir-school in 1836, 23–4; 47–50, 53, Hale's plan to increase choir, 55, 67–8, voluntary choir, etc., 81, 85, 99; 95, 97–8, 124, 129–31, 136–7, 148–61, 209, 221, 234–5

NATIONAL Guinea Subscription, 82
Nelson, Viscount, funeral, 41, 74, 78
Nepotism, 9, 34, 203
Newbolt, Canon W. C. E., 188, earlier career, 223–4, pastoral work, 224 ff.
Newman, J. H., 13, 92, 117, 202, 204

ORGAN, 10, 25, 55, 63, 80, 83, second and unsuccessful, 84, choir, 85, great, 85; 86, voluntary, 96; 125, 132 ff., 143, 207, 217
Organist, 4, 6, *and see* Attwood, Cooper, Goss, Martin, Stainer

PAN-ANGLICAN Congress, 1908, 234
Parris, E. T., artist, 82
Paul's Cross, 234
Penrose, F. C., Surveyor, 62, 84, 86, 111, 114, 131, 144, 217, his career, 218–19
Plainsong, 159
Pluralism, 13, 15, 31, 32, 39–40, 61, 62, 94, 120–2, 224
Preachers and preaching, 11–12, 19, 62, 162–4, 200, 238
Prebendaries, 5, 9, 63–4, 105, 128, 166, 174
Prebends, 9, 32, 35, 63–5, 68, 123
Precentor, 9
Property and environment, improvements in, 89–90, 109–11, 208–9
Property, leases on, 71
Puritanism, modern, 213
Pusey, Dr, 13, 36, 101, 121, 194

RANDOLPH, Dr, and his namesake, 128–9
Reform Bill, 1831, 1, 31
Reorganization of Cathedral, plan for by "A Clergyman", 1839, 134–8
Repairs, *see under* Embellishment
Reredos, 84, 100, 211–14
Retreats for laymen, 225
Richard II, King, 6
Richmond, G., R.A., 139
Richmond, Sir W., 214, 216, 217
Ritual and Ritualists, controversy, 107–8, 187, 201–2, 235, 238
Royston Heath, 90
Russell, W., Succentor and headmaster of choir school, 158–9, 169 ff.

"SACRED AREA" round Cathedral, protected by law, 241
Sacrist, 6
St Dunstan's chapel, 10, 225
St Faith's chapel, 165, 207
St Michael and St George, Order of, spiritual home, 233
St Paul's Cathedral Fund, 82
St Paul's Fund, 82–3
St Paul's Lecture Society, 224

St Paul's School, 150, moved to Hammersmith, 210
Sancroft, Archbishop, 130
Saturday Chapter (*see esp.* 121), 81, 122
Seating, 86, 94, 102, 136
Sellon, W., Receiver, 91, 209
Services and special services, 2–3, 10 ff., 67–9, 73 ff., 79–81, 84, 85, 94, Gregory's notes on deficiencies in, 97–8; 99, 100, 101, 102, 105, 106, 143, 154–5, 164–7, 232–4
Shuttleworth, H. C., 169 ff.
Simpson, J. S., Librarian and Succentor, 87–8, 127, 133, 153–4
Sinclair, Archdeacon, 210, 222, 232
Sinecures, 9, 10, 31, 35
Smith, Nowell C., *Letters of Sydney Smith*, 249
Smith, Sydney (*see esp.* 17–38, 39–57), admitted to canonry, character, 1–2; 3, feud with minor canons, 8, attempts at reform, 11, 12, regularity, 14, Somerset and London, 15–16, Milman on, 19–20, 59, administration, 26 ff., brush with Home Office, 29–30, *Letters to Archdeacon Singleton*, 33, 249, opposes reforms of Eccl. Commission, 35–6; 48, rigorous defence of canonical rights, 56; 57, 135, letters, 249–56
Smithfield, 89
Societies, visiting, 167–8, 233
Society for Promoting Christian Knowledge, 102, 231
Society for the Propagation of the Gospel, 231
Sons of the Clergy, 31, 234
Staff, maintenance (*see also* Virgers), 24, 43, 99, 116, 168, 171
Stainer, J., organist, 50, duties, 85; 150 ff., 238
Stevens, A., sculptor, 79
Stone Gallery, 242
Street, G. E., architect, 139–40
Stubbs, Canon W., 119, 121, 187, 188, 203, 209
Sub-Dean, 6
Succentor, 6, 21
Survey of the Fabric (*see also* Cockerell, Penrose, Clarke, Macartney), 25, 52, 138

TAIT, Archbishop, 74, 80–1, 91, 100, 188, 201, 202
Tate, Canon J., 14, 52, 55
Temple, Archbishop, 98, 210, 213, 221
Thefts, etc., 183–4
Therfield, 90
The Times, 242
Thornhill, Sir J., artist, 82, 211
Tijou, Wren's craftsman, 213
Tillingham, estate bestowed by K. Ethelbert of Kent, 28–9, 124, 208, 220
Tractarians, 117, 202, 204
Treasurer, 9, 109
Trophy Room, 88, 225, 227

VICARS-CHORAL (*see also* Cupola Fund), 5–6, Warden of, 6, 11; 21 ff., struggle with Chapter, 43–7, 53 ff.; 56, 67 ff., 76, 85, 94, 95, additional, 96; 97–9, 103, 115, commutation, 124–5; 149, 151–3, 159 ff., 167, 174, 179
Victoria, Queen, 18, 132, 142, 143, Jubilee, 228, Diamond Jubilee, 228–31, Requiem, 232
Victorianism, 237, 238
Villiers, Canon H. M., 61
Virgers (*see esp.* 174–83, *and see* Cupola Fund), remuneration, 29; 44, 45–6, 53 ff., 56, 67, 68, 99, 106, 115, 168
Visitors, *see* Worshippers
Vivian, Dr, minor canon, 97, 127

WALTON-ON-THE-NAZE, estate at, 208–9
Wandsmen, 81–2
Wellington, Duke of, funeral, etc., 9, 41, 70, 74–9, 118, 207–8, 233, 235

Whispering Gallery, 43, 56, 76, 183, 215
William III, King, 130
Willis, "Father" H., 86, 143, 207
Winnington-Ingram, bishop-canon, 123, 227, 245
Wiseman, Dr, 135
Worship, continuous, 198–9, Public Worship Regulation Act, 1874, 201–2; 225
Worshippers and visitors, 3, 29–30, 55, 56, 60, 67, 68, 76, 101–2, 106–7, 115, 136, 138, 140, 163, 167–8, 214

YOOL, Mr, Actuary to the Eccl. Commissioners, 114, 124
Young people, religious provision for, 107, 164, 168–9, 171–3, 225 ff.